ROADMAP TO LIBERTY

PUBLISHING INFORMATION

Author: Lucas Vincent

Publisher: Lucas Vincent Publishing
          Part of Lucas Vincent Holding Limited

Publisher Address: Unit 905, 9/F, Kowloon Centre, 33 Ashley Road
          Tsim Sha Tsui, Hong Kong, Hong Kong

First Published: November 1, 2015

Print Edition 1.6

GO FURTHER

Also visit www.RoadmapToLiberty.com

To get notified when I release a new book, accompanying website or video series → sign up here: http://eepurl.com/btwL8v

Feel free to email me at LucasVincentHolding@iCloud.com.

WELCOME

You probably purchased this book to get an overview on how to address the political issues of our time. Or you are simply looking for quick facts and arguments on libertarian positions. Maybe you were searching for a comprehensive introduction to libertarianism and the principles of liberty. This is why I will keep this foreword short.

I have often been frustrated by the fact that there is no comprehensive, easy-to-read guide to the workings of our current economic and political system, that also addresses how we can reform it in a liberty-friendly way.

I, and I am sure you, too, have limited time reading lengthy books or listening to endless podcasts. This is why I made all efforts to:

1. Make this book as concise as possible, getting straight to the facts without lengthy discussions

2. Address and summarize all major concepts about liberty and most major political issues, so you do not have to consult dozens of books and websites

3. Split the book into relatively short chapters, ordered by issue, which can be read in any order

4. Suggest multiple steps of "reforms" for cornerstone issues such as health care and infrastructure. Less far-reaching "liberty-friendly" reform proposals will be more realistic to achieve, and are

contrasted with more "idealistic" proposals that are more difficult to get through.

I am confident that this book will allow you to get a good overview on libertarianism in general and how we can reform government in a "liberty-friendly" way. I can assure you that even if you are an avid reader, a determined libertarian, or a political science graduate you will learn something from every chapter.

In order for you to benefit most from this book I recommend you to start with chapter 1 - Principles of Liberty. After that feel free to skip to and switch between chapters in any order.

Thank you,

Lucas Vincent

P.S.: You will find all the relevant sources at the end of the respective chapters.

TABLE OF CONTENTS

PRINCIPLES OF LIBERTY

CHAPTER 1

"One has the right to do whatever one likes to do, unless one infringes on the same right of others or harms people."

- The Law of Liberty

The "Law of Liberty" constitutes the foundation of libertarianism — a political ideology that puts an individual's right to self-ownership above everything else. The beauty of libertarianism is that based on this single law, we can answer all imaginable economic, political and social questions.

The "Law of Liberty" stands in stark contrast with today's political system, in which one piece of legislation alone, the Affordable Care Act (Obamacare), along with its accompanied regulations, account for 11,588,500 words or 10,535 pages. How can we truly claim to be a country of liberty, when only one of the thousands of pieces of legislation is longer than what many people will read in their lifetime?

Along with the "Law of Liberty," libertarianism is based on the "Principle of Causation" and "Voluntaryism." Throughout this book, we will come back to these three pillars of liberty in our quest to determine the liberty approach to some of today's most pressing issues. Let us look at the principle of causation and voluntaryism in more detail:

The Second Pillar - The Principle of Causation

The Principle of Causation states that whoever has actively caused an outcome should be taken responsible for it. This rule works both for positive and negative outcomes. In its simplest form, it states that an individual has the full right to the fruits of his/her labor, while a criminal has the responsibility to rectify his/her wrongdoings. While it may appear trivial, or maybe even obvious, this principle has been violated in almost any conceivable form in human history.

The Third Pillar - Voluntaryism, or the "No-Force Principle"

Voluntaryism states that all forms of human interaction should be based solely on the voluntary consent of all involved participants. Just as a sales transaction between a store and customers requires the voluntary consent of both parties, so do two partners have to agree to a marriage. However, while taken for granted in many situations, voluntaryism, too, is often violated, with conscription and taxation being prominent examples.

These three pillars of liberty are closely related to natural rights. Let us take a closer look at them, too:

Natural Rights

The three pillars of liberty just discussed can be referred to as "natural rights."

The concept of natural rights assumes that all rights enjoyed by humans were granted by god, or for our atheist readers, are inherent to human morale. For this reason, natural rights are unalienable and do

Illustration 1.1 The Law- and Principles of Liberty

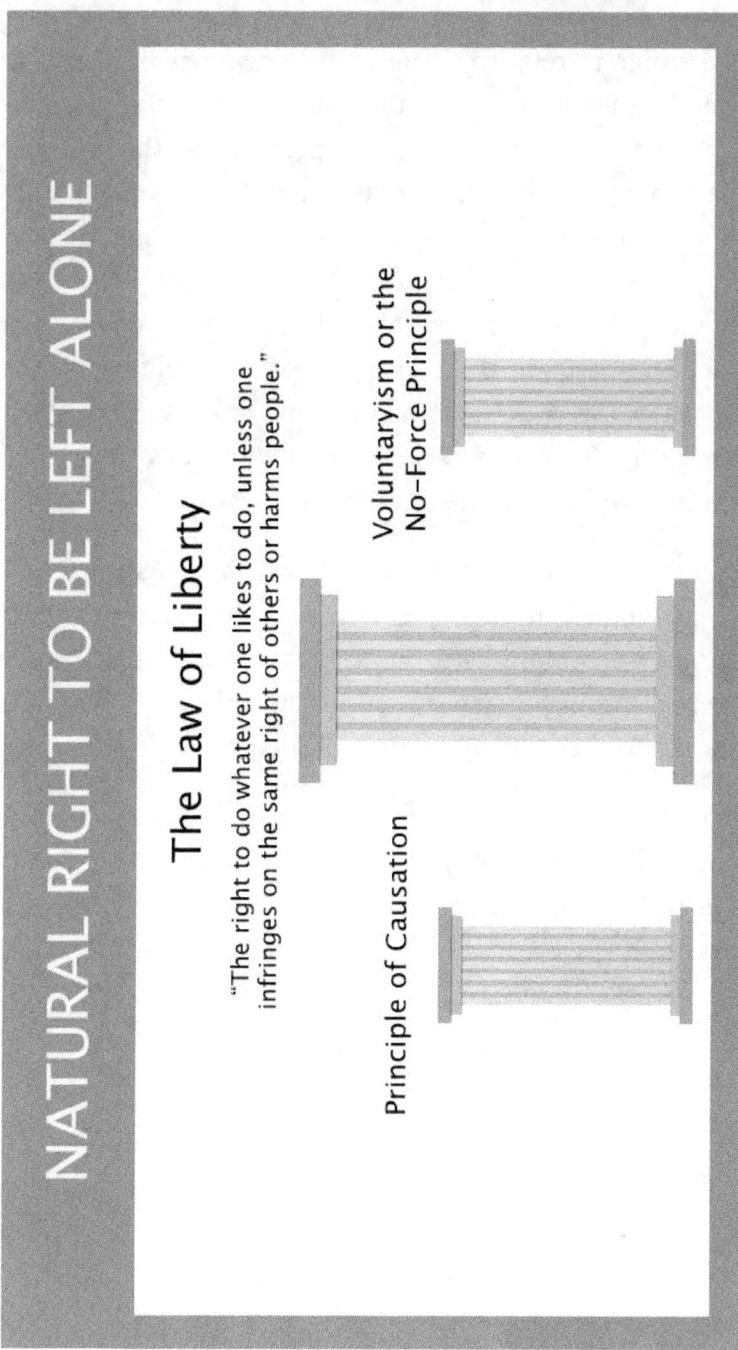

The law- and principles of liberty fully conform to what many call our "only human right" - the right to be left alone. As the law- and principles of liberty apply the natural right to everyday human interactions, we will use them to outline the liberty-approach to government. Image: own work by author not depend on governments approving them by order.

And while it is possible to refer to the law- and principles of liberty as natural rights, there is also the view that there is just one natural right, namely the "right to be left alone." From this perspective, the law- and principles of liberty are secondary to, but are still derived from and fully comply with this single natural right. Think about it: voluntaryism in its essence comes down to your right to be left alone. You are free to interact with others, but do not have to. Similarly, you cannot force others to interact with you, as they, too, possess the right to be left alone. A similar reasoning applies to the principle of causation. When you cause harm to somebody, you violated that individual's right to be left alone, and in turn you have to make up for it.

The flip side of natural rights are legal rights, which are granted and can be taken by government decree. Legal rights do not have to — and often simply do not — comply with human morale. In essence, they represent the popular opinion of those currently in power — be it a single dictator or the 51% of the population in a democracy.

Since the right to be left alone is often considered as being abstract, with an apparent lack of applicability to real life situations, this book is mainly based on the law and principles of liberty. These are used to apply the natural right to everyday human interactions ranging from consumption (principle of causation) to exchanges (voluntaryism = no-force principle).

The Definition of Liberty Matters

Ironically, the terms "liberty" or "freedom" are often used in very different contexts. Organizations such as the Afghan Taliban claim to be "freedom fighters" while at the same time, the United States fights the group to "advance the freedom" and "civil liberties" of the Afghan people.

The reason for this apparent paradox — the different use of the terms freedom and liberty by inherently opposed people — lies in the contradiction between "negative liberties" and "positive liberties".

Negative liberties describe the *freedom from* force and coercion — in the sense of the "Law of Liberty" and the two principles of liberty we just discussed. Negative liberties also fully comply with the natural right "to be left alone." The philosophy of negative liberties is followed by Ron Paul, Milton Friedman, as well as this book, and is in accordance with free market capitalism.

Positive liberties, on the other hand, present the *freedom to* have the economic resources and opportunities to fulfill oneself. When Occupy Wall Street activists or Marxist rebels in South America call for "freedom" they usually refer to "positive liberties." Examples of "positive liberties" include rights to free education or health care.

It should be emphasized that in the context of liberty, the terms "negative" and "positive" do not mean that some liberties are "bad" and others are "good." "Negative" simply means "freedom from," while "positive" refers to "freedom to."

As their names suggest, negative and positive liberties are opposites and cannot be reconciled. Negative liberties require the violation of positive liberties, for example, by stopping the redistribution of wealth (i.e., enacting a negative liberty) there is a lack of money to finance government handouts (i.e., ending a positive liberty). The same is true the other way around. Forcing people to pay taxes (i.e., violating a negative liberty) provides the financing of government-sponsored health care (i.e., instituting a positive liberty).

The difference between negative and positive liberties is also the underlying reason why pro-life and pro-choice activists claim to advance freedom and liberty, while advocating for the opposite. Pro-life advocates defend negative liberties (i.e., unborn infants should be "left alone" — the infant's *freedom from being aborted*), while pro-choice advocates support positive-liberties (i.e., advance the opportunities of a woman even if this requires the death of an unborn — the *freedom to abort another individual*).

For clarification, when someone claims to have the right to free healthcare, which is a positive liberty, one is really referring to one's supposed right to have somebody else pay for one's intended medical treatment. This is why positive liberties, while packaged as "freedom" and disguised as rights, may also be considered as the suppression of a select group of people.

Imagine a car thief justifying the theft with his right to personal mobility, an argument not far-fetched when keeping in mind the long list of demands socialists place on other people's property. The only difference between a single thief making the argument that he has the right to personal mobility and the right to free education or health care is that the latter was officially legalized through a process in which politicians write the personal desires of their constituencies on a piece of paper and sign with their name below.

Why Liberty Is Important

Everyone would agree that stealing from a friend or colleague at work is immoral, and that people who are caught should be penalized.

It would be inappropriate for your neighbor to tell you at which minimum wage you should accept a job, or who you should be allowed to marry.

But replace your friends, colleagues and neighbors with politicians you don't know, sitting in a room thousands of miles away, and all of a sudden it is fine for them to steal from (tax) you, set a minimum wage and tell you whom you are allowed to marry.

Whatever the reason these politicians are in power — be it because they are the successors of revolutionaries like in China, or because they were voted into government by your friends and neighbors, there is no justification for their yearning of power over you.

Think about it: in Western democracies, politicians are simply the extension or tools of the majority of your neighbors and colleagues.

If 60% of the people living in your area want a new community swimming pool, but you don't because you can't swim and won't use it, they do not have the right to force you to financially contribute to its construction.

However, if the same proponents in your neighborhood choose a representative, stage an election and gain the majority, it will suddenly be fine for them to force you to pay (after all, they've won your municipal election!)

Chapter 1: Principles of Liberty

Stealing is wrong. Telling others how to live their personal lives is wrong. The matter of fact doesn't change just because the act is done by a powerful dictator or a majority of people in your area.

--- A Kind Reminder ---

Feel free to read the following chapters in whatever order you like. While I recommended you to read them in the suggested sequence to allow you to make most sense of the various arguments, it will not cause much harm to start with whatever topic you are most interested in. Enjoy!

--- Sources ---

1. Length of The Affordable Care Act - "11,588,500 Words: Obamacare Regs 30x as Long as Law." CNS News. Penny Starr. http://cnsnews.com/news/article/penny-starr/11588500-words-obamacare-regs-30x-long-law. Retrieved July 28, 2015.

POLITICAL IDEOLOGIES

CHAPTER 2

We already defined libertarianism, but how does liberty compare to the other political ideologies out there?

All the seemingly countless political leanings ranging from conservatism to socialism have traditionally been placed on a right-left scale. The right-left scale is believed to have its origin from the first National Assembly convened after the French revolution in 1789. Factions loyal to the impeached monarchy were seated to the right of the chair, while revolutionaries were seated to the left. Typical parliamentary configurations found in the US and continental Europe are shown in illustration 2.1. "Left leaning" parties are seated to the left of the half-circle seat layout and vice-versa.

We were taught the right-left spectrum in school and college, while the mass media do a great job in repeating it on a daily basis. Because we have become indoctrinated by the right-left stigma, it is difficult for many to see its fatal shortcomings. Shortcomings which, among other reasons, form the main obstacles to a widespread understanding and acceptance of libertarianism. Let me explain why.

We have been programmed by governments and the media to believe that National Socialism on the far right and Communism on the far left are each other's opposite and, therefore, are placed at the opposing ends of the right-left scale. Few people question this representation.

Let us compare some of the characteristics of both these supposedly "opposed" systems and see for ourselves how "different" they really are. Following table lists various political issues and the respective views of National Socialism and Communism. For reference, I included the stances of Western democracies and Libertarianism.

Illustration 2.1 US and European Parliament Layouts

US Parliament
(Here House of Representatives)

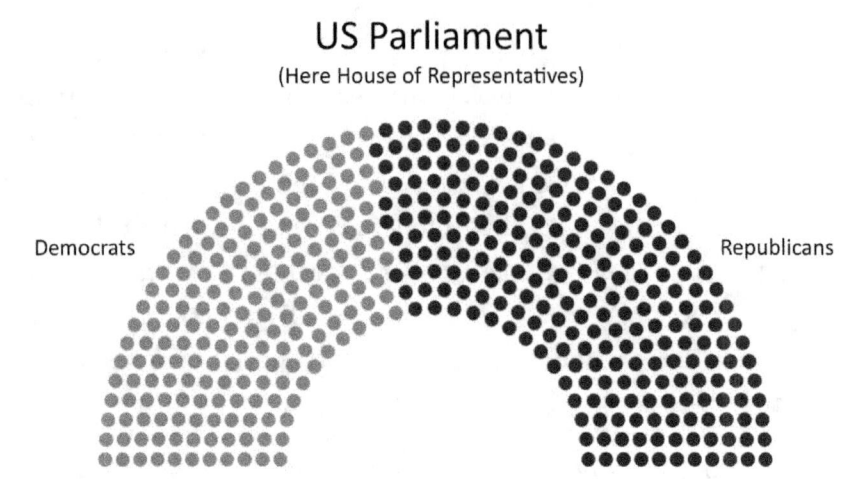

Democrats   Republicans

Democrats are seated to the left, Republicans to the right of the half-circle seat layout.

Continental European Parliament

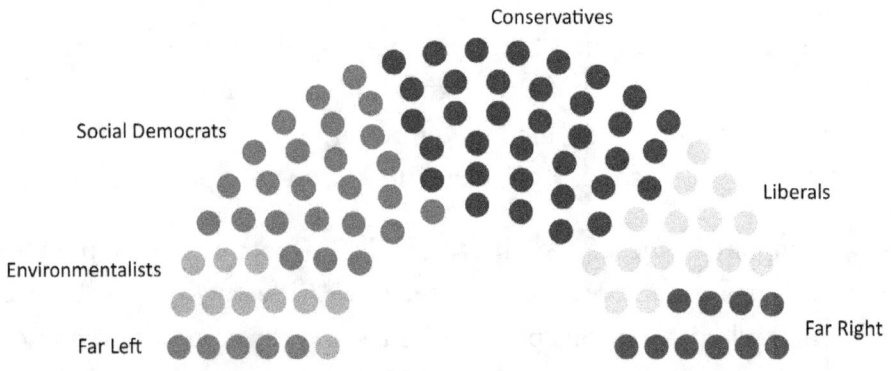

Conservatives

Social Democrats

Liberals

Environmentalists

Far Left   Far Right

European democracies have a much more fragmented political landscape than the US. Please note that "European liberals" are different to "US liberals" as will be outlined later in this chapter. The British Parliament (the House of Commons and House of Lords) follows a rectangular layout. Images: own work by author

	Communism (Soviet Union)	Naziism/National Socialism/Fascism (Nazi Germany)	Western Democracies (US, Europe)	Libertarianism (Based on the "Law of Liberty")
Cult Around The Leader	Hitler and Stalin are both revered as great leaders		Little to no leader cult	No leader cult
Religious Freedom	Religion is openly considered an enemy to both regimes. While Stalin "abolished" religions altogether, Hitler tried to win support of and control the church to his benefit		Fully respected	
Social Welfare	Provided exclusively by the government	Provided almost exclusively by government, with few private programs available (e.g., company pensions, charity)	Provided mostly by governments, though free market options are available	Provided by the free market

	Communism (Soviet Union)	Naziism/National Socialism/Fascism (Nazi Germany)	Western Democracies (US, Europe)	Libertarianism (Based on the "Law of Liberty")
Military Spending	Around 20% of GDP in the 1980s	More than 10% of GNP in non-war times (1936, before the Second World War)	Ranging from around 3.5% of GDP (US) to around 2% (EU countries)	State-funded military is non-existent (replaced by self-defense)
Imperialism (See Appendix for Detailed List)	Invaded 30 countries (36 countries based on today's borders)	Invaded 25 countries (32 countries based on today's borders)	No long-term/prolonged occupation of another country since Second World War	A small or non-existent state-funded military means no invasions of other countries
Censorship of Media	All media controlled by the state (for propaganda purposes)		Very limited government censorship of media (depending on country and type of media)	No government censorship of media

Property Rights	Communism (Soviet Union)	Naziism/National Socialism/Fascism (Nazi Germany)	Western Democracies (US, Europe)	Libertarianism (Based on the "Law of Liberty")
	Non-existent	Exist, but are frequently violated by the government or non-existent for dissidents and other enemies of the state	Property rights are respected in most situations, though government expropriations do happen (through eminent domain)	Being a cornerstone of libertarianism, property rights are not violated by the state, not even for the "public good"

	Communism (Soviet Union)	Naziism/National Socialism/Fascism (Nazi Germany)	Western Democracies (US, Europe)	Libertarianism (Based on the "Law of Liberty")
Discrimination Against Certain Ethnic Groups	Between 1927 and 1952 (under Stalin) around 20mill civilians (on top of 20mill combatants) were killed by the Soviet leadership. These include 6-7mill killed through artificial famine, mostly ethnic Ukrainians and nomad Kazakhs along with other ethnic minorities from central Asia.	The Nazis killed 11mill people in the Holocaust, including 6mill Jews and 5mill people from various other backgrounds including Slavs and Roman Gypsies	Discrimination by anyone against ethnic minorities deemed unacceptable and made illegal by law	Discrimination by government unacceptable, but allowed between individuals.

	Communism (Soviet Union)	Naziism/National Socialism/Fascism (Nazi Germany)	Western Democracies (US, Europe)	Libertarianism (Based on the "Law of Liberty")
Treatment of Dissidents	Dissidents are incarcerated in concentration camps and Gulags respectively		Dissidents are free to articulate their views	
Taxation	Progressive taxation is a cornerstone of Communism. However, it should be mentioned that formal tax rates are not representative of the tax burden, as all wages are set by the government and, therefore, include "indirect taxes" through lower wages	Progressive taxation used	Progressive taxation employed in most countries	Taxes are non-existent. Government services are either voluntary or privatized

	Communism (Soviet Union)	Nazism/National Socialism/Fascism (Nazi Germany)	Western Democracies (US, Europe)	Libertarianism (Based on the "Law of Liberty")
Allocation of Economic Resources	Resource allocation is done by the state. All companies are state-owned and controlled	Allocation occurs both through the state and to a smaller extent through private businesses. While large corporations exist, they have merged with the state in what is called fascism. Even if these corporations are owned privately, their actions are heavily influenced by the government	Done mostly through the free market mechanism, with distortions resulting from subsidies and taxes	Done through the free market mechanism

Chapter 2: Political Ideologies

As shown, the ideologies of Naziism (National Socialism) and Communism share almost identical approaches to issues ranging from the economy to religion. The only major difference may be Nazi Germany's focus on merging the state with large corporations such as Krupp in traditional fascistic fashion, while the Soviet Union nationalized all industries.

In light of the apparent similarities between the two ideologies, commentators have (successfully) tried to persuade us that there is a "crucial" difference between the two. One is a form of "national" socialism, systematically favoring its own (ethnically homogenous) citizens, while the other one is a form of "international" socialism, supposedly being more accepting of people from other ethnic backgrounds.

Nothing could be further from the truth. Both Nazi Germany and the Soviet Union invaded dozens of countries each (more so for the USSR), while relocating and murdering inhabitants of the newly occupied regions. As mentioned in the comparison table, Nazi Germany is estimated to have killed 11 million civilians (most of them ethnic minorities and Jews), while Stalin murdered 20 million civilians, including 6-7 million through artificial starvation, most of which were comprised of Ukrainians and ethnic minorities from central Asia. Both Nazi Germany and the Soviet Union killed millions in the countries they took over. Be it the 6 million Jews in Poland killed by Hitler or the 5+ million ethnic Ukrainians intentionally starved to death by Stalin between 1932 and 1933 in what has been referred to as Holodomor (literally "Extermination through Hunger"). The countries both regimes invaded either became puppet states, protectorates or satellite states — executing the occupier's commands.

Chapter 2: Political Ideologies

The core of both Naziism (National Socialism) and Communism is to advance the power of those in control by taking over foreign countries and "harvesting" their citizens. Government control and surveillance over all aspects of life are meant to create a population submissive to the state. Simultaneously, both Nazis and Communists employ socialism to:

(1) make the masses dependent on government handouts (leaving them to support the state and current leaders)

(2) eliminate the threat of upcoming non-establishment figures and businessmen by regulating and taxing them out of business. A poor government factory worker who lacks the permit to leave his small home town and move to a large city has little chance to lead a successful revolt against the tyrannical ruling elite.

We will discuss in detail how governments (and big business) use socialism to stifle competition and keep themselves in power in chapter 3.2 - Special Interests.

The political similarities between National Socialism and Communism as well as their shared quest for unrivaled, socialist world domination were pointed out by Hitler himself. In a 1941 speech he proclaimed "basically, National Socialism and Marxism are the same." He went on to explain the only major difference between National Socialism and Marxism as practiced by the Soviet Union. Hitler believed "industrialists" should be spared from execution and rather be "used" to support the working class (merging big business with the state), while Soviet Marxism completely removed the capitalist class through industry nationalization.

There is a problem with placing these almost identical "socialist" philosophies on the opposite ends of the right-left spectrum. As a result, any ideology placed in between the two — by definition — may only represent a variation of the two supposed extremes. This leaves the entire right-left spectrum solely with variations of socialism. Libertarianism and other non-socialist ideologies are left out.

The one-dimensional representation of political ideologies can in part be thanked for why most people think within the socialist paradigm that it is the government's responsibility to collect taxes, provide health care, build infrastructure etc. All political ideologies that are part of the right-left spectrum share these socialist "big-government" characteristics.

When libertarians talk about cutting regulations and taxes they are quickly labeled as "right-wingers." And when advocating more far-reaching proposals such as the abolishing of the income tax or the Fed, the mainstream media is ready to isolate us by calling libertarians "right-wing extremists" — a term usually reserved for National Socialists, which ironically championed the all-powerful state.

While the Tea Party movement and, in general, more open discussion about free market ideas have helped the term "right-wing extremist" get more accepted (and detached from its historical association with Naziism), this is not the case in Europe. Tea Party activists holding signs reading "I am a right-wing extremist" are the norm in the US, but would be socially unacceptable in countries such as Germany or France. In fact, the German term for "right wing extremist" — Rechtsextremist — and the label "Neo-Nazis" are used interchangeably by national media.

Intolerance towards any political idea which does not conform to socialism or fits on the right-left scale means that libertarianism is nearly unheard of in many parts of Europe. Not to mention that even if you want, voting for a libertarian party is impossible as there are simply none. When the German anti-euro party "Alternative für Deutschland" (Alternative for Germany) dared to propose the abolishment of the mandatory public broadcasting fees, they were quickly labeled "Rechtsextremisten" (right wing extremists) and thus put to silence.

It is the prevalence of the right-left spectrum and the inaccurate association of free market capitalism with the historic notion of right-wing extremism that makes it so difficult for libertarianism to get momentum.

Socialists in power depend on the right-left mantra to keep free market ideas out of the public's perception. Their control over the media and public education system as well as people's fear of being reprimanded by others for "extremist" viewpoints is what makes Europe a society of (socialist) consensus, at least on the surface.

Mapping Political Ideologies

A far more accurate way of mapping political ideologies is to use a two-dimensional chart with economic freedom on one axis and personal freedom on the other axis. A visual mapping based on these two criteria is also known as "Nolan Chart," named after its creator David Nolan.

Both National Socialism and Communism are located at the bottom left of this chart — sharing the characteristics of little to no economic- and personal freedom. They both represent forms of authoritarianism.

Conservatism, as it is known in the US, is found in the bottom right of the diagram — placing a strong emphasis on economic freedom (low

Illustration 2.2 Nolan Chart of Political Ideologies

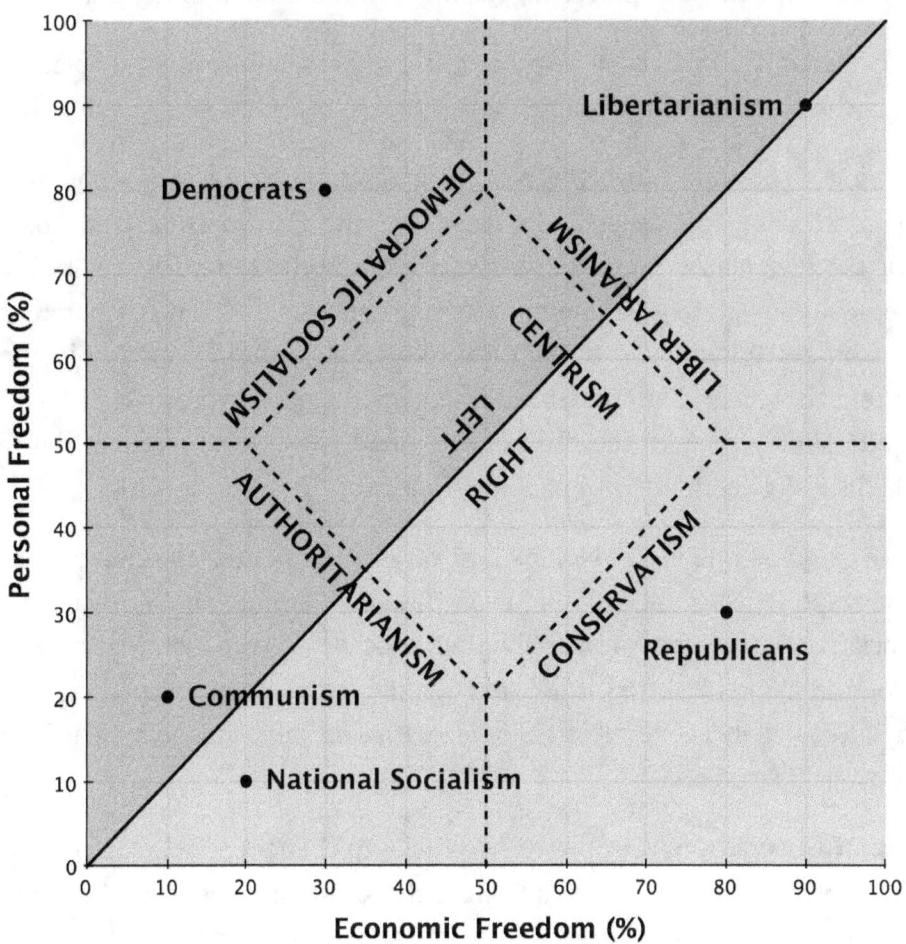

National Socialism and Communism are both types of authoritarianism. Image: own work by author

taxes and few regulations) while limiting personal freedoms (such as gay marriage, drug use and immigration). Liberalism in the way it is understood in the United States (equivalent to social democratic and environmentalist parties in Europe) limits economic freedom, while emphasizing personal liberties, placing it in the top left of the diagram.

Libertarianism joins both — economic and personal freedom — placing it in the top right of the graph.

"Being right-wing" involves placing greater importance on economic freedom compared to personal freedom, with the opposite being true for the left. Naziism and Conservatism are both referred to as "right" because they place greater emphasis on economic freedom compared to personal freedom, even though the two ideologies differ greatly in the extent to which they offer those freedoms. In other words, "right" and "left" simply refer to the ratio of economic to personal freedom, NOT the levels of economic and personal freedom.

The diagonal line in the Nolan chart divides the political landscape into right and left. As can be seen, even though Communism and National Socialism are very similar in their social and economic policies, Communism is referred to as "left" as it grants slightly more personal freedoms than economic freedoms, with the opposite being true for National Socialism.

The Nolan chart, in my opinion, is crucial to changing public opinion in favor of libertarianism. It emphasizes the similarities between National Socialism and Communism while distancing libertarianism from the "far-right" stigma.

Liberalism in the US and Europe

The term liberalism as understood in the US is very different to how it is used in continental Europe. Liberalism in France or Germany is related to classical liberalism. The German party FDP, also called "Die

Liberalen" (or "the liberals"), for example, is the most free market oriented party in the country. However, it should be stressed that because of Europe's left-leaning tendencies, even the most "libertarian" parties are usually more socialist than right-leaning Democrats such as Bill Clinton.

A personal (and admittedly, not fully scientific) theory of why Europe is more left-leaning than the US is based on two arguments:

1. The 1800s and early 1900s had significant waves of immigrants coming to the US, mainly originating from Germany, Ireland and the UK. These immigrants had in common a strong work-ethic and most important of all a desire to improve their own fate in a country without the social, political and economic constraints of old Europe. In the process, the migrants left their socialist neighbors and acquaintances behind - increasing the proportion of left-wingers in Europe. This paved the way for the socialist overthrows of governments in Russia, Austria-Hungary, and Germany. The US, on the other hand, received an influx of (mostly) free market advocates.

2. The Founding Fathers, along with the first settlers in the new colonies, were "adventurers" who were comfortable with "being left on their own" on another continent and creating their own destiny. It is this mentality which, at least to some extent, is still anchored in many Americans. People residing in Europe, on the other hand, are culturally (yet unconsciously) entrenched in the old mindset that a local king or landlord was there to care for his "subjects." This mentality continues today with Europeans looking to government to provide protection, jobs, and social welfare.

As time passes and new generations with little to no attachment to history are born, the cultural and political differences between the US and Europe will vanish. Already taking place, conservative US media have dubbed this process the "Europeanization" of the United States.

--- Learn More ---

- An overview of some of the economic and cultural policies of Nazi Germany, including tax rates, can be found here http://tapnewswire.com/2012/02/in-hitlers-germany-income-tax-was-80/.

- [SELF-TEST] Where are you on the two-dimensional Nolan chart? Find out here https://www.politicalcompass.org/test.

--- Sources ---

1. Military Spending in Nazi Germany (1936) - "The German Economy in the Twentieth Century." Hans-Joachim Braun. Routledge, 1990, p. 85.

2. Military Spending in the Soviet Union (1980s) - "Russian Military Budget." GlobalSecurity.org. http://www.globalsecurity.org/military/world/russia/mo-budget.htm. Retrieved July 28, 2015.

3. Military Spending of US and EU countries - "Military expenditure (% of GDP)." World Bank. http://data.worldbank.org/indicator/MS.MIL.XPND.GD.ZS. Retrieved July 28, 2015.

4. People Killed by the Soviet Union - "How Many People Did Joseph Stalin Kill?" Palash Ghosh. International Business Time. http://www.ibtimes.com/how-many-people-did-joseph-stalin-kill-1111789. Retrieved July 28, 2015.

5. People Killed by Nazi Germany - "The Holocaust's Forgotten Victims: The 5 Million Non-Jewish People Killed By The Nazis." Louise Ridley. Huffington Post. http://www.huffingtonpost.com/2015/01/27/holocaust-non-jewish-victims_n_6555604.html. Retrieved July 28, 2015.

6. Hitler's 1941 Speech - "Herr Hitler's Speech of February 24." Bulletin of International News, Vol. 18, No. 5 (Mar. 8, 1941), pp. 267-269. Jstor. http://www.jstor.org/stable/pdf/25642976.pdf?acceptTC=true. Retrieved July 28, 2015.

GOVERNMENT

CHAPTER 3

Chapter 3: Government

Ask ten people about the responsibilities of government and you will get ten different answers.

However, from a libertarian perspective government's objectives are clear. Government has the sole responsibility to protect citizens' liberty — ensuring that every individual has his/her "right to be left alone" protected.

While government in its current state is the perpetrator of countless violations against liberty as shown throughout this book, in *can* be transformed into a much leaner organization. A "lean government" ensures the protection of the "Law of Liberty," while itself existing and operating in accordance with this law, the principle of causation and voluntaryism. First, let us discuss "lean government" in more detail:

The concept of a "lean government" stands in stark contrast to the way our current Western democratic governments function. In Western democracies, many people ironically argue that governments should infringe on some (called "negative") liberties, such as the right to keep the fruits of one's labor or the freedom from government surveillance in order to guarantee so-called "positive" liberties, such as security and provision of welfare.

Due to the "negative liberty — positive liberty dilemma" explained in detail in chapter 1, the supposed and often accepted government responsibilities directly violate our "negative" liberties including the "Law of Liberty."

When Western democracies represent "big" government, and the concept of "lean government" underlying this book stands for "minimal government," anarchism is the concept of having no government at all. Generally speaking, anarchism is defined as the

Chapter 3: Government

"belief in the abolition of all government and the organization of society on a voluntary, cooperative basis without recourse to force or compulsion."

It is important to note that there are widely ranging forms of anarchism, some (e.g., anarcho-capitalism) supporting free markets, while other strands are inherently socialist.

There is a heated debate among libertarians on whether "minimal government" (also called minarchism) or anarchism is the best path to the protection of individual liberties. Some argue that government — no matter how small — is inherently opposed to voluntaryism. In order to preserve true liberty, it is claimed, government needs to be abolished.

And while many libertarians would probably support this notion, others realize that it is not necessarily government, a form of power concentration, that violates liberty — it is people, specifically politicians. Abolishing government, as anarchism proposes, eliminates a way people organize and concentrate power, yet it does not prevent the same people who violated liberty in the first place to do so in the future. Without the organization of government, politicians along with criminals would come up with new forms of organization — for example, gangs and clans. These gangs, just as governments do today, would again deprive us of our economic and civil freedoms.

In order to protect liberty, we need to come up with a way to restrict the portion of society who yearns for the property of and authority over others. The only way to do this, in my opinion, is through the aforementioned "lean government" which, while ensuring protection of rights, is ruled not by those who want to benefit on the cost of others, but by the fixed law- and principles of liberty.

It is the purpose of the following two sections to outline how such a "lean government" can function.

The Path From Anarchism to Big Government - A Story

It is often argued that anarchism self-destructs in the long term, leading to the inevitable establishment of an all-present state.

Assume you (along with your relatives and acquaintances) lived in a small village in the wilderness, in a world without government, taxation, official rules or police. The community you live in is one of thousands of smaller and larger towns, all existing without government oversight.

One day, a group of thugs arrives in your village — and uses violence to steal from you and your neighbors. The thugs disappear shortly thereafter, just to return a month or two later. After several years of irregular robberies, the thugs decide to move right next to the villagers, making it even easier for them to steal from the locals.

One day, the thugs come up with the idea of giving a proportion of their plunder back to the poor. This apparent act of "kindness" wins them the trust and sympathy of the less fortunate villagers. They also provide "gifts" to the elderly and children, and after several years, hand out giveaways to everyone in the village. These apparent "gifts" make the hard working villagers more complacent of the robbers and monthly raids, even though their property loss resulting from robberies outweighs the value of "handouts" by a large margin.

One day, the villagers organize a town hall meeting — complaining about the parasitic thugs living among them. The villagers argue that the community has to stop accepting these "bribes" as they merely equal a fraction of what is stolen from them every month. One of the thugs present at the meeting answers that in fact, they were the ones who secure the villagers from criminals coming from outside the town, and that they should feel "grateful" for being "protected." The villagers' complaint is soon stifled, as no one wants to become the victim of the thugs' rage. Just days ago a villager was locked up in a cage when refusing to hand over part of his income.

In light of the potential threat from other criminals entering the village, and the violence from the thugs living among them, the villagers are finally persuaded to turn over the originally privately owned landlines, electricity generators and the local newspaper. This, they hope, allows the "thugs" to better fend off a potential outside attack.

After some time, the thugs increase the frequency of their thefts from the villagers, while slightly raising the "bribes" to keep them complacent. In fact, they start offering "free" education to the village children. The thugs exploit this opportunity to teach the youngsters to view the thugs as protectors and providers of services. They tell them to use terms like "taxes" instead of theft, and "government" instead of thugs.

New generations grow up becoming more dependent on the "thugs" and internalizing the view that they are their protectors. Those who still question those in power are increasingly labeled "lunatics" and "extremists."

Then, one day, the thugs have another idea: let the villagers elect one of several pre-approved thugs to become the governor of the area. The villagers' reception of the proposal is overwhelming. In the illusion that these "elections" put everyone into power, the majority of villagers simply start ignoring those who challenge this form of "mass indoctrination." The villagers even argue that disagreement with their new "ordered" way of life should be expressed at the voting booth.

Most villagers become so used to this new "government" that they themselves start protecting the interests of the state. Those who openly criticize those in power, and have the courage to call "government" for what it is — a group of thugs — are attacked by their neighbors and fired from their jobs. Under the protection of this "societal consensus," there is simply no need for the thugs to continue bothering about dissidents of the state. After all, it makes for so much better publicity to let "indoctrinated" villagers cast "contrarian thinkers" aside, than beating them to death as was common practice in the past.

--- Learn More ---

- [Video] The Path From Anarchism to Big Government in Video Format https://www.youtube.com/watch?v=NbNFJK1ZpVg.

--- Sources ---

1. Definition for Anarchism - New Oxford American Dictionary. Copyright © 2010, 2013 by Oxford University Press, Inc. All rights reserved.

PASSING LAWS

CHAPTER 3 - SECTION 1

Depending on the type of government system, laws are passed in two major ways:

1. **In Democratic Systems**

   There are representative and direct democracies. In a representative democracy, lawmaking is restricted to voting by representatives, which themselves are elected by the public. Direct democracy consists of citizens voting on issues directly in referendums, also called plebiscites. There is not a single "pure" direct democracy in the world today.

   While most countries are representative democracies, many allow referendums. Though from a global perspective, these are rare, with those countries where referendums are legally possible only performing them in special circumstances. Plebiscites are usually used to adopt a new constitution or for a region to secede as a separate country, as occurred in South Sudan and in Scotland.

   The few places where direct democracy is a regular part of the law making process are limited mostly to a number of US states and

Switzerland. 27 US states and Washington D.C. allow varying degrees of citizen-led initiatives, though the majority of these have taken place in just six states — Arizona, California, Colorado, North Dakota, Oregon, and Washington State. Colorado's 2014 deregulation of marijuana is a prominent example of a passed state-level referendum.

Probably the only country in which federal-level referendums are common is Switzerland, where voters decide directly on around a dozen issues every year. The alpine country let its citizens vote on an increase in the central bank's gold reserves (failed), a ban on the construction of new minarets (passed) and even the proposal to limit a top earner's salary to 12 times of that of the lowest earner working in the same company (failed).

2. **In Autocratic Systems, Specifically Absolute Monarchies and Dictatorships**

The theoretical difference between an absolute monarchy and a dictatorship is that the leaders of a monarchy are chosen based on heredity. A monarchy's ruling family usually claims the divine right to rule the country, with the written law requiring the nation's leaders to be from the ruling family.

In dictatorships, rulers are selected on a non-hereditary basis. Despite this differentiation, both terms are often used loosely, and several countries fit both definitions to varying extent. North Korea's leader is chosen based on heredity, for instance, and in 2013 the country's laws and the ruling Worker's Party's statutes were amended to require "eternal" leadership by the Kim family. Despite the North-East Asian country's resemblance to an absolute monarchy, it is almost exclusively referred to as a dictatorship by Western media.

Absolute monarchies are not to be confused with constitutional monarchies, which, while sharing a name have delegated all law-making powers to parliament. Prominent constitutional monarchies include the BeNeLux countries, Denmark, Norway, Spain, Sweden, the United Kingdom, and Thailand. On the other hand, there are only six absolute monarchies — Brunei, Oman, Qatar, Saudi Arabia, Vatican City and Swaziland. We may add the United Arab Emirates, which is a federation of seven absolute monarchies (including Dubai and Abu Dhabi) of which the rulers form a national parliament.

In absolute monarchies, laws are passed based solely on the ruler's (and his/her advisors') discretion.

Almost all dictatorships are comprised of a de facto single-party system of which the leader — the dictator — possesses all law-making authority, or depending on the country, shares this power with a small body of party officials. Most dictatorships have national parliaments and even allow the presence of "puppet" opposition parties in order to pretend the existence of political freedoms. Such "rubber-stamp" parliaments exist in various forms in Belarus, China, Cuba, Vietnam and arguably in Singapore. In the past, they were found in Nazi Germany and the Soviet Union. Even North Korea officially allows its citizens to vote for one of three different parties, with the ruling Worker's Party of Kim Jong-Un accounting for about 90% of the parliament's seats. Nonetheless, opposition parties have to pledge allegiance to the ruling party and are members of the "Fatherland Front" — an organization led by the Worker's Party and used to control any opposition.

Making Sense of the Law Making Process

Before asking how to pass laws in a liberty-friendly manner, we should ask ourselves whether introducing new laws is reasonable in the first place.

The 113th US Congress, which lasted for two years from January 3, 2013, to January 2, 2015, enacted a total of 296 laws. Let me ask you: how many of these laws do you recall?

Similarly, have the additional ~3000 laws enacted since 2000 really improved our lives?

The vast majority of these laws are not only unconstitutional but do not comply with the "Law of Liberty" or the principles of liberty. For reference, a link to a constitutional analysis of all recent bills is included in the "Learn More" section at the end of this chapter.

The few laws which actually comply with an individual's "right to be left alone," such as tax decreases or the Airline Deregulation Act signed into law by Jimmy Carter in 1978 are merely reversals of previous unconstitutional government power grabs.

A truly "lean government," based solely on the principles of liberty does not need new laws to be passed. Once government is restructured into an organization whose first priority it is to protect liberty, a precedent is set which limits government to exactly that. Any new laws and regulations — such as tariffs or the regulation of marriage — would only diminish this liberty. The "Law of Liberty" is sufficient to make any new, absolutely necessary policy decisions — without the need of a parliament.

Let us make the hypothetical assumption that in several decades a company will invent a technology that beams humans from one location to another. The invention is new and therefore not 100% safe. From time to time, humans get "lost" in the process of beaming.

From a traditional view, legislators would come up with new regulations restricting the use of the technology, perhaps authorizing its use for animals and objects only, or maybe even banning it outright.

In a "lean government," on the other hand, no new laws are passed — there would be no parliament. Regulating new technologies such as beaming would be relegated to the free market. Most people will be reluctant to "get beamed" in the first place, based on our natural dislike to try out things we are not used to. Of the few who voluntarily sign up for the service, one or two might get missing — fueling a public controversy. Those who are willing to take the risk are free to do so — nobody is forced to be beamed.

In order for the inventor of the technology to recoup his upfront investment, he has to make reliability improvements and potentially partner with other companies to return consumer trust. Once the death rate resulting from beaming falls below that of conventional modes of transport, for example air travel, the technology is likely to become widely accepted by the free market. Technology regulates itself based on the force of customer demand — no big brother is needed!

What if a foreign country attacks us? Even this situation can be dealt with in a way that does not require parliamentary authorization of military power. In a "lean government," a military would continue to exist, but for the sole purpose of defending against foreign intruders. As soon as the US is attacked (as happened in Pearl Harbor), our constitution permits the military to counter-attack — no presidential or parliamentary approval needed. As foreign interventions, such as Nato's attack on Libya, do not conform to the principles of liberty, they should not take place, and no government figure or parliament is needed to make the decision of whether to intervene in far-away conflicts. For more on the military read chapter 10 - International Security.

My point is that a "lean government" — whose objective is to protect its citizens' liberty — does not require the passing of new laws or the presence of a parliament. A piece of legislation which violates the law and principles of liberty, for example a tariff, should not be passed in the first place. And a law which conforms to liberty, e.g., a free speech amendment, would be covered by the "Law of Liberty" underlying the constitution anyway.

It certainly appears extreme to abolish the legislative, including government committees and positions of autocratic rule. Yet this is the only way to prevent new laws that restrict our right "to be left alone" from being passed.

Does this mean we should continue to have a president or cabinet members? Yes, but their duties are different. In a "lean government," these officials do not have the task or power to propose and enact new laws. Instead, it is their sole responsibility to ensure the judiciary's and executive's complacency with the "Law of Liberty." For more on this read chapter 8 - The Judiciary and chapter 9.1 - Police Force.

Illustration 3.1 Government Without Parliament?

The notion of abolishing parliament seems radical, but is essential to preserve liberty. What should we do with the Capitol in Washington D.C.? Sell it to private investors and use the receipts to pay down part of our national debt. Image: kropic, Bigstock

The Legislative, Democracy, and Dictatorships

Any law not in compliance with a human's right "to be left alone" by definition constrains liberty. It does not matter how such a law comes into existence, be it because it represents the personal opinion of a dictator, the view of a committee made up of unelected bureaucrats or the majority of the people.

Democracy is hailed by many in the West as "freedom" — allowing citizens to rule themselves. However in essence, democracy is not different to a dictatorship or single party state. In a dictatorship the opinion of one person counts, and in a single party state that of a small group of officials. In a democracy, the opinion of a group of people which happens to make up more than 50% of the population is considered "sacred."

The 51% could simply rule as a dictatorship, coming up with whatever laws they please, without asking the other 49% for their opinion. Yet by allowing everyone including opponents to vote on issues creates the illusion that the minority has a say in determining its destiny.

Just because a king, a government committee or a random group of people that makes up a majority has a strong opinion, morally speaking, does not entitle them to enforce their views on everyone else.

Liberty makes the assumption that moral values are objective truths, and that every human has the right to determine his or her own life. Any law or regulation, no matter how many support it, violates this unalienable right "to be left alone."

As Benjamin Franklin apparently said (the originator is disputed): "Democracy is two wolves and a lamb voting on what to have for lunch. Liberty is a well-armed lamb contesting the vote."

Regulations That Violate Liberty Are "Institutionalized Discrimination"

Any government order, be it a law or regulation, that does not comply with the right to be left alone represents a form of "institutionalized discrimination."

Take the example of a tariff. Assume steel producing businesses successfully lobby the government to ban cheaper steel imports from China and India. Because many people are wary of job losses, the majority of the population supports the ban.

On the other hand, you have businesses dependent on steel, ranging from car manufacturers to large-scale property developers. It is these businesses, the people they employ and the consumers buying their products that suffer. Car manufacturers face higher production costs, reduced profits and, as a result, lower dividends paid to shareholders and pension funds. Employees whose salaries depend in part on company profits make less disposable income. Consumers have to pay more for cars. The additional money paid to domestic steel producers has to come from somewhere — in this case from regular consumers.

While the ban on Chinese and Indian steel imports *artificially* improved the economic situation of local steel producers, it made domestic steel consumers pay the price. How is this "institutionalized discrimination" of government legislation against a selected portion of the population justified?

Most laws inherently advantage one group of people, while disadvantaging another. If government is meant to represent its citizens equally, how can it discriminate when passing laws?

It does not matter how many people support a piece of legislation. Robbing and murdering others is always wrong, even if it is supported by 51% of the populace.

Ironically, had the proposal to ban foreign steel imports been accompanied by a paragraph on the consequences on steel consumers it would have been unlikely to find widespread support. In this context I highly recommend you to watch a short video on Walmart shoppers, the link to which you can find in the "Learn More" section.

--- Learn More ---

- Database tracking all resolutions passed in Congress and laws enacted. https://www.govtrack.us.

- Constitutional analysis of bills and voting index on congressmen, prepared by the New American magazine http://www.thenewamerican.com/freedom-index.

- [Video] Will Walmart Shoppers Support "Every Day High Wages?" https://www.youtube.com/watch?v=LLr5oWfoWRY

--- Sources ---

1. North Korea's Leadership Succession - "North Korea rewrites rules to legitimise Kim family succession." Audrey Yoo. South China Morning Post. http://www.scmp.com/news/asia/article/1296394/democratic-peoples-monarchy-korea-north-korea-changes-ruling-principles. Retrieved July 28, 2015.

2. Resolutions Passes by Congress - GovTrack. https://www.govtrack.us. Retrieved July 28, 2015.

SPECIAL INTERESTS

CHAPTER 3 - SECTION 2

One important reason why abolishing the legislative is crucial to protecting liberty is the influence of special interests.

In today's America, most if not all bills are lobbied by special interests, ranging from trade unions to corporations and private individuals. Organizations spent more than $3.2 billion on lobbying in 2015 alone, more than twice as much as in 2000.

Almost $500 million in 2012, and another $243 million in the first 6 months of 2013 were spent just on lobbying health care related issues, including amendments to the Affordable Care Act (also known as Obamacare). The stock market was so enthusiastic about mandatory health coverage and government collaboration with major health care providers that gains of the S&P Health Insurance Index outperformed the market by a factor of 2 to 1 in 2013.

Similarly, the TPP (Trans-Pacific Partnership), a trade deal to be enacted between 12 Pacific-rim countries, is advertised to be a simple free trade agreement. However, if this is the case, why does the agreement require thousands of pages? Cannot we simply agree on a 40-word statement like the one I came up with below?

Illustration 3.2 Total US Lobbying Expenditure

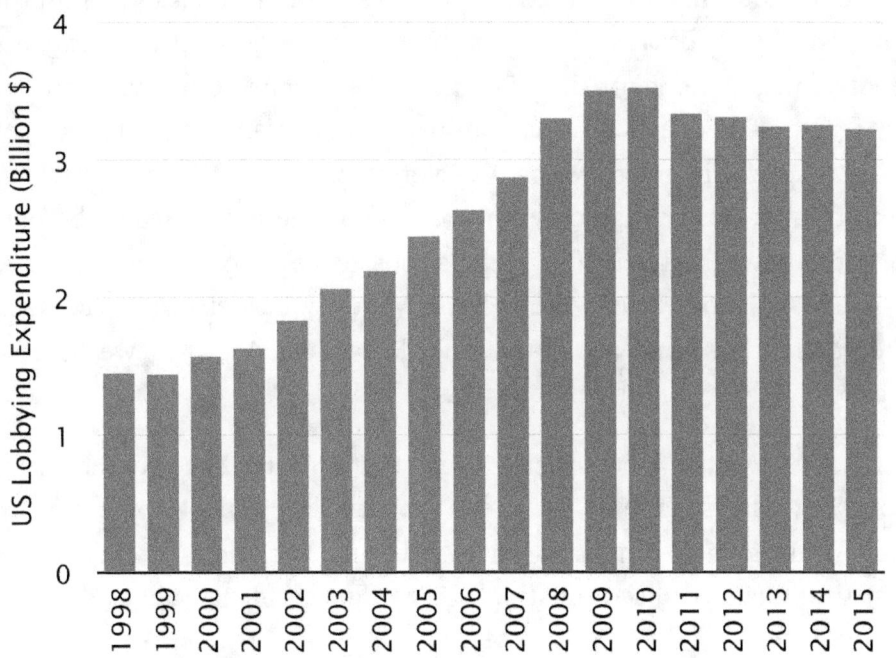

Total US lobbying expenditure skyrocketed by 124% in the 10 years between 2000 and 2010 from $1.57 billion to $3.52 billion, before leveling off. Image: own work by author; data from OpenSecrets.org

"Businesses and individuals residing in TPP member countries have the right to freely trade goods and services with each other, unrestrained by tariffs, government fees, and safety-related regulations. The only goods excluded from this agreement are counterfeit products and weapons."

The problem with the TPP and many other pieces of legislation is that under the guise of a genuine cause, such as free trade, these agreements try to authorize favors for special interests. Special interests want to protect their businesses from competition while ensuring receipts of government subsidies. This is why the TPP (and every other major piece of government legislation) is hundreds, often thousands or in the case of the Affordable Care Act more than 10,000 pages long. Of course, negotiations for the TPP and the Affordable Care Act are done in secret — between a select number of politicians and a few of the largest special interest groups. Everyone not part of the inner circle of government power may only find out about the new taxes to be paid and the new liberty-violating regulations to be followed once a bill is passed. As Nancy Pelosi, Democratic Minority Leader of the House of Representatives, said about the Affordable Care Act "[...] we have to pass the bill so you can find out what is in it [...]."

Any laws written by a special interest group and enacted thanks to lobbying efforts naturally have the intention to benefit some parties, and disadvantage others. As a result, any such laws are forms of "institutionalized discrimination" by the government against some of its citizens.

And as radical as it sounds, the only way to end a system which allows special interests to gain favors on the back of the general public is to abolish the practice of passing new laws altogether, and have government based solely on a fixed set of liberty-based laws.

Billionaires Can Be Socialists

People usually assume that billionaires, by definition, are capitalists. After all, didn't they benefit from the free market to become wealthy in the first place?

This common misconception is due to people's (including billionaires') different views on *who* should enjoy free markets.

Almost everyone — at least those who do not appreciate to be servants to others — wants a "free market" for him- or herself, even socialists. The basic definition of free market simply entails that there is no government involvement in your personal and business life. Everyone wants to enjoy the right to be left alone and freely follow his/her personal beliefs, or engage in economic interactions with the people of one's choice. A person not having the desire to make own decisions would essentially prefer to be controlled by others. And while there are such people out there, they constitute the minority.

However, people differ substantially in their beliefs of whether *others* should have "free market" rights to make their own economic and social decisions. Free market libertarians, for instance, believe that every individual has the right to make his or her own choices as long as they do not infringe on the same right of others or harm people.

Socialists, on the other hand, and totalitarian socialists like Hitler or Stalin in particular, believe that people should not have the right to choose their own way of life. The government is to define what people learn, where people travel, and which mandatory government services they have to buy. Interestingly, it is always the socialists in power — the inner circle of officials for both the National Socialists and Communists — who possess all "rights" and "power" to make up laws as they wish. Socialist leaders can do and live however they feel, say whatever they want and make economic exchanges with whomever they desire. And when government officials are strip-searched by police just like their "subjects," as happened to Indian diplomat Devyani Khobragade in New York, there is a huge outcry. Similarly, US officials preach the importance of strict traffic fines and enforcement while in the US, but could not care less about traffic safety when it comes to them speeding abroad. Between 2003 and 2013 the US Embassy in London, UK alone amassed £8,172,245 in unpaid traffic fines (US$12,5 million at FX £1=

$1.53) based on almost 71,000 individual offenses. This translates to more than 19 fines a day! Thanks to the 1961 Vienna Convention diplomats enjoy immunity and won't be required to pay up anytime soon. As these examples hopefully make clear, government officials love granting "free market" rights and liberty to themselves and their inner circles, while denying everyone else basic freedoms. Note that this does not imply that ignoring traffic rules equals liberty, for a more general discussion about the regulation of personal lifestyles read Chapter 15.3 - Individual Lifestyles.

There are various billionaires (though certainly a minority) who, while insisting on all personal freedoms imaginable for themselves (just like Hitler or Stalin), want to deny the same for everyone else. John D. Rockefeller, founder of Standard Oil (known today as the three separate companies Esso, ExxonMobil, and Chevron) along with his descendants are probably the best example of these "socialist billionaires." By the time he deceased in 1937, his oil empire had become industry dominating through the use of aggressive free market business tactics. He had bought up oil barrels and chemicals required for oil refinery to force competitors out of business. Yet while embracing the free market system for themselves, the Rockefeller family wants to impose socialism on everyone else. The rationale behind this is that once powerful and wealthy, it is easiest for them to keep their wealth and power by:

1. blocking off likely competitors (e.g., other industrialists) through high taxes and regulations

2. using government connections to lobby for the creation of loopholes that protect their own wealth from the adverse effects of the anti-business regulations they just lobbied for.

This is why Rockefeller welcomed anti-trust legislation of the early 20th century: the value of the split-up Standard Oil company was valued two to three times more than the original firm, further increasing his wealth. At the same time, upcoming firms were prevented from ever becoming as dominant as Standard Oil, missing out on economies of scale.

Similarly, the latest Rockefeller to have served in the US Congress — senator John (Jay) Rockefeller of West Virginia, a great-grandson of the oil tycoon — has voted against liberty and in favor of socialism on every imaginable issue. This includes voting to increase taxes on those earning more than $1 million and voting against death tax exemptions. He even voted in favor of repealing previous cuts of the capital gains tax and spending the estimated increase in revenue of $47 billion on the military. As could be expected, Jay Rockefeller also voted against the Bush tax cuts.

The public policy think tank Citizens for Tax Justice (CTJ) rated him as voting in favor of progressive taxation 100% of times. Progressive taxation is a tax system that taxes individuals with higher incomes at disproportionally higher tax rates, and is one of the 10 key demands made by Karl Marx in his Communist Manifesto. The various forms of income taxes will be discussed in more detail in the upcoming chapter 4.2 - Income Tax.

The New American Magazine's "Freedom Index" has assigned him a cumulative score of just 13% for his last 15 years in Congress, labeling him as a congressman with one of the most "unconstitutional" voting patterns.

The Rockefellers are so deeply entrenched in global power politics that the site of the United Nations building in New York was donated by John D. Rockefeller, Jr., the only son of the Standard Oil co-founder. He even went so far as to suggest building the UN headquarter not in Manhattan, but on his private estate known as Kykuit or John D. Rockefeller Estate, located about 30 miles (48 km) northeast of the current UN site. It is naive to think that the family that donated the land of the UN headquarter does not have political influence, which it uses to advance family interests.

There are many apologists of the Rockefeller family, arguing that the tax increases they support and global political influence they possess benefit the less fortunate. Look at any of the Rockefellers' profiles and you will keep seeing them described as "philanthropists." Yet if the Rockefellers are so caring of others as is claimed, why did their family name become synonymous with the ruthless business practices that eliminated countless Standard Oil competitors — and the livelihoods that were dependent on them? Or why did the "philanthropist" John D. Rockefeller Jr. lead the 1914 Ludlow Massacre, which involved setting fire to an accommodation tent of striking workers and the resulting death of 26 people including 11 children?

Free markets and competition are the only force that can lift people out of poverty, as happened in China. Yet John D. Rockefeller famously said that he thinks that "competition is a sin" — except of course when he represents the "competition."

He, the once wealthiest man in the world with an inflation-adjusted net worth of around $350 billion at its height is in favor of free market practices when they benefit his family, but, along with his offspring, does everything in his power to prevent others from amassing similar wealth.

Illustration 3.3 United Nations General Assembly Hall in New York City

As of 2015, the United Nations has 193 member countries. Even North Korea is a UN member. Three prominent countries that have been bared from membership are Kosovo, Morocco-occupied Western Sahara and Taiwan (with the UN officially recognizing the People's Republic of China in place of Taiwan since 1971). The Vatican City and Palestine are non-member observer states. Image: United Nations Official Website

Please do not call a family which uses its wealth to buy politicians and increase taxes on anyone who could become a competitor "capitalist." Capitalism is a belief system that says that anyone should enjoy economic freedom, not just those in power. It is socialism that limits freedoms to the elite. Denying others free market rights is what socialists — be it the Rockefellers or communist dictators — regard as essential in order to enrich themselves on the back of others.

Safety Locks and ISBN Numbers

Special interests flex their power wherever you look. You are probably familiar with the ubiquitous TSA safety locks found on virtually all luggage. TSA locks, while differing slightly in design from luggage to luggage, can be opened with a TSA master key. Did you know that a private company called Travel Sentry developed these locks, and partnered with the US government, specifically the TSA (Transportation Security Administration, an agency of the U.S. Department of Homeland Security), which officially approved their system?

Ever since Travel Sentry has been granted the right to set TSA lock standards, luggage manufacturers worldwide have to ask them for approval of their TSA lock designs. Travel Sentry is the de facto monopolist in a market in which only one other lock company — Safe Skies Luggage Locks — has recently been approved by the TSA. Travel Sentry licensed their locks to virtually all luggage and travel lock producers in the world. Besides the TSA, customs agencies in Canada, Germany, Israel, Japan, the Netherlands, South Korea, and the UK, among others, have started using their patented system.

Imagine the profits generated from a technology which the US government officially made the de facto global lock standard.

The ISBN system (ISBN standing for International Standard Book Number) is similarly controlled by a single, private company — at least in the US. Originally, the ISBN system was developed by the non-governmental International Organization for Standardization (ISO), based in Geneva, Switzerland. Once the numbering system was developed, its administration was passed on to the organization's member countries.

This led to differing processes on how ISBNs are administered and assigned to books. In Canada, for instance, the system is overseen by the government and an author can apply for an ISBN for free.

In the US, the government decided to pass this privilege over to a privately owned company called Bowker, meaning whenever you want to get an ISBN for a book, you need to apply for it through this company. Due to Bowker's monopoly it can charge $125 for a single number, $225 for 10 numbers and $575 for 100 numbers. Large publishing houses may buy numbers in bulk (up to one million), which reduces the ISBN unit cost to fractions of a dollar.

What is the profit margin on a single ISBN? We won't know, as Bowker is private. Though we could estimate it, since, in order to get an ISBN, you merely have to type the title and a description of your book into an online form, which soon afterwards provides you with a computer-generated number.

Whenever government colludes with private businesses, for example, to grant them monopoly status, we have fascism, something everyone should be opposed to. It is fine if a company invents a new type of lock and patents it, but it is not okay for government to use its power to make it the de facto only type of lock their security agents accept.

I often wonder, when you invent a lock, how do you convince the government or, in this case, the TSA to make it the only standard they accept. I bet if you or I tried to call or mail them about our invention we would face nothing but closed doors.

--- Learn More ---

- Locks officially approved by the TSA - http://www.tsa.gov/traveler-information/baggage-locks.

- Bowker, the company which assigns US ISBN numbers - https://www.myidentifiers.com.

--- Sources ---

1. Total Lobbying Expenditure - "Lobbying Database". Open Secrets. http://www.opensecrets.org/lobby/. Retrieved June 26, 2016.

2. Health Care Lobbying - "Health care industry spent $243 million in 2013 lobbying Obamacare." Mike Flynn. Breitbart. http://www.breitbart.com/big-government/2013/09/23/health-care-industry-spent-243-million-already-in-2013-lobbying-obamacare/. Retrieved July 28, 2015.

3. S&P Health Insurance Index Performance in 2013 - "ObamaCare Enriches Only The Health Insurance Giants and Their Shareholders." Robert Lenzner. Forbes. http://www.forbes.com/sites/robertlenzner/2013/10/01/obamacare-enriches-only-the-health-insurance-giants-and-their-shareholders/. Retrieved July 28, 2015.

4. Nancy Pelosi Quotation - Brainyquote. http://www.brainyquote.com/quotes/quotes/n/nancypelos411981.html. Retrieved July 28, 2015.

5. "Parking fines incurred by Diplomatic Missions and International Organisations in the UK." Mark Simmonds. UK Government. https://www.gov.uk/government/speeches/parking-fines-incurred-by-diplomatic-missions-and-international-organisations-in-the-uk--2. Retrieved July 28, 2015.

6. John (Jay) Rockefeller Voting Record - On the Issues. http://www.ontheissues.org/Economic/John_Rockefeller_Tax_Reform.htm/. Retrieved July 28, 2015.

7. New American Magazine Freedom Index - New American Magazine.
    http://www.thenewamerican.com/index.php?
    option=com_content&view=article&id=38&Itemid=828&nameid=R000
    361. Retrieved July 28, 2015.

TAXATION

CHAPTER 4

Chapter 4: Taxation

Let's look at following definition:

"[An] act in which property belonging to another is taken without that person's consent."

Most readers will agree that above statement accurately describes the term taxation. However, this is not the definition for taxes. It is the definition of *theft*.

A common definition of taxation — "a compulsory contribution to state revenue" — sounds less aggressive, yet its essence is the same as that of stealing.

Well, you might argue, taxes are used to support the basic functions of government such as infrastructure, security, and utilities. The state collects taxes to return them back to us in the form of universal services.

But do these circumstances really make a difference to the fact that taxes are a form of forceful expropriation? Imagine Ford Motor Company placing a 10-year-old Focus in front of your garage and, without asking you, deducting a $10,000 bill from your bank account. You may consider this theft, but your friends may tell you that Ford just wants to care for your mobility. The problem: you already own a car and planned to use the $10,000 for a down payment of a new house. Even if you planned to purchase a car from the money, you might have preferred buying a Toyota Corolla rather than a Focus.

If Ford were involved in such practices the company would be charged with theft, yet people continue to find excuses for government officials doing and advocating the same on a daily basis.

Any forced purchase of goods and services which you would not have voluntarily agreed to if you had the chance, reduces your wealth. Be it government provisions such as infrastructure and police or a used Ford being placed on your front yard, if you do not voluntarily engage in an exchange, you value the money you have to give up more than what you receive in return.

Every time a central planner decides what you should get for your earned income your net worth as measured by the total value you place on all your tangible and intangible possessions diminishes. The extent to which government stole from you can be quantified by subtracting the value you place on government services from the taxes you pay. Even when government provisions cost more than what you pay in taxes, central planners may be stealing from you. As long as *you* place less value on the services that you receive than you value your tax dollars, you are being robbed. Let us make this clear through an example. Imagine government takes $100 from you, then borrows an additional $100 from a bank and provides you with $150 worth of horse meat. While the cost of what you get may be more than what was stolen from you, the value *you* place on horse meat is still lower — leaving you with a lower net worth. Now add that you or your children will have to pay back the $100 the government borrowed plus interest, and you will end up losing even more.

If government services were valued more than what people pay in taxes, no force would be needed to collect taxes.

The *forceful* taxes-for-services exchange is worsened by the fact that governments are monopolies, and thus vaporize large portions of the taxes they collect in administration and bureaucracy. Just take what Western media outlets have dubbed the "world's most expensive road." The 25 mile (40 km) road was built at a reported cost of $8.6 billion in the Russian resort town of Sochi, connecting the venues of the 2014 Olympic Winter Games in the mountains with the Olympic sites on the shore of the Black Sea. To put this number in perspective, the road cost the equivalent of the annual GDP of the Bahamas. More accurately speaking, the inefficiencies of the state monopoly do not "vaporize" tax money, but redistribute it to a group of corrupt politicians, corporate cronies and other beneficiaries (such as construction firms).

This is why "taxation" is basically a "euphemism for theft."

--- Sources ---

1. Definition for Theft - West's Encyclopedia of American Law, edition 2. Copyright 2008 The Gale Group, Inc. All rights reserved.

2. Definition for Taxation - New Oxford American Dictionary. Copyright © 2010, 2013 by Oxford University Press, Inc. All rights reserved.

3. World's Most Expensive Road - "Tunnels and tarmac: How to make the "world's most expensive road." Ben Wyatt. CNN. http://edition.cnn.com/2014/02/23/sport/road-expensive-sochi-2014-winter-games/. Retrieved July 28, 2015.

4. Bahamas GDP - "GDP by Country." CIA World Factbook. https://www.cia.gov/library/publications/the-world-factbook/fields/2195.html. Retrieved July 28, 2015.

TYPES OF TAX SYSTEMS

CHAPTER 4 - SECTION 1

Tax systems vary widely by country, one being less fair than the other. Generally speaking, we can categorize all tax systems by two factors: tax incidence & reach. Let's explain them in more detail.

Tax incidence measures the percentage tax on the underlying item (e.g., a car, property, wages), as the value of the underlying item increases. There are three types of tax incidents: progressive (tax rate increases with increasing item value), proportional (tax rate is fixed) and regressive (tax rate decreases with increasing item value).

For example, under a progressive income tax system you will have to pay higher tax rates as your income increases. Under a proportional income tax system your tax rate remains constant, while under a regressive tax system your tax rate decreases as you earn more. Under a regressive system one may be charged a fixed amount of income tax, e.g., $10,000, independent of income. As income rises, the percentage share of the $10,000 as part of total income becomes smaller — reducing the effective tax rate.

Illustration 4.1 outlines the three types of tax incidence, both in terms of the change in the percentage tax rate and the amount of tax paid as the item value (e.g., income) changes.

Illustration 4.1 Types of Tax Systems (right)

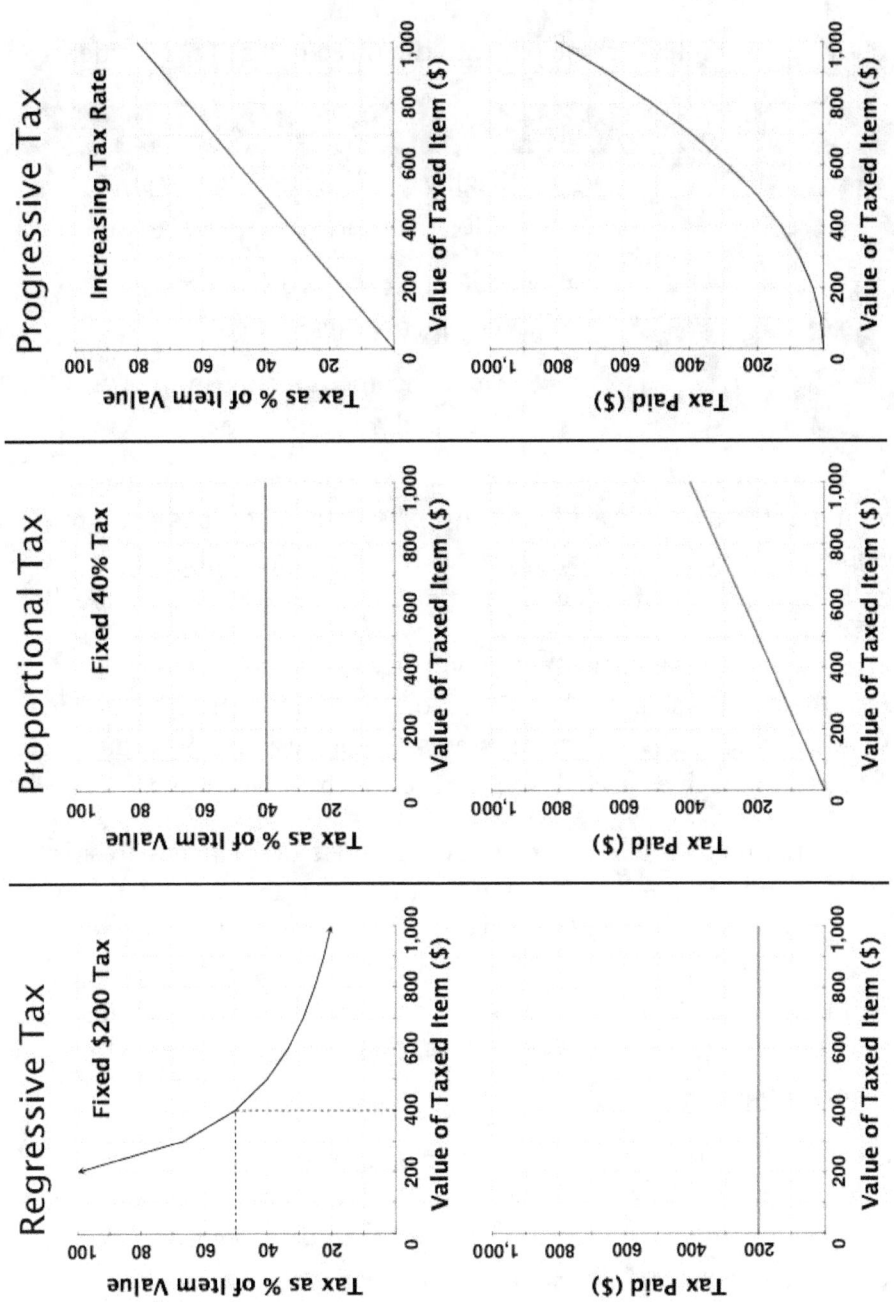

Tax systems are classified by tax rate (top row of diagrams) and amount of tax paid (bottom row of diagrams). Image: own work by author

Chapter 4 - Section 1: Types of Tax Systems

Following examples may help clarify the three types of tax incidence:

Tax Type	Example
Regressive Tax	Highway toll ticket at $10/car, fixed airport departure fee
Proportional Tax	Value-added tax (e.g., 10% of good's value), flat income tax (also called "Fair Tax")
Progressive Tax	Stepped income tax rates in the US and most of Europe

What I refer to as "reach" of the tax system describes the group of people affected (i.e., taxed) by a tax system. There are three types of reach: territorial, residential, and citizenship-based.

Territorial reach means that any activity taking place within the territory of a jurisdiction is taxed. Hong Kong, Singapore, and Panama employ territorial income tax systems. If you reside there, you will not be taxed on income derived from outside their jurisdictions.

Residential reach refers to a country's practice of taxing its "residents." The residential *income* tax system is the most common in the world, used by almost all countries in Asia, Europe, South America as well as Australia, Canada, and New Zealand. If you are resident in one of these countries, your income will be taxed according to local tax rates, irrespective of whether the income was earned inside or outside of the country's borders.

Along with most income tax systems, many value-added tax (VAT) systems fall into this category. In most instances, VAT applies to the products bought by a country's residents, independent of where those goods were bought. For example, US residents have to pay VAT on locally bought goods and services, while tourists residing outside of the country are eligible for VAT refunds. Similarly, US residents purchasing high-value goods in Europe are required to pay customs on any products they bring back home.

The citizenship-based tax system is the least common of the three and practiced only to tax income in the United States and the East-African country of Eritrea (where it is only partly enforced). A citizenship-based income tax system taxes income of its *citizens*, irrespective of whether these reside in the country of citizenship or where the income was earned. Imagine an US-American born in Singapore who has never lived nor stepped a foot onto US territory. Under the US citizenship-based tax system he/she would be obligated to report his/her income to the IRS and may be taxed twice, as at the point of writing there is no income tax treaty between the two countries.

Below matrix visualizes the two categories of tax systems, along with naming prominent examples.

Tax Systems by "Reach"	Tax Systems by Incidence		
	Regressive	Proportional	Progressive
Territorial	Highway Tolls	Hong Kong income tax	Malaysia income tax
Residential	Annual car registration fees	Estonia income tax, most value-added taxes	UK income tax
Citizenship-Based	-	-	US income tax

--- Learn More ---

- A comprehensive list of all countries by their tax system (territorial, residential, citizenship-based) can be found here www.financialfreedomindex.com/international-taxation.html.

- An overview of tax rates, including income-, corporate-, capital gains-, consumption- and inheritance taxes is available on http://www.financialfreedomindex.com/taxation.html

- The official list of countries with which the US has income tax treaties is available here www.irs.gov/Businesses/International-Businesses/United-States-Income-Tax-Treaties---A-to-Z.

Chapter 4 - Section 1: Types of Tax Systems

INCOME TAX

CHAPTER 4 - SECTION 2

The income tax is probably the most controversial of all taxes, not only because it violates the "Law of Liberty" and principles of liberty, but due to its shaky legal ground and unfair progressive implementation in the majority of the world's countries. Let us discuss both these issues in more detail.

1. The US income Tax Is Not Legal

The first US income tax was introduced in 1861 in order to pay for the American Civil War. However, the 3% rate charged on all annual income above $800 (around $21,000 in 2015 USD) was soon repealed after the war was over. The Wilson–Gorman Tariff Act followed in 1894, reducing US import tariffs and in turn introducing the first peacetime income tax. The tax constituted a 2% rate on all annual income above $4,000 (around $110,000 in 2015 USD).

Our current income tax system originates from the Sixteenth Amendment to the US Constitution, adopted on February 3, 1913. The Sixteenth Amendment reads:

"congress shall have power to lay and collect taxes on incomes, from whatever source derived, without apportionment among the several States, and without regard to any census or enumeration."

Upon introduction, income tax rates ranged from 0% to 7%, but were soon raised, reaching a top rate of 15% in 1916, and a whopping 67% in 1917. In 1918, the rate further increased to 77%. Numerous tax decreases and increases later we are left with our current progressive income tax rates.

There are numerous arguments why critics deem the US government's collection of income taxes unconstitutional. Let us address the main talking points below:

A. Wages Are Not Income

This concept argues that wages are merely what workers receive in exchange for their time. Time is a gift from our Creator. When we work, we "exchange" this gift for money — in the form of wages.

Why should we pay a tax on a gift that we exchange for something else? The exchange itself, or what we call "earning wages," does not result in the use of government services, and should therefore not be taxed to fund them. The principle of causation states that government provisions should be financed directly on a usage basis, for example, through tolls for roads and voluntary social security contributions for those that opt-in to a government pension scheme.

Because some people naturally prefer leisure time, and others exchanging time into money, those with long working hours and high incomes are not necessarily better off than those with short hours and low salaries, and vice versa. Everyone is free to decide for himself/herself how much time to exchange for money. If time and money can be freely exchanged, why do we tax people who exchange their time for dollars, but not those who value leisure time more than a high salary?

Either income taxes are replaced by usage taxes, or people earning wages are charged the same taxes as those with lots of free time.

In this context, the income tax arguably taxes an individual's existence, whether one uses public services or not.

Instead it is argued that "real" income consists of proceeds from rent, capital gains (profits) and corporate profits — everything that does not originate from a mere exchange of a gift from our Creator.

B. Progressive Income Taxes Are Discriminatory

The progressive income tax system used in the US and most other Western countries taxes those with high incomes at higher rates. Why this is unfair will be discussed shortly. As a result of being discriminatory to high-income earners, it has been suggested that the income tax violates the Fourteenth Amendment, which guarantees every citizen equal treatment before the law.

C. The Income Tax Law

Some claim that the Sixteenth Amendment was never correctly ratified by all states. In this context, the proclamation "Show me the Law" has become synonymous with the tax-resistor movement. Their argument is that there is no law demanding citizens to pay an income tax.

These three and dozens of additional arguments would require a separate book to be discussed properly. For your reference, here are some details on the two opposing sides:

1. Irwin Schiff is a prominent proponent of the income tax protestor movement. He was sentenced to prison in a show-trial — based on tax evasion charges — in which the judge denied him the right to present his extensive collection of evidence. Schiff outlines his arguments in his book "The Federal Mafia - How the Government Illegally Imposes and Unlawfully Collects Income Taxes." He has made the book free for download as PDF on his website http://www.paynoincometax.com/federalmafia.htm, where you will also find detailed documentation on his trial.

2. The IRS has prepared a list of numerous anti-income tax arguments and rebuttals. Be warned that this list includes many, but not all anti-tax arguments and be vigilant when assessing the validity of the IRS's rebuttals. The PDF document can be found here http://www.irs.gov/pub/irs-utl/friv_tax.pdf.

Furthermore, it should be mentioned that numerous authors have discussed the "coincidence" of Congress having passed the federal income tax and the Federal Reserve Act in the same year of 1913. It is claimed that the main purpose of the income tax was to generate additional revenue to allow the government to pay interest to the newly established Fed. The creation of a central bank barred Congress from minting interest-free money and required it to issue interest-paying treasury notes instead.

Contrary to this argument, in fiscal year 2015 the US government paid "only" 229.2 billion in interest on outstanding debt, compared to the 1,478 billion it collected in individual income taxes. Nonetheless, it should be noted that the federal government currently enjoys historically low interest rates. Interest payments would increase significantly, if interest rates rose to the long-term average.

2. The Progressive Implementation of the Income Tax Is "Unfair"

Imagine three triplets, born on the same day, to the same parents. All three enjoyed the same upbringing and education. After having completed high school, the three take up the same jobs as mechanics.

The difference between the three is how many hours they are prepared to work. As a result, they earn very different incomes:

Triplet	Working Hours / Week	Annual Income ($20/h)
One	25	$26,000
Two	40	$41,600
Three	80	$83,200

All three decide to purchase condominiums next to each other in a new three-apartment complex.

After several years, the roof starts leaking. The three decide to have it repaired at a cost of $10,000. The question is how they should split the cost. There are three options, all of them mirroring the three types of tax incidence we discussed earlier:

A. Regressive Tax System / Tax Incidence

This type of tax system is by far the most straightforward and "fair." It follows the principle of causation in that it assumes that every taxpayer should only pay for the services he or she consumes. In our example, the benefit of repairing a leaky roof which covers all three apartments clearly benefits all three of the triplets equally. As a result of each of them receiving a third of the benefit, everyone contributes $3,333 or 1/3 to the cost of the repair.

The reason why this system is called "regressive" is because the higher the income of the (tax)payer, the lower is his effective *tax rate*, as shown in following table.

Triplet	(Tax)Payment	Annual Income	Effective Tax Rate
One	$3,333	$26,000	12.8% (3,333/26,000*100%)
Two	$3,333	$41,600	8.0%
Three	$3,333	$83,200	4.0%

While the higher effective tax rate for lower income people may seem "unfair" at first, it is the direct result of lower income and in this case personal work habits — not because low-income earners pay a higher absolute amount of tax.

Similarly, imagine two siblings with the same background earning different salaries as a result of their different work ethic. Sibling one earns $50,000 a year, sibling two earns $100,000. Both decide to buy a Chevrolet Malibu at $25,000. As a result of their different income, the cost of the car represents 50% of the first sibling's earnings and just 25% of the second sibling's income. Is it fair that the first sibling pays a higher percentage of his income on the car? — Of course! Again, the reason why the car makes up a larger percentage of the first sibling's income is because of his poorer work ethic. The absolute price of $25,000 is the same for both. If the first sibling wants to be able to afford more, he has to work more, just like his brother.

B. Proportional Tax System

Under the proportional tax system, every triplet pays the same percentage amount of his income for the repair of the roof. Let us calculate that rate based on the repair's $10,000 cost. $10,000 makes up 6.63% of the total income of the three, which is $150,800. We use this flat tax rate to charge the siblings. 6.63% of the first triplet's income of $26,000 is $1,724 and so on as shown in below table.

Triplet	Annual Income	(Tax) Payment
One	$26,000	$1,724
Two	$41,600	$2,759
Three	$83,200	$5,517
TOTAL	$150,800	$10,000
COST OF REPAIR	$10,000	
(TAX) RATE	6.63%	

The proportional tax system is less fair than the regressive tax system because although all three siblings receive the same benefit from the roof repair, those with higher income pay more. To collect the $10,000 for the roof repair, with the condition that everyone pays the same (tax)rate, the first triplet has to pay just $1,724, while his high-income brother chips in three times as much at $5,517.

The absurdity of this system becomes clear when looking at a hypothetical situation where everything we have to pay for — not just military defense, infrastructure, and government welfare etc. — was priced according to a flat rate based on income. Let us assume a car was priced at 25% of an individual's annual income. This would mean that however much you work, whether it is just one hour per year earning you a total of $10, or thousands of hours, earning you $100,000, you would always be able to afford the car. The first individual in our example would pay just $2.50 for the vehicle (25% of $10) while our high-income earner would pay $25,000.

Now assume all goods including food and apartments were priced at fixed rates of income. Working overtime would be senseless, as the amount you make in additional income will be required to pay for the proportional increase in prices for the goods you consume.

The proportional tax system is the equivalent of the "flat tax" or "fair tax" often advocated by fiscal conservatives. The reason why it is called "fair" despite its shortcomings is that it appears reasonable compared to the worst of all tax systems — progressive taxation.

C. Progressive Tax System

Under a progressive tax system, the tax rate increases as an individual's or company's income increases. These tax rate increases or tax brackets, as they are properly called, are arbitrary and have changed much over the last hundred years, ranging from 0% to 93.6%.

We will apply (arbitrary) progressive tax rates to our triplets to pay for the roof repair as outlined in following table.

Under our progressive tax system, the first triplet contributes nothing to the repair, while the third sibling shoulders almost 80%. The reason why this tax system is the least fair and most absurd is that working less and earning less effectively increases your purchasing power.

In comparison, under the proportional tax system purchasing power remains constant, while under the regressive system purchasing power decreases with lower income.

Triplet	Annual Income	Progressive Tax Rate (Arbitrarily Chosen)	Tax Paid
One	$26,000	0%	$0
Two	$41,600	5%	$2,080
Three	$83,200	9.52%	$7,920
TOTAL			$10,000

If all goods and services were priced based on the progressive system, a car may cost 50% of income for a high-income earner, but only 20% for a low-income person. As a result, an individual earning less could actually afford to buy more cars than a high-income earner in a pure progressive system.

The progressive income tax is the reason why the top 10% in the US pay 68% of all federal income taxes, while only earning 45% of all income. In comparison, the bottom 50% merely pay 3% of all federal income taxes, but make 12% of national income.

Summary

Income taxes are a violation of the "Law of Liberty," the principle of causation and voluntaryism.

The progressive income tax, in particular, screams of injustice, allowing people with less income to "buy" more than those with higher incomes.

A discussion on progressive taxation would be incomplete without mentioning its brainchild — Karl Marx. While income taxes have existed in some form or another for thousands of years — ranging from Mesopotamia to the feudal systems of Europe — Marx made it popular to tax high-income earners at higher rates. He also listed the progressive income tax as one of the ten planks of communism — set out in his "Communist Manifesto" of 1848.

Do we really want to run our government based on an ideology which failed everywhere it was implemented?

The notion of using the proportional or progressive systems to price cars or real estate is absurd, so why is it accepted to use progressive taxation to price government services?

If we were to return to the federal government's spending level of the year 1985, we could eliminate the individual income tax *and* reduce the budget deficit.

In 1985, the federal government spent $946.3 billion or 2,098.8 billion in 2015 dollars. This compares to our 2015 spending level of $3,758.6 billion — an inflation-adjusted spending increase of $1,659.7 billion. In 2015 the federal government collected $1478.1 billion in income taxes. This means if we returned to the inflation-adjusted spending level of 1985, saving us $1,659.7 billion annually, we could scrap the individual income tax *and* reduce our annual budget deficit by $181.6 billion.

Cut spending down to Ronald Reagan's level and we can easily afford axing income taxes and the reduction of the federal budget deficit.

--- Learn More ---

- Calculate your effective tax rate based on the year between 1913 and 2012. http://qz.com/74271/income-tax-rates-since-1913/.

- Does the US meet 90% of Karl Marx's Demands? - http://www.wnd.com/2011/07/319117/.

- The effect of rising interest rates on the federal debt - http://www.thefiscaltimes.com/Articles/2014/01/08/Rising-interest-rates-will-slam-Federal-Budget.

- [Video] The Progressive Income Tax: A Tale of Three Brothers - https://www.youtube.com/watch?v=S6HEH23W_bM.

--- Sources ---

1. US Constitution - Archives.gov. http://www.archives.gov/exhibits/charters/constitution_transcript.html. Retrieved July 28, 2015.

2. US Historical Income Tax Rates - TaxFoundation.org. http://taxfoundation.org/article/us-federal-individual-income-tax-rates-history-1913-2013-nominal-and-inflation-adjusted-brackets. Retrieved July 28, 2015.

3. "Top 10 Percent of Earners Paid 68 Percent of Federal Income Taxes." The Heritage Foundation. http://www.heritage.org/federalbudget/top10-percent-income-earners. Retrieved July 28, 1015.

4. Inflation Calculator - US Bureau of Labor Statistics. http://www.bls.gov/data/inflation_calculator.htm. Retrieved July 28, 2015.

5. Fiscal Year 2015 Federal Government Revenues - USGovernmentRevenue.com. http://www.usgovernmentrevenue.com/year_revenue_2015USbn_16bs1n_1011G0#usgs302. Retrieved July 28, 1015.

6. Federal Government Spending by Year - USGovernmentRevenue.com. http://www.usgovernmentspending.com/total_1985USmt_16ms5n. Retrieved July 28, 1015.

CONSUMPTION TAX

CHAPTER 4 - SECTION 3

A consumption tax — depending on country also known as value-added tax (VAT) and goods and sales tax (GST) — usually refers to a flat tax rate applied to all final sales. Tariffs and excise duties are similar, with the main difference being that tariffs apply to imported goods and excise duties are paid on special groups of goods, such as cigarettes and luxury goods.

Proponents of the abolishment of the income tax often suggest to account for any tax revenue shortfalls by increasing consumption taxes, tariffs, and excise duties.

The reason why many libertarians including Ron Paul are in favor of consumption taxes is their assumption that an individual's level of consumption of goods and services is proportional to one's use of public resources. According to theory, this makes consumption taxes comply with the "Principle of Causation." Consumption taxes also try to approximately link the timing of when taxes are paid (when the good or service is paid for) with the moment public resources are used (e.g., when a good is produced and transported). This allows an individual with high income (but low consumption) to pay less in taxes than an individual with the same or slightly lower income, but with higher levels of consumption.

Nonetheless, assuming that every individual spends about the amount one earns in one's lifetime (with variations in the timing of spending), tax revenues generated through consumption taxes are merely delayed, not reduced, compared to income taxes. When comparing a 20% income tax with a 20% consumption tax, for example, an individual would either spend the 20% in tax upfront under an income tax regime, or spend the same taxes over time as all income is eventually spent on consumption. As all income is spent at some point, the revenue generated from a 20% income tax equals the revenue generated from a 20% consumption tax (ignoring the time value of money, i.e., the fact that the government may earn interest on taxes it collected earlier).

A frequently cited advantage of consumption taxes is that they are much more difficult to avoid than income taxes, thus also making foreign visitors, the unemployed, and illegal immigrants pay for the public resources they use. They also allow someone planning to retire in a foreign country to pay fewer taxes in the country in which he/she lives and works at the moment.

While consumption taxes are "fairer" than income taxes in that they try to link tax payments with the use of public resources, they are not perfect. The main downside is the fact that they merely "try" to link taxes with public resource use — something that does not always work, especially in today's mostly service-based economies. For example, is a more expensive car, say a BMW, really linked to the use of more public resources than an economy car, say a Toyota Corolla? If not, why should the BMW buyer pay several times the amount of consumption tax than the Corolla owner?

Furthermore, the production and consumption of many products and services are hardly linked to the use of public resources, if at all. For example, assume you hire somebody online to build you a website. Should you pay consumption tax on that? There is no increase in the use of public resources when a person builds the website for you, compared to you taking your own time to complete the task. Both scenarios result in the same economic activity, and use the same level of public resources. Yet in one case you have to pay a tax while in the other case you don't.

While sharing many attributes with the proportional income tax, consumption taxes have the advantage to make illegal immigrants and tourists pay. However, the problem of linking actual tax payments with the use of public services — in accordance with the principle of causation — persists.

Chapter 4 - Section 3: Consumption Tax

PROPERTY TAX

CHAPTER 4 - SECTION 4

Property taxes are usually charged based on a percentage value of the underlying piece of real estate. They tend to be collected by municipal governments and are used to finance local schools, public services such as the police and fire services as well as local infrastructure including roads and the sewage system. If property owners owe property-, income- or any other taxes, the government is free to seize their property.

Property taxes violate both the principle of causation and arguably the US Constitution. Let us look at both these issues in detail:

1. Property Taxes Defy the Principle of Causation

According to the principle of causation, government services should be paid for by those who use them. Property taxes may be an easily manageable way to share the bill for public resources, but are they fair?

The following non-exhaustive overview lists services paid for by property taxes and the factors determining their level of use.

Type of Service/Cost	Used/Caused by	Cost Factor / Unit
Education (School, College)	Children/Students	Number of Students
Fire Services	People Causing Fires/ Accidents	Number of Fires/ Accidents
Police	Troublemakers/ Criminals	Violations/Crimes
Road Provision and Services	Vehicle Drivers, Pedestrians	Mi/Km Driven + Basic Maintenance
Sewage Disposal	Residents	Gallons/Liters of Sewage

The main problem of property taxes is that the valuation of real estate, based on which property taxes are charged, is only vaguely, if at all, correlated to the usage of government services.

Let us take following example. Imagine two families, both with the same annual income and the same number of children. Both families live next to each other, the first family residing in a more expensive house than the other. Due to the different home values, the first family pays twice the property tax than the second. How is this fair? After all, each of the families sends two children to the same school, and uses public resources such as the sewage system and police to the same extent.

According to the demographic-economic paradox, as a country accumulates more wealth, its fertility rate — measured in births per thousand women — decreases. The same is the case for families within a country. Low-income families get more children, earlier in life. As shown in the following chart, the birth rate is highest for households with an annual income below $10,000, at 98.3 births per 1,000 women per year. Families with household income above $75,000, on the other hand, have the lowest birth rate at just 54.8 births.

Illustration 4.2 Birth Rates Decrease With Increasing Household Income

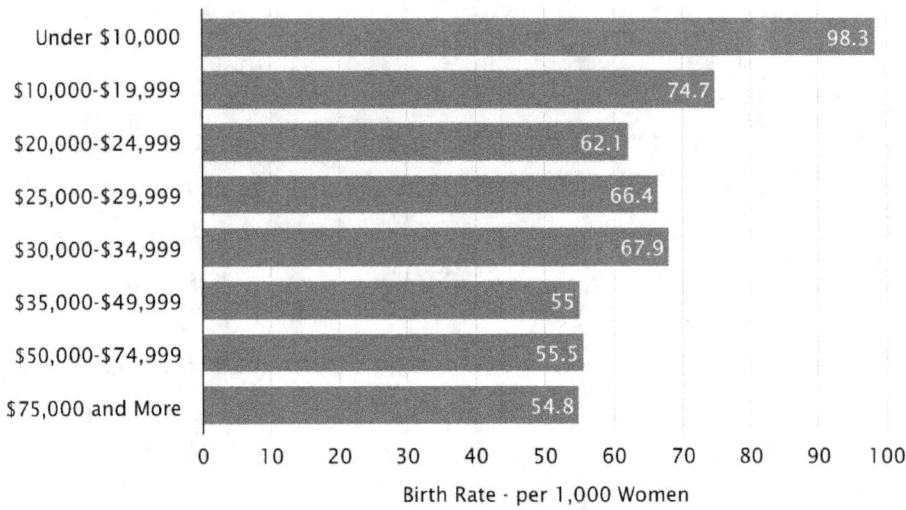

Image: own work by author; data from Statista.com

Families with higher income naturally reside in more expensive properties, even though their average household size is smaller. As property taxes are based on property value and size, depending on region, and not the number of residents, smaller households end up paying more in absolute and per-capita terms.

Furthermore, the most expensive properties are often owned as secondary homes, with their owners using them only a few times a year. Yet these are the properties on which local governments charge the highest property taxes — contrary to intuition that taxes should be paid in accordance with usage of public utilities.

The same is the case for vacant properties held by their owners for investment purposes. If an apartment or house is unused, why should its owner pay taxes for local public schools, the sewage system or — in case the property is located in a gated community — for police and local roads?

Illustration 4.3 More Expensive House - Higher Property Taxes

Why should you pay higher property taxes on the same piece of land just because you built a more expensive house, assuming the number of residents stays the same? Image: Franck Boston, Bigstock

Property Taxes in Washington D.C.

Washington D.C. sets property taxes for vacant properties at more than five times the rate (5%) for regular residential real estate (0.85%). D.C. obviously wants to discourage out-of-town property investors, but why? Reducing the number of investors may sound good for locals, but it really is not. Imagine a new property developer planning to build an apartment complex. For any unit that is not handed over to a buyer from day one of completion (which is the norm), the property firm will have to pay the 5% property tax rate. As a result, fewer property developers will start construction, leading to less supply of real estate, higher prices and, on average, older units in the market. Even if discouraging property investment would financially help locals, any benefits gained by local residents would equal the losses experienced by other investors. It is the government's job to protect property rights, not to pick winners and losers in the property market.

Illustration 4.4 Paying Property Taxes for Abandoned Houses

Nobody wants to invest in the well-known $1-houses in Detroit because the city decided to calculate property taxes not based on purchase price, but a government valuation. Property taxes for abandoned houses like the ones shown here — located not far from downtown Detroit — may be as much as $5,000 to $10,000 per year. Image: own work by author

2. Property Taxes May Violate the US Constitution's Fifth Amendment

The Fifth Amendment states that government should not:

"deprive [a person] of life, liberty, or property, without due process of law; nor shall private property be taken for public use, without just compensation."

The Amendment can be interpreted widely, with some arguing that property taxes are a violation of the principle that people should not be deprived of their property. A property tax, over the long term, results in the entire value of the land or house being redistributed to the government, with the property owner being forced to pay a percentage of the real estate's value every year.

On the other hand, there are those who argue that while the property tax is a form of deprivation, it occurs under "due process of law," as required by the Constitution. Due to the vague wording of the Amendment, the government would theoretically be free to take all people's property, as long as it complies with the law.

We know that in 1796, one year before George Washington stepped down as President of the United States, local governments in 14 out of the 15 US states taxed property. So even if property taxes are constitutional, what they appear to be, they also have been supported or at least tolerated by the Founding Fathers.

Conclusion

The main reason why people acquire real estate is to free themselves from rent. However, mostly in part due to property taxes property owners often end up paying almost as much in taxes, homeowner association (HOA) fees, and other maintenance expenses as they would pay in rent. How can a government which prides itself to protect "liberty" tax (and thus punish) the ownership of property?

Whether the Founding Fathers supported them or not, property taxes violate the principle of causation and as a result liberty. They should be replaced by other means to finance public services — in ways we will discuss in the upcoming chapters.

--- Learn More ---

- Interesting discussion on the demographic-economic paradox and whether it still holds true http://www.economist.com/node/14164483.

- The official list of countries with which the US has income tax treaties is available here www.irs.gov/Businesses/International-Businesses/United-States-Income-Tax-Treaties---A-to-Z.

--- Sources ---

1. US Constitution - Archives.gov. http://www.archives.gov/exhibits/charters/constitution_transcript.html. Retrieved July 28, 2015.

2. US Birth Rate by Household Income - Statista.com. http://www.statista.com/statistics/241530/birth-rate-by-family-income-in-the-us/. Retrieved July 28, 2015.

3. Property Taxes in 1796 - "Taxation in American Cities and Towns, 1888." Ely, Richard T. Page 116-127.

4. Washington D.C. Property Tax - "Real Property Tax Rates." Office of Tax and Revenue. DC.Gov. http://otr.cfo.dc.gov/page/real-property-tax-rates. Retrieved July 28, 2015.

CONCLUSION

CHAPTER 4 - SECTION 5

Taxes are inherently opposed to the "Law of Liberty," the principle of causation and voluntaryism. In order to comply with liberty and everyone's "right to be left alone" we should replace the current tax-based system of government with one based solely on the principle of causation — pay-as-you-go style.

How this is to be achieved depends on the specific tax and the services they currently finance.

The following chapters will discuss the most important government services currently financed through taxes — ranging from welfare to infrastructure, to education, the police, the judiciary, and defense.

Keep in mind that there are many ways government services can be reformed. For this reason, most chapters on government provisions outline a number of possible reforms, ranging from realistic and mostly uncontroversial to idealistic and far-reaching. Reforming government is a complicated process, with many people being opposed to change. And while this book on one side covers realistic approaches to how we can make government more liberty-friendly, it also intends to outline how a purely libertarian world may look like.

Chapter 4 - Section 5: Conclusion

SOCIAL WELFARE

CHAPTER 5

Generally speaking, social welfare is "any government system that provides monetary assistance to people with an inadequate or no income." Social welfare programs vary from country to country and may include pensions, unemployment benefits, health insurance, and assistance to the poor. In the US, the similar term "Social Security" is used to refer specifically to financial benefits provided to retirees.

The United States has one of the most complex social welfare systems in the world. As of 2011, there were 79 means-tested welfare programs which cost the federal government $929 billion per year, including $210 billion allocated by Congress to the states. The Social Security and Medicare programs cost an *additional* $1.25 trillion according to a 2013 Heritage Foundation report.

The combined social welfare spending of $2.3 trillion allocated by Congress made up around 62% of the federal government's 2013 budget of $3.684 trillion. US welfare programs can be categorized into following four groups:

1. **Pensions:** The "Old-Age, Survivors, and Disability Insurance (OASDI)," commonly referred to as "Social Security" was introduced by Franklin Delano Roosevelt in 1935. The program was developed to support elderly people which lacked family support and failed to secure places in so-called "poor houses."

2. **Unemployment Insurance:** The amount of unemployment benefits and the period for which they are paid largely vary by country. In the US, unemployment insurance is sometimes included under the umbrella term "Social Security."

3. **Health Care:** About 60-65% of health care provisions and spending in the US are covered by government programs, including

Medicare, Medicaid, TRICARE, the Children's Health Insurance Program, and the Veterans Health Administration.

- Medicare is a public health insurance system targeted for those aged 65 and above as well as the disabled.

- Medicaid is a subsidy program provided to low-income people and meant for medications and health-related services.

- TRICARE is another US-specific program providing civilian health care benefits to military personnel and their dependents.

- The Affordable Care Act (Obamacare) requires every US resident to acquire health insurance. Health care plans may be purchased directly from a private insurance provider, or through one of the health care marketplaces set up by the government. On the marketplaces, individuals can buy pre-approved health care plans from private insurance companies. This system is different to many European countries like the UK and Germany, where the government itself is a provider of health care through government-owned insurance companies like the NHS in the UK. Nonetheless, individuals may still purchase private health insurance.

4. **Means-Tested Programs:** As mentioned before, means-tested social programs include at least 79 different schemes. The "means-tested" rule requires recipients to show that they pass one or more requirements in order to qualify for a benefit. Means-tested programs include public housing subsidies, food stamp programs, child benefits, school lunches, educational grants and energy subsidies provided to low-income families.

Insurances Versus Subsidies

Broadly speaking, we can categorize social welfare programs into insurances and subsidies.

Insurances such as pension plans ("Social Security" in the US) and health insurance are usually mandatory for all employees. Employees (often in combination with their employers) pay monthly dues to become eligible for insurance payouts should one reach old age or get sick. In the US, Social Security as well as unemployment insurance are mostly paid for through payroll taxes, while health insurance coverage is paid for through monthly premiums by the insured individual.

Subsidies, which include many of the means-tested programs in the US such as food stamps and public housing allowances, are paid out directly to qualifying recipients. Their difference to insurances is that recipients are not first required to pay into the system to get covered.

The Libertarian Perspective

Let us look at the ways welfare programs violate libertarian principles:

Welfare Insurances:

1. **Voluntaryism** - Most if not all government-promoted insurance schemes ranging from pensions to health insurance are mandatory, forcing people to buy a service even if they prefer not to. This application of force is a direct violation of the "No-Force Principle," also called voluntaryism.

2. **Principle of Causation** - The way people pay into public insurance schemes is not correlated to how benefits are received. We will look at this in more detail in the following sections.

Welfare Subsidies:

1. **Voluntaryism** - The "No-Force Principle" is violated because various forms of taxes are used to redistribute income from productive people to those which are subsidized. This redistribution of income is involuntary and accordingly indistinguishable from theft as discussed in chapter 4 - Taxation.

2. **Principle of Causation** - Even more prevalent for subsidies than for insurance schemes is the disconnect between who pays for the benefits — taxpayers — and who receives it — usually those paying little to no income taxes.

In the following four sections, we will look in more detail at the various welfare systems, how they violate liberty and how to reform them in accordance with everyone's "right to be left alone."

Illustration 5.1 Welfare and the Elderly

Most welfare spending is meant to help the elderly. However, retires can just be as well off under a privatized welfare system as will be shown in chapter 5.1. Image: monkeybusinessimages, Bigstock

--- Sources ---

1. Definition for Social Security - New Oxford American Dictionary. Copyright © 2010, 2013 by Oxford University Press, Inc. All rights reserved.

2. "Examining the Means-tested Welfare State: 79 Programs and $927 Billion in Annual Spending." Robert Rector. Heritage Foundation. http://budget.house.gov/uploadedfiles/rectortestimony04172012.pdf. Retrieved July 28, 2015

PENSIONS

Government-run pension schemes are common in most Western countries. America's government pension scheme is known as "Social Security."

In this section, we will first look at how mandatory pension schemes violate liberty, before discussing how to reform them.

Mandatory government pension schemes result in following moral hazards:

1. Most Pension Plans Are Mandatory

While it is understandable — at least to some extent — why one is forced to financially contribute to causes such as defense and infrastructure spending, this cannot be said for pension plans. Defense and infrastructure benefit everyone in some form or another, yet the pension system is meant for individuals to first pay in and in return get fixed monthly payments later in time.

Why is everyone forced to be covered by a pension scheme, especially if one prefers to save his/her "retirement money" in one own's bank account? As outlined before, forced purchases such as pension insurance are a form theft. If you are covered by Social Security *against your will,* which may or may not be the case, it is likely that you value your pension benefits less than your contributions.

It is often said that pension plans were invented for those who lack the discipline to plan ahead for retirement and save enough money for the future. Yet why should those who are disciplined enough to care for themselves be treated the same — and as a result be *punished* for other people's lack of organization?

When one has the choice not to enroll in a pension scheme and fails to save enough money for retirement, it is one's own problem. Just because some people I do not even know have never put in the effort to learn how to budget, does not entitle the government to manage *my* retirement savings. Otherwise, my fiscal responsibility would entitle the government to force everyone not to get any form of pension. I do not have the right to prevent others from signing up for a pensions scheme, nor do others have a right to force me to get one.

Similarly, the argument that everyone is part of a "social contract" to care for one another is bogus. I never agreed to or signed a social contract, making any such "illusive" contract invalid according to contract law.

2. Your Pension Contributions Do Not Match Your Benefits

Completely contrary to the "Principle of Causation," those people who pay significantly more in Social Security taxes only receive fractions back in benefits. Similarly to the progressive income tax system, high-income earners receive fewer pension benefits for every tax dollar than low-income people.

High income and low-income earners alike are taxed a flat 6.2% of their income in the form of payroll taxes, with an additional 6.2% being contributed by employers. This means that as income increases, Social Security taxes increase proportionally. However, increasing income will result in a less than proportionate rise in benefits. To be exact, one will receive 90% of monthly income up to $826 in monthly benefits, 32% of monthly income between $826 and $4890 and just 15% of any income above $4890.

The progressive income tax system taxes higher incomes at higher rates, while keeping benefit levels in the form of defense and infrastructure the same. The Social Security system, on the other hand, taxes proportionally, while progressively reducing benefit rates at higher incomes.

This is best shown through following diagram, which illustrates that any increases in pre-retirement income (x-axis) result in ever lower increases in benefits (y-axis)

Illustration 5.2 Relationship Between Pre-Retirement Earnings and Social Security Benefits (US)

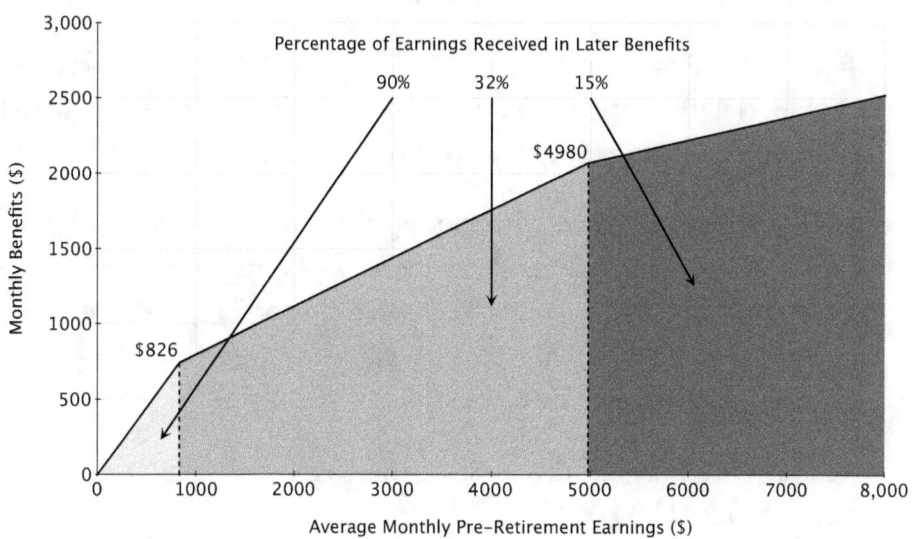

People with low incomes get 6 times as many benefits (90%) out of every additional $1 income they earn than high-income earners (15%). Image: own work by author; data from the Social Security Administration

3. Many Are Better off Placing Their Money in Savings Accounts

The Social Security system is used to redistribute money from high-income earners to the poor — not to "help" people save for their retirement. A study by the Urban Institute has calculated and compared Social Security taxes paid and benefits received for average-wage earners. A single male earning the average wage (44,600 2012 dollars) and retiring in 2030 will receive $65,000 fewer benefits than he paid in Social Security taxes. If this individual is female, the difference between taxes and benefits equals a "personal deficit" of $40,000.

The same is true for two-earner couples, with both earning the average wage. Upon retirement, their combined benefits are $125,000 less than what they paid in.

If you earn above the average $44,600, the "loss" you experience from Social Security increases exponentially, as every additional dollar spent in Social Security taxes results in fewer future benefits.

While the Urban Institute has not provided figures for high-income singles, they estimated numbers for a two-earner couple with one person earning the average wage and the other person earning above average at $71,400 per year. The estimated "loss" of such a couple equals a whopping $225,000.

We can only imagine the losses suffered by a couple where each partner makes $300,000.

It turns out that if you make significantly less than average, you will receive slightly more in benefits than you paid in. A couple retiring in 2030, with one person making the average wage and the other one earning $20,000 per year will receive $8,000 more in Social Security benefits than they paid in taxes.

For the majority of people retiring in the decades ahead, saving Social Security contributions in a personal savings account or even in cash under a mattress would turn out to be more favorable than paying into the system. The reason for the discrepancy between taxes and benefits lies mainly in older generations currently "raiding" the system at the cost of future generations, as will be outlined under point 8.

4. **Work More - Pay More**

The legal retirement age in the US ranges from 62 to 66 (increasing to 67 for those born in 1960 and later). Should you decide to retire at full retirement age (currently 66), you will receive the full amount of the scheduled monthly retirement payments. Retirement at an earlier age (earliest at 62 years) will reduce monthly benefit receipts.

For those deciding to apply for pension payments early, for example at age 62, while continuing to work, the government reduces benefits by $1 for every $2 earned. This means if you earn $1,500 per month, your benefits will be cut by an additional $750 compared to those who choose not to work and receive benefits early. This "rule" exposes the pension system's intention to assist poor retirees on the cost of others — under the clever disguise of helping you to "save" for retirement.

5. **Payroll Taxes Are High**

While the payroll taxes you currently pay may "only" represent 6.2% of your paycheck, you should not forget that your employer has to chip in an additional 6.2%. Most people fallaciously assume that just because your employer is the one who transfers part of the tax to the government, the taxes do not affect you. Basic economics shows that whether a tax is levied on the seller (the worker in this case) or the buyer (the employer) is irrelevant. The tax incidence — meaning who will pay for it at the end — depends solely on the employer's price elasticity of demand for labor and the employee's price elasticity of supply.

Infinite price elasticity of demand for labor means that even a minimal increase in wages results in an infinite drop in demand for workers and thus layoffs. If an employer's price elasticity of demand for labor is infinite, the employee will bear 100% of any taxes levied on labor. Whether this tax is formally levied on the employee or the employer is irrelevant. Why? If wages increased by only 1% in the form of taxes, workers would lose their jobs. Thus, in order to remain employed, employees have to bear 100% of the burden of any payroll taxes.

Do not forget that even if the employer bears some of the payroll taxes as infinite price elasticity is unlikely, they will be passed on to consumers in the form of higher prices.

Companies are people. Any corporate income will eventually be remitted as wages and dividends to regular citizens. As a result, any payroll taxes paid by employers hit everyone just as much as the taxes paid by employees. Those who are self-employed already know this, as they have to pay the combined 12.4% in Social Security taxes.

6. **Gender Discrimination**

Believe it or not, but numerous countries all over the world allow women to retire earlier than men. Some of these countries including their respective retirement ages for men and women are displayed in following table. The United States does not have different retirement ages for the two genders.

Country	Retirement Age - Men	Retirement Age - Women
Austria	65	60
China	60	50-55
Colombia	62	57

Country	Retirement Age - Men	Retirement Age - Women
Croatia	65	60
Czech Republic	63	59-63
Greece	67	60-67
Israel	67	62
Italy	66	64
Poland	65-67	60-67
Romania	64	59-63
Russia	60	55
United Kingdom	65-66	60-66
Vietnam	60	55

The largest of these "gender gaps" is probably found in China, where female factory workers can retire as early as 50 (at 55 for public sector workers), while men's retirement age is 60. Now add that women in China have a life expectancy of 77 years at birth, 3 years higher than that of men at 74 years, and you will realize that women on average receive benefits for up to 13 years longer.

Similarly in Austria, one of the few Western countries where the public pension system still discriminates by gender, women retire 5 years before men. Add the 5 years longer average life expectancy of women (78 years for men versus 83 years for women) and females on average receive benefits for 10 more years. For Austria, this means that an average female retiree will receive €87,000 ($104,000 at FX €1=$1.20) more in pension payments than the average man.

However, this difference in benefits still ignores the fact that women on average pay fewer taxes than men. Women would enjoy an even larger advantage when comparing men and women with identical jobs.

Though even in a country like the United States, where the retirement age is the same for men and women, male retirees are discriminated against — simply because they live shorter. The US Social Security Act itself is written in gender-neutral terms, stating that if a man and woman pay in exactly the same over their working careers, they will receive identical monthly benefits. US women live 5 years longer (76 for men versus 81 for women), resulting in them receiving more benefits.

This was also reflected in the previously discussed study by the Urban Institute, which showed that a male single retiring in 2030 will receive $65,000 fewer benefits than he paid in Social Security taxes, while for a female the difference is "only" $40,000.

Technically speaking, women should retire later than men, not earlier.

As a result of women's higher life expectancy and career choices, they pay in only 41% of Social Security taxes in the United States, while receiving 49% of benefits. Of benefit recipients aged 85 and older, women make up 68%.

7. You Have a Shorter Than Average Life Expectancy? - Bad Luck!

Assume you are 55 years old and are diagnosed with final stage brain cancer. You are expected to perish within the next 6 months. Because the earliest retirement age in the US is 62, you will never receive the benefits you paid hundreds of thousands of dollars for. If you had the choice to manage your own money, you would now be able to bequeath your retirement savings to you children, allowing them to stay in university as the family's only breadwinner perishes.

Instead, because government prevents you from accessing your own retirement savings, you need to continue to work — and pay Social Security taxes — until you pass away. Your children will have to quit university, and you are prevented from spending a portion of your retirement contributions on enjoying the remaining months of your life.

8. The Social Security Taxes You Pay Do not Finance Your Retirement

The Social Security taxes you currently pay will not be used for your retirement — they pay for the current generation of retirees. When you retire, your pension is going to be paid by the succeeding generation and so on. The problem with this pyramid scheme is that in numerous advanced economies, foremost Japan, most European countries, and the US, people are having fewer children to pay for an aging population.

While in 1935 there were 16 workers for every Social Security recipient, this ratio has plummeted to an alarming 3 workers today. As fewer workers need to pay for more retirees, Social Security taxes continue to go up, while benefits are reduced.

The problem is that your Social Security taxes are not benefitting you, but the current retiring population. If this population happens to be larger than the succeeding population, future generations will have to cut back, while current retirees benefit.

9. **The First Generation of Social Security Recipients "Scammed" Their Grandchildren**

Social Security was introduced in 1933 by Franklin Delano Roosevelt to financially support those aged 65 and above. A contributing factor why Social Security is essentially a pyramid scheme is that this first generation of recipients never paid any Social Security taxes to finance their benefits. The same is the case in all major European countries.

Because the first generation of recipients were supported by the second generation and so on, it is impossible to end the scheme without leaving the last generation penniless.

Millennials are expected to be content to pay ever increasing payroll taxes, while retiring at a later age with smaller benefits. At the same time, younger generations are expected to "honor" the generation that "scammed" them, and at least in Europe started two world wars and was responsible for the rise of Naziism and Communism.

There are dozens of nations with much younger populations (and lower taxes) than the West, all of which happily accept people of all ages moving there. Be it Panama, Malaysia, the Philippines or Thailand. I recommend moving there early in life to escape the socialist financial disasters waiting to wreak havoc in the entitlement societies of the West. Nonetheless, I need to add that if you happen to be a US citizen, this suggestion will be of little help to you unless you are willing to give up your citizenship. As discussed in chapter 4.1 - Types of Tax Systems, the US citizenship-based income tax system otherwise only shared by Eritrea makes emigration to an economically freer country senseless.

The scam that is Social Security can be quantified using the tax-benefit analysis used earlier in this chapter. While those earning average wages and retiring 2010 or later lose out in the current system, generations which retired decades earlier stroke it big.

A single male retiring in 1960, for example, received more than 6 times the amount of benefits he paid in taxes. A single female earning the average wage and retiring in the same year received more than 8 times what she paid in taxes. Older generations spent more than what they earned — and future generations will have to pay for it.

Illustration 5.3 Benefit Analysis for a Single Man and Woman Earning the Average Wage (2012: $44,600), by Retirement Age

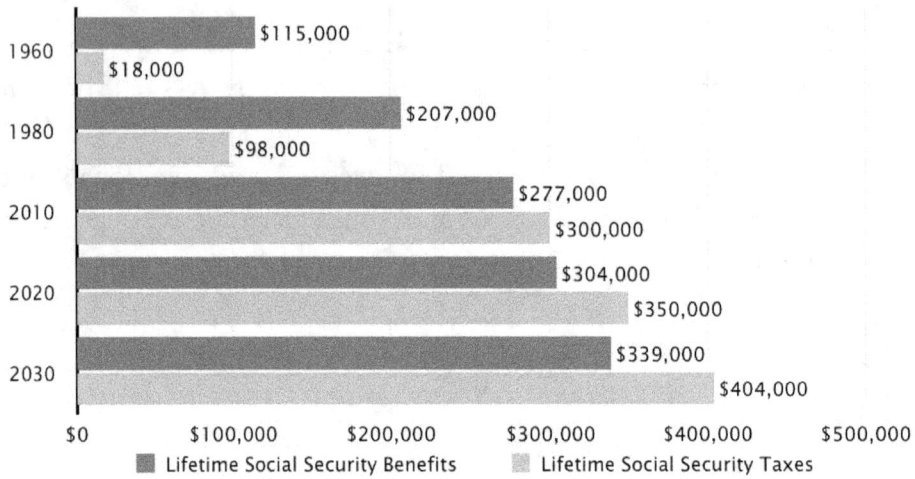

Social Security Benefits VS Taxes - Single Men

Social Security Benefits VS Taxes - Single Women

Due to their longer life expectancy, women receive more benefits for every Social Security tax dollar paid compared to men. This is just one of the reasons why the

pension system is discriminating against men. Losses for individuals earning above the average $44,600 are significantly higher than shown here. Images: own work by author, data from the Urban Institute

Solutions

There are two options to make the Social Security system more compatible with voluntaryism:

1. Continue to offer a public Social Security program, but make it optional. Let people decide whether they want to opt-in. Yes, this may lead top-earners to leave the program, but this is what you get when one portion of the population wants to live off of the other portion. Just because supporters of Social Security are in the majority does not entitle them to force other hardworking folks to subsidize their retirement in Florida. Forcing people who want to remain uninsured to buy insurance is equivalent to theft and violates an individual's right "to be left alone." If people wish to manage their retirement savings on their own — so be it.

2. Allow private opt-in pension schemes. Private pension programs already exist in most countries, however, they may not replace public pension schemes. This has to change. People should be allowed to invest their own money wherever they wish, whether this means giving it to the government or a private pension provider. Those who pay into a private pension scheme should be free to opt-out of Social Security completely.

--- Learn More ---

• [Video] How does Social Security really work? https://www.youtube.com/watch?v=p2hwO3y2Q4s.

--- Sources ---

1. "What happens if I work and get Social Security retirement benefits?" Official Social Security Government Website. https://faq.ssa.gov/link/portal/34011/34019/Article/3739/What-happens-if-I-work-and-get-Social-Security-retirement-benefits. Retrieved July 28, 2015.

2. Social Security Benefit Amounts - Official Social Security Government Website. http://www.ssa.gov/oact/cola/piaformula.html. Retrieved July 28, 2015.

3. Social Security Benefits Versus Taxes Comparison - "Social Security and Medicare Taxes and Benefits over a Lifetime - 2012 Update." C. Eugene Steuerle and Caleb Quakenbush. The Urban Institute. http://www.urban.org/sites/default/files/alfresco/publication-pdfs/412660-Social-Security-and-Medicare-Taxes-and-Benefits-Over-a-Lifetime--Update.PDF. Retrieved July 28, 2015.

4. Age Expectancy at Birth, by Gender - World Health Organization. http://apps.who.int/gho/data/node.main.688?lang=en. Retrieved July 28, 2015.

5. [German] Gender Discrimination for Pensions in Austria - "OECD-Rüge für die Pensionsreform." Wiener Zeitung. http://www.wienerzeitung.at/nachrichten/wirtschaft/international/272383_OECD-Ruege-fuer-die-Pensionsreform.html. Retrieved July 28, 2015.

6. Women Receive More Benefits from Social Security Than They Pay in - "Women's Stake in Social Security." National Academy of Social Insurance. https://www.nasi.org/learn/socialsecurity/womens-stake. Retrieved July 28, 2015.

UNEMPLOYMENT BENEFITS

CHAPTER 5 - SECTION 2

In the United States, unemployment benefits usually make up 40-50% of a laid-off person's previous pay and are paid for up to 6 months. Unemployment benefits are mostly financed through federal and state payroll taxes paid by employers. Because benefits are administered by states rather than the federal government, they, along with the taxes which pay for them, vary by state. During severe recessions, Congress may extend the standard 6 month period for which benefits are paid. This is what happened during the 2008/2009 financial crisis when the eligibility period was extended to 99 weeks.

Most European countries, on the other hand, do not limit the period for which unemployment benefits are paid. Nonetheless, an active search for work is still a requirement to receive benefits.

As with other government programs, unemployment insurance has shortcomings:

1. **Free Markets, not Unemployment Insurance Are Needed**

   The best way to reduce unemployment is by eliminating work-related regulations, such as the minimum wage.

In a pure free market, employers would be allowed to make whatever employment offers they wish to the general public — be it a job with above-average compensation and unemployment protection or with a basic $5 per hour salary. As in any unregulated market, the forces of supply and demand lead to a market equilibrium at which every willing individual is employed. Unemployment is just another form of resource oversupply. As people are searching for jobs, they reduce their wage expectations, and as a result, more employers are interested in hiring them. At some stage, wages have dropped to a level at which every individual finds employment, even if that means that one has to work for $5 an hour.

Price controls for goods such as bread and milk have failed everywhere they were implemented, yet the government still controls the minimum level of wages.

The minimum wage eliminated many low-wage jobs, such as that of the gas-station attendant, and condemned the people who previously performed them to unemployment. As a result, we now have to fill up our cars on our own and pay for welfare for the unemployed gas station attendant.

What gives the government the right to prohibit someone to work for a few dollars an hour at a gas station?

Requiring employers to pay for an employee's unemployment insurance — as any other government regulation such as a minimum wage — increases employment costs and thus discourages firms from hiring, resulting in unemployment. Imagine your business needed a short-term worker for a couple of weeks while one of your regular employees is on vacation. In the free market, you could easily hire someone for that period of time. Yet in our highly regulated economy, the number of documents to be filed and regulations to be followed may very well make it more worthwhile to run the business without additional help.

Unemployment insurance is another mandatory government program forced on every employer and employee, while self-employed individuals usually do not have to pay and cannot qualify for payments. Just like the other government-run insurance schemes, mandatory unemployment insurance goes against voluntaryism. If an employer wants to save on his employees' unemployment insurance payments and instead raise wages slightly — why not? Just as an employee can set "his/her price" in the form of wage expectations, so should an employer be free to make whatever employment offer he desires. It is then up to both parties to agree or not to agree on a work arrangement. Who is the government to interfere in that process and set requirements a work arrangement must fulfill?

2. **The Disconnect Between Payroll Tax Payers and Benefit Recipients**

As mentioned before, unemployment insurance is financed through the employer's payroll taxes. Because this tax is proportional to income, employers make more contributions for top executives than for easily replaceable factory workers. However, it is the factory worker who suffers more frequent and longer periods of unemployment, and as a result, receives most of the government's unemployment benefits.

Easily replaceable factory workers are laid off regularly when the economy contracts. After all, their low requirement for training means a company can easily hire new workers once demand picks up.

Demand for executives, on the other hand, fluctuates much less with the economy's boom and bust cycles. Due to a top executive's extensive knowledge of a firm's operations he/she is more difficult to replace — making a firm reluctant to lay him/her off.

3. An Incentive Not to Work

From a theoretical perspective, the short 6-month time period during which unemployed benefits are paid represents a strong incentive for people to search for work. However, even after unemployment benefits end, not working can earn you more than minimum wage in 35 US states. Benefits still paid out after unemployment benefits end include public housing allowances, food stamps, and energy subsidies. In 13 US states, welfare benefits can earn you up to $15 per hour, significantly more than what you earn in an entry-level position at a fast food chain or supermarket.

Simply raising the minimum wage to a level higher than welfare spending will not solve this problem. First, at $15 per hour, some people will continue to prefer staying at home than working all day for just $1 or $2 more. Secondly, the increase in minimum wage, depending on the state, would need to be significant, leading to the loss of many of the jobs the currently unemployed were meant to get.

Nonetheless, I want to stress that in order to earn $15 per hour from welfare one has to qualify for half a dozen welfare programs, which may not be possible for everyone.

In Europe, the combination of higher unemployment benefits and the lack of a time limit on benefit payouts means that millions are long-term unemployed by choice. It is no wonder countries such as

Spain and Greece have unemployment rates of around 25%, with about 50% of youths searching for jobs.

A big contributing factor to this problem is large shadow economies. Especially in Southern Europe, people, including the unemployed, earn a living by working underground, not paying taxes and receiving benefits. The shadow economy is particularly large in Italy and Greece, where it accounts for 27% and 27.5% of the economy respectively. In comparison, in the United States the shadow economy accounts for slightly more than 8% of the economy.

An official job may earn less than unemployment benefits and a tax-free income from illicit work. Unless entitlement systems change, there is little reason to expect unemployment in Southern Europe to fall below double digits.

Solutions

There are numerous ways to deal with unemployment in an economy, while still complying with the "No-Force Principle."

1. Abolish the payroll tax used to finance unemployment insurance. Instead, establish a public, but voluntary opt-in unemployment scheme. Such a program needs to be run like a private insurance to be financially viable, while being denied access to any other government funds. Employees can enroll by paying a monthly fee, and may choose between various plans. Some hypothetical plans may look as follows in terms of logic:

   a. Basic Coverage Plan: pay in $100 per month to receive benefits of $1000 per month for one year once unemployed. In order to avoid an unemployment insurance funding gap, monthly payments are adjusted to account for the average frequency of national unemployment and financial benefits withdrawn.

    b. Advanced Coverage Plan: pay in $100 per month to receive benefits of $1000 per month for 2 years + agree to pay into the plan at least until the benefits are repaid like a student loan.

2. Eliminate any employment-related regulations. Reasons why businesses are not hiring in recessions include their inability to lay off people at will, or pay a salary below minimum wage. Another factor may include the requirement for employers to contribute to an employee's health care costs. Repealing red tape removes the risks for companies to hire — reducing unemployment. Fewer regulations mean that the long-term unemployed receive a chance to re-enter the job market and move up the career-ladder. There are literally millions of jobs that could be created through the elimination of the minimum wage.

3. Deregulate the insurance industry and allow new startups to offer private unemployment insurance. Federal regulations currently prevent virtually anyone without hundreds of millions of dollars to start a new insurance company. Deregulating this market will allow new insurance providers to fill the niche of unemployment insurance.

4. In a free market world, with little to no taxes and almost no regulations people would have more money in their pockets to donate to and support the unemployed on a voluntary basis. Private donations and charitable spending already make up $1.6 trillion annually in the US alone, a number that would rise with people's higher disposable incomes. Do not forget that in the 19th century, when the US economy was much less regulated than it is today,

people did survive without unemployment benefits, so why should it not be possible today? Note that the modern world's first unemployment insurance was only introduced in 1911 in the United Kingdom.

--- Learn More ---

- [Video] Milton Friedman on Welfare https://www.youtube.com/watch?v=bJWZ27OT16M

--- Sources ---

1. "The Work Versus Welfare Trade-Off: 2013." Michael Tanner and Charles Hughes. The Cato Institute. http://object.cato.org/sites/cato.org/files/pubs/pdf/the_work_versus_welfare_trade-off_2013_wp.pdf. Retrieved July 28, 2015.

2. Size of the Shadow Economy by Country - "Shadow Economies All over the World." Friedrich Schneider et al. World Bank. https://openknowledge.worldbank.org/bitstream/handle/10986/3928/WPS5356.pdf?sequence=1. Retrieved July 28, 2015.

3. Unemployment Rate in Greece - Eurostat. http://appsso.eurostat.ec.europa.eu/nui/show.do?dataset=une_rt_m&lang=en/. Retrieved July 28, 2015.

HEALTH INSURANCE

CHAPTER 5 - SECTION 3

Government health care programs vary from country to country. With the Affordable Care Act (commonly known as Obamacare) health insurance coverage became mandatory in the US, just like in most other Western countries.

In the US, consumers can choose between private health insurance providers or a pre-approved health care plan offered through the government's health care exchanges. Most Europeans have the choice to get private insurance or be insured by a government-run insurance like the National Health Service (NHS) in the UK.

As in the other sections, we will first look at how mandatory health insurance schemes violate liberty, before discussing health care reforms.

1. Health Care Coverage Is Mandatory

Why should one be forced to get health insurance if one prefers to be self-dependent? It should be your choice whether you want to be insured or save your money on your own terms.

Even if there are people out there wishing to spend their health insurance premiums on a new car or a vacation instead — so be it. There are people who value other things such as consumer goods or a personal investment fund more than a health plan. People's preferences are naturally different.

Allowing a majority of people who desire health insurance to force those who have other spending preferences to get insured violates liberty just as much as if those who dislike insurance forced everyone else to be uninsured.

Whether health insurance is "good" or "bad" depends on an individual's preferences. And as long as these preferences do not harm others one has no right to force another individual to comply with one's own belief system.

Not to mention that "forced" health plan purchases represent a form of theft for those who would prefer to remain uninsured — simply because these individuals value their money and the things they can buy with it more than mandatory insurance.

If health insurance was voluntary, some of the people who opt-out would without question be unable to pay their medical bills. However, this is by no means an argument to force everyone to become insured:

1. The uninsured who spend their money on consumption rather than saving for unexpected medical bills are responsible for any later shortfalls. Nobody — including the government and doctors — should be forced to help them. After all, forcing doctors to help the uninsured would in itself constitute a violation of the "No-Force Principle." One should not be pitiful

for those who refused to care for their health and, as a result, end up sick and penniless.

China shows us how such a system can work in reality. When you call an ambulance you will not be picked up unless you show the paramedics proof of insurance or pay them on the spot in cash. The same is the case in Chinese hospitals: treatment will not start unless you are insured or you (or an acquaintance) pays upfront.

2. Just because there are some irresponsible people who are uninsured and do not plan ahead does not mean there aren't uninsured people who have started a private health care savings fund. People wishing to save for unexpected health problems and remain uninsured should not be forced to buy health insurance just because there are irresponsible individuals.

3. Even with insurance, bankruptcies due to unexpected medical bills are common. In fact, medical bankruptcies have surpassed bankruptcies resulting from credit card and mortgage debt to become the number one reason for personal insolvency in the US. And 78% of medical bankruptcies are experienced by people which *have* insurance. Technically speaking, insurance does not really "insure" you against large medical bills, as many plans do not cover extraordinary expenses or have large deductibles. Why be insured, if the hundreds of dollars you pay in monthly premiums merely go to the once a year flu vaccine or dental cleaning?

2. Earn More - Pay More

As with almost all government programs, when you earn less, you have to pay less for the same services used by those with high incomes. Under the Affordable Care Act, earning less than $46,680 in a single household means you may qualify for discounts on premiums. The irony of this policy is that people with lower incomes, in particular, suffer more diseases ranging from heart conditions to diabetes and obesity. These diseases are mostly the result of lifestyle choices such as refusing to work out, excessive alcohol consumption and a diet rich in fats and sugars. Technically speaking, low-income earners with unhealthy lifestyles should pay more than wealthy individuals, not less. After all, they should make up for their higher-than-proportionate dependence on medical services. The government's redistribution of wealth to low-income individuals by offering them lower premiums does not incentivize them to switch to healthier lifestyles.

Germany goes even further with adjusting premiums to income. When insured through one of the hundreds of government-owned insurance companies, total premiums always make up at least 14.6% of income (shared by employee and employer). If you are a company health insurance fund operating more efficiently than a government-owned provider and want to reduce your prices to attract customers — you are prohibited from doing so. This is what happened to my father's insurance a few years ago when he resided in Germany. A letter he received from his health insurance stated that the government prohibited them to lower rates based on the surplus they generated that year. Instead, they had to remit the "profits" to government-owned insurance providers to help balance their financial statements.

Because German premiums are based on a percentage of income, a person earning ten or twenty times more than another individual has to pay ten or twenty times more for health insurance. Where is the incentive to work hard, take risks and innovate if the cost of basic services you use increases by the same proportion as your income?

3. I Live a Healthy Lifestyle

There is a fair number of people who eat healthily, do not drink or smoke, work out regularly, and avoid hazardous activities such as skiing or cycling in the city. Many of these "healthy" individuals rarely see their doctor.

Why should these people be forced to pay into a health care fund which also pays for those who drink, smoke, eat unhealthy food and never work out? If a government is to get involved in people's lifestyles at all, it should promote a healthy way of life. Yet it is doing the opposite by forcing responsible individuals to "subsidize" those who eat unhealthily.

Many health plans used to take into account preconditions such as smoking and obesity-related diseases when calculating premiums, though the Affordable Care Act has significantly reduced the extent to which insurers are allowed to do this. This is why the vast majority of people is now required to pay more for health insurance — while those with irresponsible lifestyles pay less.

Even if insurers were free to charge higher rates to those with unhealthy lifestyles, personal activities such as skiing would still not be accounted for. How can it ever be justified that safety-conscious gym-visitors have to subsidize the risk-taking sportsman who is prone to costly injuries?

Illustration 5.4 People Are Responsible for Their Health - at Least to a Large Extent

If someone rides down a ski slope by night, break his legs and as a result needs to go to an emergency room, it is his fault. You should not have to pay for that. Image: bren64, Bigstock

4. Heavy Users Should Pay More

Men smoke more, drink more, do riskier sports and live shorter lives than women. However, they are far less likely to visit a doctor than women are. A study by the Centers for Disease Control and Prevention (CDC) shows that men are 80% less likely than women to use a regular source of health care, for example, by visiting a doctor. Furthermore, according to research by the American Academy of Family Physicians (AAFP), 36% of surveyed men only visit the doctor "when they are extremely sick." Men also do far fewer health check-ups than women. Similarly, News-Medical.net reports that women were found to visit a doctor three times more likely than men on a regular basis.

Despite enjoying better health, women make more use of medical services, simply because they visit the doctor for small issues men do not bother doing a check-up for.

Since women use medical services more often, shouldn't they pay more for health insurance? This is how it was before the Affordable Health Care Act was passed. Women paid higher premiums on 92% of health plans. With Obamacare, gender-based premium differences in health care programs were outlawed. While gender-neutral premiums appear fair, they are not, as they charge men more and women less than what would be appropriate for their gender-specific usage patterns. Men, who already live shorter, are now required to subsidize and thus further improve women's health.

For those who consider it men's fault that they do not visit the doctor more frequently — consider this:

1. Visiting notoriously overworked doctors for minor colds or bruises as done by women distracts doctors from seriously ill patients. If men were to visit the doctor as often as women do, not only would average premiums go up for everyone, but seriously ill patients would suffer even longer wait times, potentially costing lives.

2. How would you feel about a new "meal plan?" A 300-pound football player and you pay in $50 each per day to buy lunch for both of you. When you complain that you only eat a salad and

desert costing a total of $20, while the football player eats $80 worth of food, he responds that it is your fault that you do not eat more.

This is how many men feel about gender-neutral health care pricing.

5. **Insurance Was Invented for Unexpected Expenses, not Check-Ups and Vaccines**

When the first modern health insurance schemes were introduced in the middle of the 19th century in the UK and Germany they were meant to pay for unexpected expenses. These could relate to extraordinary work accidents or sickness preventing a person from coming to work.

The term "insurance" is defined as *"providing protection against a possible eventuality (i.e., a risk)"* quoting the New Oxford American Dictionary. Insurances protect individuals from improbable, but potentially costly events ranging from accidents to natural disasters, fires, and theft — at least so goes the theory.

Today's health insurance works differently — paying for any regular health-related expenses such as health checkups and vaccinations just as much as for unexpected expenses. If you already know you have a dental cleaning twice a year and that you get an annual flu shot in October, why not pay for it yourself? There is a great loss of efficiency by first sending the money to an insurance, which then subtracts administration fees, wages for its employees, office rent and taxes, before paying for your predictable routine expenses. The people maintaining this system could do more productive tasks such as contributing to innovation in tech and robotics, or help invent new food products.

Look at it this way: do you have car insurance which pays for worn down tires or oil changes? Of course not, because these expenses are predictable and do not require risk hedging — the originally intended purpose of an insurance.

Illustration 5.5 What Insurance Was Meant For

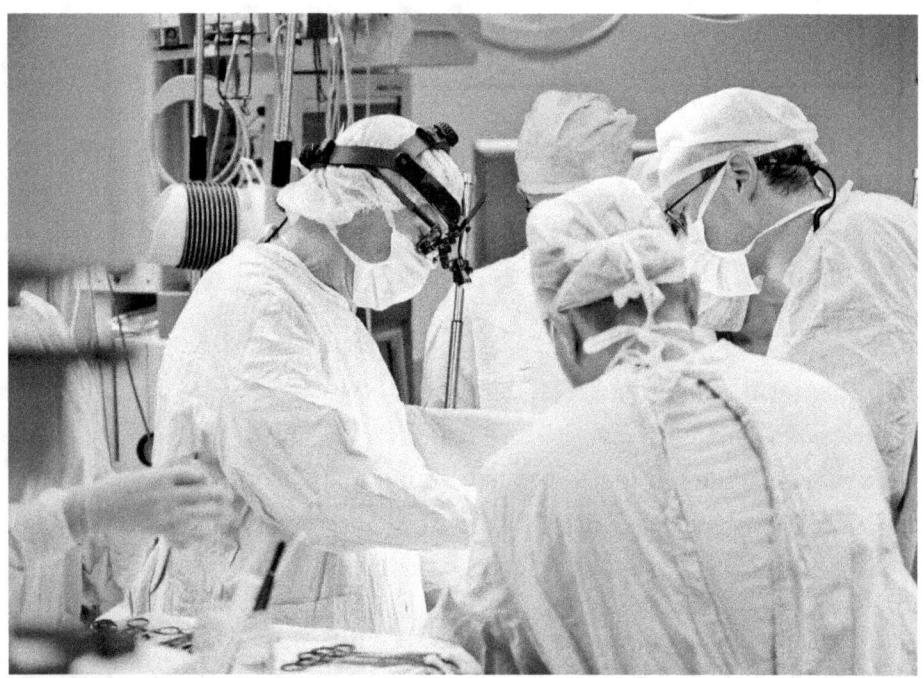

Health insurances were first introduced to cover unexpected expenses, for example for a heart surgery as shown in the picture — not to cover the cost of the annual flu shot. Image: kadmy, Bigstock

6. I Do Not Want to Pay for Other People's Birth Control (or Vaccines)

Health insurance, depending on plan and country, includes coverage of controversial practices such as abortions, birth control, and vaccinations. Irrelevant of whether a majority or minority of people are against these practices, based on religious faith and personal values, nobody should be forced to pay for something he or she cannot morally support. Not to forget that forcing somebody into a transaction itself represents a violation of the "No-Force Principle."

7. Health Insurance Premiums Are High - Insurances and Governments Are Inefficient

Whenever government nationalizes an industry, prices increase (directly or indirectly through taxes) while quality deteriorates. Since the Affordable Care Act became effective, health care premiums have increased in all but 6 US states. Premium hikes of more than 80% were reported in Arkansas, Iowa, Mississippi, Nevada, New Mexico, North Carolina and Vermont. On average, premiums increased by 49% nationwide. The Obamacare Website featuring the enrollment system alone has famously cost $2.1 billion to set up.

The efficiencies lost through government involvement in health care are passed on to consumers in the form of higher premiums. It is that simple.

However, even private insurers waste billions of dollars on administration alone. When you pay your health care fees, a large chunk of that money is used to pay for wages, prestigious office towers and billions in advertising. The same money could be spent on actual health care if people were allowed to save their money privately instead of spending it on premiums.

As a result, being *uninsured* pays off for the vast majority of people practicing *reasonably healthy* lifestyles.

Solutions

There are several reforms which can make the health care system conform to voluntaryism and everyone's natural right "to be left alone":

1. Continue to offer a public health insurance program, but make it optional. Let people decide whether they want to opt-in. While this may lead "healthy" individuals to leave the insurance, it is more than fair. People making unhealthy lifestyle decisions have no right to force more disciplined individuals to subsidize their poor habits. Government should be prohibited to subsidize public health care through other means such as income taxes, and instead adopt market principles to make the insurance scheme financially independent. Such market principles may include charging smokers and obese individuals higher premiums.

2. Allow people to have no health insurance at all. Allowing people to choose whether to get health insurance is essential for voluntaryism to be respected. At the same time, we should stop requiring doctors and other health-professionals to help out people in need in order to prevent "free-loading" and respect their very own right to voluntaryism.

--- Sources ---

1. Medical Bankruptcies on the Rise - "Medical Bankruptcies are Still a Problem, Here's What to Expect." Fox Business. Donna Fuscaldo. http://www.foxbusiness.com/personal-finance/2014/02/18/medical-bankruptcies-are-still-problem-here-what-to-expect/. Retrieved July 28, 2015.

2. "Medical Bills Are the Biggest Cause of US Bankruptcies." Dan Mangan. CNBC. http://www.cnbc.com/id/100840148. Retrieved July 28, 2015.

3. Low-Income People Can Save Under the Affordable Care Act - "Income levels that qualify for health coverage savings." HealthCare.gov. Retrieved July 28, 2015. https://www.healthcare.gov/lower-costs/qualifying-for-lower-costs/.

4. [German] Health Care Premiums in Germany - "Krankenversicherung Beitrag Beiträge 2015." IMACC.de. http://www.imacc.de/lohnabrechnunggehaltsabrechnung/sozialabgabenarbeitgeber/krankenversicherung/index.html. Retrieved July 28, 2015.

5. Men Have Riskier Lifestyles Than Women - "Why don't men do what the doctor orders?" Rowan Walker. The Guardian. http://www.theguardian.com/lifeandstyle/2009/jun/10/men-doctors. Retrieved July 28, 2015.

6. The Affordable Care Act Eliminates Gender-Specific Pricing - "Stop sex discrimination in health plan costs." Marcia Greenberger. CNN. http://www.cnn.com/2012/03/20/opinion/greenberger-health-premiums-gender-gap/. Retrieved July 28, 2015.

7. Men Visiting the Doctor Less Often Than Women - "Men and Doctors: Understanding the Disconnect." Chris Iliades. Everyday Health. http://www.everydayhealth.com/mens-health/men-and-doctors-understanding-the-disconnect.aspx. Retrieved July 28, 2015.

8. "National survey finds women more likely to see doctor on regular basis than men." News Medical. http://www.news-medical.net/news/20110609/National-survey-finds-women-more-likely-to-see-doctor-on-regular-basis-than-men.aspx. Retrieved July 28, 2015.

9. Definition for Insurance - New Oxford American Dictionary. Copyright © 2010, 2013 by Oxford University Press, Inc. All rights reserved.

10. "No, Obamacare Has Not Reduced Insurance Costs." - Yevgeniy Feyman. Forbes. http://www.forbes.com/sites/theapothecary/2014/08/06/no-obamacare-has-not-reduced-insurance-costs/. Retrieved July 28, 2015.

11. "Obamacare Website Costs Exceed $2 Billion, Study Finds." Alex Wayne. Bloomberg. http://www.bloomberg.com/news/articles/2014-09-24/obamacare-website-costs-exceed-2-billion-study-finds. Retrieved July 28, 2015.

ASSISTANCE TO THE POOR

CHAPTER 5 - SECTION 4

In the United States, the poor are financially assisted through at least 79 government sponsored, means-tested programs. These vary from public housing to food stamps, child benefits, and energy subsidies. Most of these programs were initiated by Lyndon B. Johnson's vision to create a "Great Society" during his presidency between 1963 and 1969. The "Great Society" also included various other initiatives concerning civil rights, education, and the environment.

The failures of Johnson's "War on Poverty" are numerous. They are the main reason why we need urgent welfare reform.

We Spent $22 Trillion While Poverty Has Remained Constant

The US government has spent $22 trillion on poverty — enough to repay the current national debt of $18.3 trillion (as of July 2015) and still have $3.7 trillion left. Not included in this calculation are the hundreds of billions of interest we could have saved *every year* by focusing on balancing the budget instead of welfare spending. Over the next 10 years alone the government expects to spend another $14 trillion — putting total spending on the War on Poverty to a staggering $36 trillion by the mid-2020s.

The irony is that while the US poverty rate as a percentage of the population declined from 22.4 in 1959 to 14.7 in 1966, just *before* the War on Poverty started, poverty has remained stagnant at 14.5% ever since Johnson's welfare programs were introduced.

Little was achieved in improving upward mobility and self-sufficiency. Lyndon Johnson wanted to transform the poor into taxpayers, making them pay for the benefits they originally received. Instead, welfare created dependency which locked people into poverty. The poor's dependency on benefits is so large that around 48 percent of Hispanics and 47 percent of Blacks live in households receiving social welfare.

Poverty From an Absolute and a Relative Perspective

The official government poverty statistics are based on the concept of absolute poverty. Absolute poverty refers to people living below a certain standard of living. The government determines poverty by comparing "pre-tax cash income against a threshold that is set at three times the cost of a minimum food diet," where the cost of the food diet is annually adjusted for inflation. In 2015, this meant that a single earning less than $11,770 annually is considered to be living below the poverty line.

The other way of looking at poverty is the measure of "relative poverty." Depending on the definition used, somebody is considered "poor" when earning less than a certain percentage — for example 20% — of median income in a society. This way of looking at poverty is usually used by critics of income inequality. When top-earners significantly increase their income, while low-income people experience only slight wage raises, income inequality increases. In terms of absolute poverty, the poor would still improve their living standards and be better of. In terms of relative poverty, however, it appears that the poor get poorer, simply because their "relative" income decreases compared to that of top-earners.

The problem with relative poverty is that it ignores the living standard of the poor and instead concentrates on whether others have it better than them. Relative poverty (and income inequality) would actually decrease even if the poor experienced a 20% drop in income, as long as top-earners suffered a larger decrease, for example, by 30%. Similarly, if the "poor" would drive new BMWs, they would probably still resent those with fleets of Rolls-Royces.

"Relative poverty" and income inequality are a direct result of different work habits and risk taking — and neither should nor can be eliminated.

While income inequality is a result of different work habits and risk taking under capitalism, it is to a large part a direct result of government corruption and suppression in socialist nations. Whenever government is powerful, a country's leaders and their cronies are free to exploit the general population. This is why socialist countries such as Brazil — now run by former Marxist guerrilla fighter Dilma Rousseff — have higher income inequality than the US.

Communist governments' sole intention to exploit their citizens is probably best shown by East Germany's practice to only allow those that have reached retirement age to permanently migrate to the West. Until 1987, East Germans below retirement age were only permitted to visit West Germany for significant family events relating to a parent or grandparent — for example, a marriage or a funeral. A visitor also had to leave behind one's spouse and child as "collateral" to ensure his/her return to East Germany. Of course, if you decided to move to the West for retirement, you had to give up any pension receipts you paid for the majority of your life.

Many Poor Are Not Materially "Poor"

We are often obsessed with the definition of "relative poverty" when talking about the poor. While the "poor" only make a fraction of high-income earners, it is a long stretch to consider them poor from a material perspective, or poor in absolute terms.

About 75% of Americans below the poverty line reported that they owned at least one car, while 80% of "poor" households have air conditioning. In comparison, only 2% of all German households (poor and non-poor) have air conditioning.

Similarly, an average American living below the poverty line has more living space than the average non-poor person in many European countries including the UK, France, and Germany.

Types of Poverty

When people talk about poverty, they mainly refer to the lack of financial means to buy food, shelter or other goods and services. It is often overseen that poverty can also refer to a lack of free time or emotional satisfaction.

Wages are what we get in exchange for our time, resulting in most people either ending up time-poor and (relatively) money-rich, or time-rich and money-poor. While there are people advocating the redistribution of monetary wealth, nobody has proposed redistributing time wealth from the unemployed to those who work 70h+ per week.

Everyone is born with the same gift of time and free will. You are free to exchange as much of your time and your effort into income. Any redistribution of income or time between individuals is theft.

The Destruction of the Traditional Family

Today's poor have it worse than 50 years ago from a variety of perspectives, one of them being the rise in out-of-wedlock births. While only 7% of children were born outside of marriage in the mid-60s, this figure has risen to an alarming 41% today. Blacks — who ironically were meant to be helped by the Great Society — are most affected by this problem. A whopping 72% of Black babies are born out of wedlock. With the rise in out-of-wedlock births, the proportion of children living with a single parent or no parent at all has increased from just 13% in 1960 to 39% in 2013.

This destruction of the traditional family is a main driver of perpetual poverty and the poor's dependence on welfare.

An increasing minority of single parents earns more when not working, meaning that their children not only lack the stability of a married household, but are shown from birth how to depend on the welfare system. Of those working, single fathers and mothers earn less than their married counterparts. 88% of married fathers have full-time jobs (80% for women), while only 69% of single dads do (60% for women). As a result, single parent households are not only left with one instead of two bread winners, but the remaining parent earns less, too. Lack of household income means that children are often left unable to afford college. Instead, the youth becomes susceptible to crime, drug use, and teenage pregnancy — continuing the perpetual cycle of poverty for the next generations to come.

Forced Charity

The money spent on the War on Poverty represents nothing more than a giant "forced charity" program. American taxpayers were made to "donate" $22 trillion. Instead of helping the poor to become self-dependent and find jobs, taxpayers have had to subsidize the poor's food, transportation, TV sets and other consumer goods.

You are free to donate to whatever charitable cause you like. But is it justifiable for you to force others to contribute to the charity of your choice? If not, how is it justifiable for the government to force others to do so?

Solutions

How can we reform the still ongoing War on Poverty in a way that it

(1) actually helps the poor to become self-sufficient and

(2) does not violate people's right "to be left alone?"

There are several options including:

1. **Eliminate Funding of Welfare Programs Through Taxpayer Money.** As a first step, ending the government's practice of forcing

taxpayers to finance other's TV sets and cars is essential in respecting voluntaryism.

2. **Eliminate Workplace Regulations.** As said many times before, an economy without minimum wage finds a job for everyone, even if it pays just $5 per hour. In addition to ending minimum wage legislation, we should eliminate payroll taxes, maximum work hours and other work-related regulations. By doing so, we remove all possible disincentives an employer may experience from hiring a worker.

   An unregulated $5/h job may be tough, but is the only way for the poor to gain experience and over time to move into higher paying positions. There is little reason why a company should pay $15 or $20 for a 10-year long unemployed individual with no workplace experience. Providing those people with tough, low-paying jobs is the only way to move them into the middle class — no financial assistance can do this as the War on Poverty has shown. Many now famous individuals started out working at minimum wage. My first two jobs paid nothing, yet I was grateful to have had the chance to work there and gain workplace experience. My third job paid a flat rate of $16 per day, mainly to cover commuting costs. Thanks to these jobs I am now able to get relatively high paying work in the private sector.

3. **Eliminate Welfare Benefits.** This seems harsh, but it pushes the poor into accepting poor-paying jobs in the private sector. As long as welfare benefits pay minimum wage or more, people will continue to lack the drive to work all day at the same rate at a local company. An unregulated market will find a job for everyone, while it makes it easier to start a business for a few hundred dollars. The poor should get jobs — not benefits.

4. **At Least Replace the Stepped Welfare Eligibility Requirements.** Many social programs pay out once an individual falls below a certain income threshold. The problem with this type of system is that people earning just slightly more than the cut-off line could increase their income by getting a lower paying job, or in some cases even by quitting work altogether. As a result of lack of discipline, some people succumb to this incentive and move down the career ladder by choice — eternally giving up on the chance to get promoted to high paying positions. This phenomenon gains media attention from time to time especially in Europe where welfare payments are comparably generous and long-lasting.

   This "barrier" can be removed by adjusting benefit payouts smoothly, for example, by granting $2 of benefits for every $10 in lower income. If you get a promotion, you won't all of a sudden become ineligible for welfare benefits — which could possibly reduce your total income. Instead, welfare benefits are reduced by $2 for every additional $10 you earn.

5. **Count on Private Charity.** Americans are already spending $1.6 trillion on private welfare every year. With the elimination of public welfare programs and the reduction or abolishing of taxes, people will be able to increase their donations. After all, charity took care of the poorest portion of society before the War on Poverty started. As mentioned before, charity and incentives to work helped reduce the percentage of people living below the poverty line from 22.4 in 1959 to 14.7 in 1966, just *before* the War on Poverty started, so why shouldn't it be possible today?

--- Learn More ---

- [Video] How does Social Security really work? https://www.youtube.com/watch?v=p2hwO3y2Q4s.

- [Video] The Great Society's triumph and tragedy https://www.youtube.com/watch?v=EClpFLDrK0g

- [Video] The war on work https://www.youtube.com/watch?v=1nN1HqAps4Y

--- Sources ---

1. Private Expenditure on Welfare. OECD. http://www.oecd.org/els/soc/expenditure.htm. Retrieved July 28, 2015.

2. US National Debt Clock - US Debt Clock. http://www.usdebtclock.org. Retrieved July 28, 2015.

3. Spending on the War on Poverty - "The Great Society 50 Years Later: How We're Failing America's Poor." Rachel Sheffield. The Daily Signal. http://dailysignal.com/2014/05/22/great-society-50-years-later-failing-americas-poor/. Retrieved July 28, 2015.

4. 2015 US Poverty Line - U.S. Department of Health & Human Services. http://aspe.hhs.gov/2015-poverty-guidelines. Retrieved July 28, 2015.

5. Measuring Absolute Poverty - "How is poverty measured in the United States?" Institute for Research on Poverty. http://www.irp.wisc.edu/faqs/faq2.htm. Retrieved July 28, 2015.

6. Countries by Income Inequality - The CIA World Fact Book. https://www.cia.gov/library/publications/the-world-factbook/rankorder/2172rank.html. Retrieved July 28, 2015.

7. Migration Between East and West Germany - "E. Germany Relaxes Curbs on Working Citizens' Visits to West." Robert J. McCartney. The Washington Post. http://www.washingtonpost.com/archive/politics/

1988/04/17/e-germany-relaxes-curbs-on-working-citizens-visits-to-west/ bf53ec1a-a4a5-4168-a171-759393155c9b/. Retrieved July 28, 2015.

8. 2013 Poverty Rate, Out-of-Wedlock Births & Standard of Life of Today's Poor - "The War on Poverty: 50 years of failure." Robert Rector. The Washington Times. http://www.washingtontimes.com/news/2014/sep/ 19/rector-the-war-on-poverty-50-years-of-failure/. Retrieved July 28, 2015.

9. Penetration of Air Conditioning in Europe - "The future environmental impact of room air conditioners in Europe." C. Pout and E. R. Hitchin. 2008. http://nceub.commoncense.info/uploads/W2008_10Hitchin.pdf. Retrieved July 2008.

10. Out-of-Wedlock Births & Reduction in Poverty Before the War on Poverty - "The Failures of LBJ's 'Great Society.'" George Will. Newsmax. http:// www.newsmax.com/GeorgeWill/LBJ-Great-Society-Eberstadt/ 2014/05/19/id/572076/. Retrieved July 28, 2015.

11. Children Living in Households With a Single or No Parent - "Less than half of U.S. kids today live in a 'traditional' family." Gretchen Livingston. Pew Research. http://www.pewresearch.org/fact-tank/2014/12/22/less-than-half-of-u-s-kids-today-live-in-a-traditional-family/. Retrieved July 28, 2015.

12. Single Parenthood in the US - "The Mysterious and Alarming Rise of Single Parenthood in America." Aparna Mathur et al. The Atlantic. http:// www.theatlantic.com/business/archive/2013/09/the-mysterious-and-alarming-rise-of-single-parenthood-in-america/279203/. Retrieved July 28, 2015.

INFRASTRUCTURE

CHAPTER 6

Chapter 6: Infrastructure

In this chapter, we will look at infrastructure, specifically transport infrastructure — roads and airports. Depending on type, the way we finance their construction and maintenance varies. Let us look at them in more detail:

Roads

The US highway system is publicly owned and paid for through a per-gallon fuel tax. The highway system is administered by the Highway Trust Fund established in 1956. The original tax was 3 cents per gallon of fuel, which today stands at 18.4 cents per gallon of gasoline and 24.4 cents per gallon of diesel. Adjusted for inflation, fuel taxes have decreased, as 3 cents in 1956 are worth $26.3 cents in 2015, more than what is currently charged for both gasoline and diesel.

Nonetheless, it should be noted that the original tax was meant to construct, and afterwards maintain the highway system, while the taxes collected today have the main purpose of repairing and maintaining our highway infrastructure. Thus, at least from a theoretical perspective, today's lower fuel taxes are more than justified.

Despite this, the Highway Trust Fund is broke and already required additional funding of $55 billion through debt between 2008 and early 2015. Bailouts of the fund are approved while fuel taxes intended for highways are in part used to finance public transport and appropriated for the reduction of the federal deficit. Ronald Reagan signed into law the appropriation of 1 cent per gallon to public transport. In the mid-1990s, 6.8 cents went to deficit reduction, which was later reduced to 2.5 cent in 1997 with the decrease of 4.3 cents being redirected to the Highway Trust Fund. This meant that between 1993 and 1997, a total of 7.8 cent or more than 42% of fuel taxes were used for purposes other than highways.

Solutions

There are two "liberty-friendly" options to properly finance the highway system and replace the current per-gallon fuel tax:

1. **Introduce Mileage- and Weight-Based Pricing**

   While a per gallon fuel tax does correlate with an individual's actual highway usage, it is not perfect. For instance, why should somebody pay more in highway taxes just because he/she has an older car and, as a result, uses more fuel? Buyers of electric cars do not only receive purchase subsidies depending on state, but are not required to contribute to the financing of the highway system, since they do not purchase regular combustion fuels.

   On the other hand, the fuel tax is also paid by those who rarely use their vehicles on highways and mostly drive within city limits, or consume significant amounts of fuel on their private properties such as farms. Why should these people pay for a highway system they are not using?

   In order for the financing of the highway system to fully comply with the "Principle of Causation," a mileage- (and weight-) based payment system is needed. In this context, the principle of causation states that actual use of infrastructure — here the highway system — should correlate 1:1 with how it is paid for.

   The main reason why many oppose such a "metered" system — besides the potential abuse of your location data — is that new charging systems usually increase out-of-pocket expenses for drivers. However, in the system proposed here, metered highway tolls would replace fuel taxes, not augment them.

Of course, in order to fully adhere to the "Principle of Causation," tolls would have to be adjusted to match actual highway expenses. No additional government funds should be appropriated for highways, nor should tolls be used for any other expenses such as public transport or national debt relief.

2. **Privatize All Highways**

An alternative to the mere replacement of fuel taxes by metered tolls would be the privatization of the highway system. Private highway operators would acquire existing highways and manage them on their terms. Highway ownership by different investors leads to competition: many metropolitan areas are served by several highways, and there are many routes a truck can take, say, to go from Chicago, IL to Dallas, TX. Especially people living in cities have the choice to use public transport to avoid highways altogether when commuting to work or traveling to another city. This choice resulting from dispersed highway ownership and different means of transport makes highway operators compete through lower prices, safer roads, shorter routes and less congestion — benefitting everyone.

Contrary to popular opinion, private highway operators cannot charge whatever they want due to the principles of supply and demand. Once tolls are too high, people will simply stay in their town to make a purchase, only order online, or move closer to their place of work.

Critics of privatization often argue that highway privatization increases drivers' out-of-pocket expenses. The Indiana Toll Road is a prominent example were this was the case. However, the main reason for higher costs is not privatization, but that tolls are added to, rather than replacing fuel taxes.

Even if private tolls replaced fuel taxes, it can be argued that privatization increases costs — at least on a superficial level. Take the $4.65 EZPass fare for the total distance of the Indiana Toll Road. It compares to $1.40 in fuel taxes for the route's 152 miles based on a 20 mpg car and the current 18.4 cent per gallon gas tax. Taking a fuel tax of 26.3 cent — equivalent to the inflation-adjusted 3 cent rate from 1956 — a driver would pay $2.00.

Yet these numbers oversee the fact that while fuel taxes almost exclusively pay for the maintenance of highways, the tolls charged by the owners of the Indiana Toll Road pay for its maintenance and de facto "construction" — *a second time*. Let me explain: the original construction of the highway was paid for through fuel taxes. Once completed, the only arising costs were for maintenance. That maintenance costs less than initial construction is obvious, so let us just assume the fuel taxes of $1.40 for a full one way route are sufficient to cover maintenance expenses.

Highway privatization should encompass the *replacement* of fuel taxes with privately charged tolls. Given the competition between highway providers, and the usually higher efficiency of private firms, tolls should equal not more than fuel taxes, and likely less. So why are tolls so much higher?

The often overlooked answer is that the consortium of investors in the case of the Indiana Toll Road did not simply take over highway maintenance. It paid the state of Indiana $3.8 billion just to be allowed to collect tolls for maintenance expenses.

So in addition to the $1.40 in tolls necessary to maintain the highway, the operating company has to incrementally pay for the $3.8 billion it paid to the state. This is where the difference between the fuel tax rate and the EZ-Pass fare — $3.25 per route — goes to. In essence, the Indiana State government made residents pay twice for the highway. First, when it was constructed through the payment of fuel taxes. Second, when drivers have to pay an additional $3.25 per route to allow the highway operator to recover the $3.8 billion acquisition costs — money that goes directly to the state.

The government first makes people pay for the construction of a highway through fuel taxes, then sells it to somebody else and keeps the proceeds of the sale to itself. Sadly, only few realize that the Indiana State government just raised taxes by $3.8 billion.

The majority of tolls goes to the state, not highway investors. Assuming that investors use 70% of the current $4.65 EZ-Pass fare to pay for the highway's acquisition, it will take around 1.17 billion full-length passenger car journeys to pay for the $3.8 billion in acquisition costs. From the remaining 30% of tolls the operator has to pay for maintenance, wages of toll booth operators, administration, and taxes.

To be exact, the $3.8 billion were paid for a 75-years lease, not the acquisition of the highway. When the current operator returns a well-maintained highway to the state as laid out in the lease agreement, Indiana can cash in another $3.8 billion or the inflation-adjusted equivalent in leasing out the highway.

Drivers will have to pay not only for the highway's maintenance, but billions to the government every time the state grants a new investor the right to maintain the road. These tax increases can then be spent on whatever vanity projects politicians desire.

Real privatization would entail the scrapping of fuel taxes, an end to billions of government bailouts of the Highway Trust Fund and competition between highway owners. The proceeds of highway sales to private investors should go to the taxpayers who paid for the highway system's construction, not the state, for example by splitting Indiana's $3.8 billion among drivers.

Government budget holes should not be financed by letting taxpayers pay twice for the same highway, recording the extra income in state revenue, and calling the new highway owners greedy for wanting to recover the $3.8 billion lease price tag it paid to the state.

Other non-highway roads are mainly paid for through property- and local income taxes. And while the current financing of smaller roads differs to that of the highway system, the same principles for "liberty-friendly" road financing apply. Many gated communities already include their own privately owned roads, paid for through homeowner associations. Now let these communities own, control and pay for sections of local roads located in front of them, and there is one reason less for the government to tax us.

Illustration 6.1 Privatization of Long-Distance Roads

Privatization of rural long-distance roads such as this one near the Dallas Divide mountain pass in Colorado helps to move the cost of maintenance to the minority of people who actually use them. Image: SNEHITDESIGN, Bigstock

Chapter 6: Infrastructure

Airports

Similar to the highway system, maintenance of US airports is financed through a tax on aviation fuels. Construction of airports, on the other hand, is mainly paid for through local government funds.

Taxes on aviation fuel are often passed on by airlines to passengers by charging a per-ticket "fuel tax." Because the tax is paid on fuel, taxes are proportional to fuel consumption of an aircraft rather than actual use of airport facilities. Assume two identical aircraft, with the same number of passengers, using identical facilities at JFK airport in New York. Both planes depart just minutes apart from each other, one heading to Anchorage, Alaska, and the other one flying to Boston, Massachusetts. Due to the Anchorage flight's higher fuel consumption (due to the longer route), the airline and passengers have to pay a tax multiple times as high as the tax charged on the Boston flight.

How is it justifiable to make the Anchorage passengers pay more tax if after all they used the same airport resources? Contrary to the highway system, the length of a flight is not related to infrastructure use. The current way of financing airport maintenance is in direct violation with the "Principle of Causation."

Similarly, the use of government funds to finance airport construction is morally questionable. There are frequent fliers, and those who rarely fly at all. Why should everyone, including those with fear of flying be asked to pay for airport construction?

Solutions

There are two options for a more "liberty-friendly" system of funding airport construction and maintenance:

1. Introduce New Types of Financing

For airport maintenance: introduce departure and arrival fees, while abolishing aviation fuel taxes. Departure and arrival fees should be flat and the same irrelevant of whether passengers fly to a neighboring city or thousands of miles away. Fees should be solely based on usage of airport facilities (e.g., by charging more on a flight using a gangway), and not flight distance. Airport departure fees are already used in some countries, including the Philippines and Indonesia.

Airport construction should be financed through the issuance of bonds (which are repaid solely from airport revenues), or better, through privatization (discussed in a moment). Independent financing without the need for local government funds ensures that people not using airports will not pay for them. Some airports, including New Orleans' airport upgrade, are already financed through bonds.

2. Privatize Airports

Airport privatization ensures that no tax dollars are being spent on them, while the owners are free to decide on how to generate revenue for airport facilities. As a result, privatization can help make the state leaner, taxpayers save money and overall make the economy more efficient, as private owners have a profit motive contrary to government officials.

There are two levels of airport privatization: privatization of management and privatization of ownership. At the moment all major US airports are publicly owned and managed, the same being true for many other world airports.

Nonetheless, airport privatization has proven successful in various parts of the world. Germany's largest and Europe's third-largest airport — Frankfurt Airport — for example, is owned and operated by publicly traded Fraport AG. And while around 50% of the company's shares are held by local governments, the same company also owns interests in countries where there is no local government involvement. Ljubljana Airport, Slovenia's largest airport, for example, is fully owned by Fraport, while the firm has majority ownerships in airports in Turkey and Peru.

Illustration 6.2 Government-Owned, Yet Market-Based - Dubai International Airport

Government-owned Dubai International Airport — one of the five largest airports in the world — is financed through a market-based model. Only 2% of Dubai's economy is based on oil, and the emirate does not collect income or property taxes which could be redistributed to the financing of the airport. The airport's income is derived mostly through airline fees, and retail. In fact, Dubai International houses the largest airport retail facilities in the world, along with its terminal 3 (shown

here) being the world's second largest building by floor space. Image: p.lange, Bigstock

Conclusion

Private companies are usually more efficient than governments. Only private ownership can lead to competition. And most importantly, privatization results in highways and airports servicing market demand, be it people's desire for cheap no-frills services, or more upscale, and expensive infrastructure.

Privatization has gotten a bad reputation because governments use it to pass hidden tax increases as we saw with the Indiana Toll Road. Let us give privatization a chance and call out the real cause of toll hikes — the government.

The American Society for Engineers (ASCE) estimates that total infrastructure investment needed until 2020 totals almost $3.6 trillion — in order to remain competitive with other countries. Our government deficit does not allow for such a huge investment, to the contrary, our current financing scheme is not even sufficient to cover basic infrastructure maintenance costs. Let's work with the private sector to make the US economy more competitive.

--- Learn More ---

- [eBOOK] The Privatization of Roads and Highways - An in-depth look at the benefits of private road ownership - https://mises.org/sites/default/files/The%20Privatization%20of%20Roads%20and%20Highways_2.pdf

- [Interactive Website] US Infrastructure Report Card - An estimation of infrastructure investment needed by 2020 - The American Society for Engineers (ASCE) - http://www.infrastructurereportcard.org.

--- Sources ---

1. Highway Trust Fund in Debt - "Politicians Claim the Highway Trust Fund is Broke, But Spend Money on Squirrel Sanctuaries and Bike Paths." Dorothy Jetter. Americans for Tax Reform. https://www.atr.org/politicians-claim-highway-trust-fund-broke-spend-money-squirrel-sanctuaries-and-bike-paths. Retrieved July 28, 2015.

2. The History of the US Fuel Tax - US Federal Highway Administration. http://www.fhwa.dot.gov/infrastructure/gastax.cfm. Retrieved July 28, 2015.

3. Inflation Calculator - US Bureau of Labor Statistics. http://www.bls.gov/data/inflation_calculator.htm. Retrieved July 28, 2015.

4. Indiana Toll Way Privatization - Indiana Business Journal. http://www.ibj.com/articles/49549-indiana-asks-tollway-firm-to-prove-financial-stability. Retrieved July 28, 2015.

5. Indiana Toll Road EZPass Fare - "Indiana asks tollway firm to prove financial stability." EZPass Indiana. http://www.ezpassin.com/traveltime/. Retrieved July 28, 2015.

6. Subsidiaries and Investments of Fraport - Fraport AG. http://www.fraport.com/en/the-fraport-group/fraport-worldwide/subsidiaries-investments.html. Retrieved July 28, 2015.

7. New Orleans Airport Upgrade - "New Orleans Airport Upgrades With New Terminal." Jim Watts. The Bond Buyer. http://www.bondbuyer.com/issues/122_79/new-orleans-aviation-board-adopts-475-million-airport-revenue-bond-sale-1050987-1.html. Retrieved July 28, 2015.

EDUCATION

CHAPTER 7

Everyone, whether childless or not, has to pay for the public education system through property taxes. In this sense, public education represents a "purchase" everyone has to pay for, even if it is never used.

However, it may also be argued that property taxes go towards paying for one's personal public education, not for that of children one does not have. Nonetheless, there are still at least three issues concerning the "fairness" of how we pay for our current education system:

1. People use public education because it is mandatory. Imagine the Ford Motor Company deducting $20,000 from your bank account and placing a new Ford Focus in front of your house. Because the money is gone, you cannot spend it on your preferred car and are left using the Ford. Does your reluctant use of the Focus make the forced purchase legitimate? I doubt it, especially when considering that it prevented you from spending your hard earned money on a better car.

   Yet forcing people to pay for public school under the threat of fines and arrest, leaving them unable to use the same money for private education, is "fine" if done by a government. If a private company, including a private school, was involved in such practices, it would be charged with duress and thievery — serious crimes.

2. The taxes an adult pays today are in no way connected to that person's public school attendance many years or even decades ago. Think about it: public schools are mainly funded through property taxes. Now assume you grew up in a neighborhood with average house prices and average property taxes. As a result, you attended a public school with average taxpayer funding.

   Today, you may live in a neighborhood with lower than average, or higher than average property prices and taxes. As a result, you end up paying less or more than would be appropriate for the education you received.

3. There are people who never attended a US public school. This number is surprisingly high as it includes people who attended private school, were homeschooled, or migrated to the US as adults. Why should they be forced to pay for something they never used?

Even if one has not attended a US public school or sent own children there, it is often argued that an education system financed by everyone incentivizes society to have children. The incentive to bear children, it is claimed, ensures that future generations are large enough to sustain the state. The logical fallacy of this argument is that more children not only equal more taxpayers, but more consumers of government services. Having a smaller future population ideally means that costs and benefits paid by government decrease proportionally.

However, this "ideal" situation is not reality, with higher birth rates being needed to pay for the unsustainable levels of spending and resulting debt of previous generations. Yet just because previous generations "overspent," this does not mean we should perpetuate the pyramid scheme and continue subsidizing education to incentivize childbearing.

Take Bernard Madoff, the investment advisor who created a $65 billion Ponzi scheme, as example. As he needed an ever increasing client base to pay off previous investors, it would have made sense for him to encourage large families. This could have been done by charging childless single investors more in administration fees than those with children. Larger future generations would have allowed him to continue his pyramid scheme indefinitely.

If Madoff had discriminated against childless investors, he would have been fined — in addition to his 150 year prison sentence for the operation of a fraudulent Ponzi scheme. Yet our government is free to discriminate against childless singles, all while perpetuating our Social Security Ponzi scheme.

It is often argued that a fully privatized education system would make education unaffordable and thus inaccessible to children living in poverty. However, when compared, average annual government expenses for the education of one child are surprisingly similar to what parents pay for private school.

In the school year 2011-12, the average government expense for elementary and secondary school students attending public schools amounted to $11,014.

This compares to $10,940 for the average private school in the same school year.

Technically speaking, society as a whole would spend approximately the same if all US students attended private school, rather than public school. Unfortunately, our monopolist government already decided for your children to attend "their" school and prospectively deducted tuition fees from your bank account. This means that if you send your kids to private school, you effectively have to pay twice for their education — once for an unused public education and another time for private schooling.

While the average expense figures for public and private schools can be easily compared, it should be kept in mind that they represent mere averages.

Public school expenses per student vary greatly not only between states, but especially between cities and districts. Districts with high home values (and thus high property tax income) usually spend more on education.

Tuition fees also vary greatly for private schools, with Northeastern schools being the most expensive. There is also a significant cost difference between religious and non-sectarian schools.

As of 2012/13, Catholic schools on average charge the lowest tuition, averaging $7,020 per year, with other religious schools costing on average $8,850.

Non-sectarian schools cost much more, with tuition fees averaging $21,910. Tuition fees, however, vary widely within school types. At the low end, non-sectarian schools only average $750 per year, while at the high end tuition costs on average $29,700.

Because public education is mostly financed through property taxes, some parents already choose between moving to a neighborhood with well-funded public schools and high property taxes, and moving to an area with lower property taxes and using the saved tax dollars for their children's private school education. Depending on the number of children a family has, the private school they select, and the savings in taxes they realize it may be possible for a family to save money by having their children attend private school. For more on this read the article listed in the "read more" section at the end of this chapter.

Options for Reform

How can we reform the educational system in a way that makes everyone pay for one's own education, in accordance with the principle of causation and voluntaryism? There are several options, some of them more far-reaching than others:

1. **Introduce a School Voucher System**

   This is probably the easiest and least controversial reform one can propose. A school voucher system assigns a voucher for every child, covering all K-12 tuition expenses. The voucher may be capped at $10,000 per year and student, approximately equaling the annual government expenditure per public school student today. A voucher system would keep government expenditure the same, yet allow parents to choose a school for their child. Private schools compete along with public schools to receive students and the income school vouchers provide.

   This "free market" of competing schools can be augmented by removing government regulation on curricula and requirements to have certain facilities. Instead, private schools are free to develop their own curricula, adopt an international high school program such as the International Baccalaureate (IB) or even work together with universities to design programs preparing students for college. Some schools might specialize in sports, others focus on science, and again other schools may emphasize on business studies.

   The competition between schools, along with the lack of requirements on how to teach, allows students and parents to choose a school which fits their own interests and preferences. Because schools need to "compete" for students to remain afloat, school quality is high and everyone can enjoy a private school environment.

There are almost endless possibilities of how schools may choose to position themselves. For example, it would not be far-fetched to think of schools which ask for an additional $1,000-$2,000 per year to offer kids even more opportunities, such as extensive field trips to other states and countries.

Another idea which might take track is a "condensed" school career. A private school may remove certain subjects from the curriculum in order to allow students to graduate with a full high school diploma in just 10 years or less. As an example, for kids who dislike sports and music this means removing those two subjects from the curriculum. Imagine the potential savings of students' time and agony, as well as the advantages of allowing kids to start and complete university two years early. A shorter school career translates into more years of working income, while reducing the government's expenditure on school vouchers.

The great thing about a voucher program is that it allows for full customization of schools to student needs and preferences. Why do we need one government-approved education model like Common Core that fits all, if we can have hundreds of choices at the same or lower cost?

A voucher system allows students from all social backgrounds to receive the opportunity to begin at the same starting point. The problem of poor inner city children is that they have no choice other than attending a run-down inner city school. Poor education perpetuates the cycle of poverty, resulting in poor paying jobs, crime, drug abuse and teenage pregnancy. With school vouchers, students from inner cities are free to attend schools outside their neighborhood or district. Additional entry interviews/exams may be used to prevent a deterioration of the classroom experience in high-quality schools.

Supporting the argument in favor of school vouchers is data coming from districts which have already implemented such programs. Washington D.C. and New York City both awarded school vouchers to low-income families. African American students which won a voucher in the DC lottery program and, as a result, had the choice to attend private school were 24% more likely to go to college than students who attended public school. A similar school voucher lottery in New York City also resulted in a 31% increase in full-time college enrollment for African Americans, though no significant impact on Hispanic students was found (too few White and Asian students took part in the study to make conclusions about them). Yet probably one of the best and most surprising results of the program was that when introduced on a large scale, the school vouchers actually *decreased* government expenses on schooling.

2. **Abolish Public Schools**

Competition between public and private schools in a voucher system only remains fair when the state discontinues supplementary funding of (i.e., subsidies for) public schools. After all, a main argument for employing a voucher system is to encourage public schools to improve to the private school level. Providing them with even more money may slightly increase their offerings to students, but in the long run only perpetuates their inefficiency.

If public schools have to compete with private schools on a level playing field — with the same amount of government (voucher) funds — there is little reason not to close them down after private schools have expanded their capacity to educate all US children.

There will always be people out there rejecting the voucher system. Be it teachers not wanting to work more, or liberal parents fearing the loss of a public style education.

However, according to voluntaryism, teachers and their unions have no right to impair the future of students by depriving them of school (and teacher) choice.

And if liberal parents prefer a public school curriculum, what hinders them from starting their own school and teaching according to the current public school standards? Let us see how many parents voluntarily choose to send their children there. Isn't it interesting that liberals complain when they are stripped of the right to force their educational practices onto everyone else, while protesting conservatives teaching their free-market view of the world?

The beauty about the voucher system (and the free market in general) is that everyone may live as one pleases — as long as one respects the same right of everyone else.

3. **Complying with the "Principle of Causation"**

The voucher system is ready to be implemented today. And while it may take a decade or two for new private schools to be built, new curricula to be designed and schools to develop their own unique identities, it will immediately lead schools to improve as a result of competition.

A more far-reaching issue to address is how to finance a government-led voucher program while complying with the principle of causation — the notion that every individual should be responsible for covering his or her own expenses.

The simplest way to achieve this is by eliminating all government funding of education in the form of public schools *and* vouchers, along with axing the property taxes currently used to fund it. People should only finance the education of their *own* children — in a direct manner, not indirectly through taxes.

The main problem with such a policy is that some parents will not voluntarily pay for their children's education, and choose to cash in the savings instead. There are several options to deal with such parents:

1. Legally require parents to pay for their children's education. Make it a legal requirement for parents to finance their children's K-12 education. If parents fail to do so, government may step in and redirect part of their income to fund their own children's education. Of course, some parents will be unable to pay 10k per year and child, especially if they have several children. But there is a solution for that, too:

2. Establish a mandatory "education fund." According to this proposal, every adult should be required to pay into a "personal education fund." Starting from the first year of employment, the government would require every individual to incrementally deposit the value of several standard school vouchers into a savings account style "education fund." Once a child is born, and both parents happen to be unable to pay for his/her education, the government taps their "personal education funds" to secure the financing of their child's education.

The education funds are used solely for one's own child(ren). People who remain childless until a certain age (e.g., 65 years) will be allowed to cash in their education fund deposits.

Again, it should be emphasized that private school tuition fees replace a large portion of property taxes that currently pays for public education. As the average private school costs slightly less than public schooling, as shown before, school expenses should decrease for the average family. Yes, you will have to pay tuition fees, but this is more than compensated for by the reduction in taxes.

What makes such a system superior to our current tax-based system is that it would stop the practice of charging those with the highest valued properties the most for education, rather than those who have children. How is it justifiable to force a childless single with an expensive property to pay more for public schooling than a large family residing in an average-value home?

While the "education fund" proposal may ensure every child receives a proper education, I am still at odds with the idea of *forcing* people who know they will remain childless to deposit money into a (refundable) education fund.

3. Charity and Adoption

The poorest of families could still rely on charitable organizations such as the churches to provide a basic level of education. After all, with the elimination of most or all taxes people will be able to spend more money on causes they care about, and some of them will relate to providing education to the poor. Not to forget that annual tuition for sectarian schools already averages only $7k per year, or about $4k less than what it costs government to provide education to the average child.

When children lack access to education financed through charity, they should be made available for adoption to more caring foster parents. After all, why should a child suffer from a lack of education just because he/she has parents who violated their responsibility of good care by birthing a child into abysmal poverty? And why should unrelated childless singles be forced to subsidize irresponsible parents and pay for their children's education?

4. Introduce background checks

This proposal may seem contrary to liberty, but why not require aspiring parents to show financial proof that they can pay for a child's education before allowing them to have a child? The same is already required for foster parents.

Conclusion

Replacing our current public education system with one based on school vouchers is easy and allows every child the same head-start. School vouchers work where they have been tried, reduce government expenditures and offer students a higher quality learning environment in private schools.

In a second step, we have to think about how to reform the way we finance education — to make it conform with the principle of causation. It is open for discussion whether simply requiring parents to pay for their children's education is sufficient, or whether a more far-reaching program such as "refundable education funds" is needed. Number one priority in this regard is to end the practice of forcing childless individuals to pay for other people's children's education — while ensuring that kids receive a proper education.

--- Learn More ---

- How sending your child to private school can save you money. http://time.com/money/3108717/private-school-public-school-costs/.

- Overview on the various types of private schools including Montessori and Waldorf schools - http://money.usnews.com/money/personal-finance/articles/2015/02/03/can-i-afford-to-send-my-child-to-private-school.

- [Video] Milton Friedman on public schools and school vouchers - https://www.youtube.com/watch?v=Syp_jR4BNBk.

--- Sources ---

1. Average Public School Expense Per Student - National Center for Education Statistics. https://nces.ed.gov/fastfacts/display.asp?id=66. Retrieved July 28, 2015.

2. Average Tuition of Private Schools by Type (Calculated based on a weighted average of grades based on the number of enrolled students) - National Center for Education Statistics. http://nces.ed.gov/programs/digest/d13/tables/dt13_205.50.asp. Retrieved July 28, 2015.

3. "A Generation of School-Voucher Success." Matthew M. et al. Wall Street Journal. http://www.wsj.com/articles/SB10000872396390444184704577585582150808386. Retrieved July 28, 2015.

Chapter 7: Education

THE JUDICIARY

CHAPTER 8

Chapter 8: The Judiciary

The two pillars of the judiciary — the court system and correctional facilities — have been flooded with cases and inmates respectively.

Both need urgent reform, not just to tackle their inefficiency, but to make them comply with the law and principles of liberty. Let us look at them individually in the following two sections.

THE COURT SYSTEM

CHAPTER 8 - SECTION 1

Our existing government-run court system is highly inefficient. As of June 2015, the average processing time for a US court case was two and a half years. The average time between a court filing and the first hearing averages 15 months, with the hearing process itself taking another 15 months.

As with all averages, some court districts perform better, while others do worse. Fort Myers, Florida, for example, suffers the longest lasting court cases, taking on average 40.1 months or 3 years and 4 months. As illustrated in the following chart, most districts reported wait times until the first hearing, and the hearing process itself to take between 10 and 20 months each — totaling 20-40 months for the entire case.

Illustration 8.1 Average Wait Times Before Hearings and Average Hearing Processing Times by US Court District (right)

Fort Myers, Florida suffers the longest court trial durations. Please note only districts for which both sets of information were available are displayed, meaning that 6 districts out of 168 have been omitted. Raw data on the "average wait time until hearing" was provided in half months only, resulting in a less precise distinction in court districts. Average processing time was converted from days to months shown here. Image: own work by author; data from the US Social Security Administration

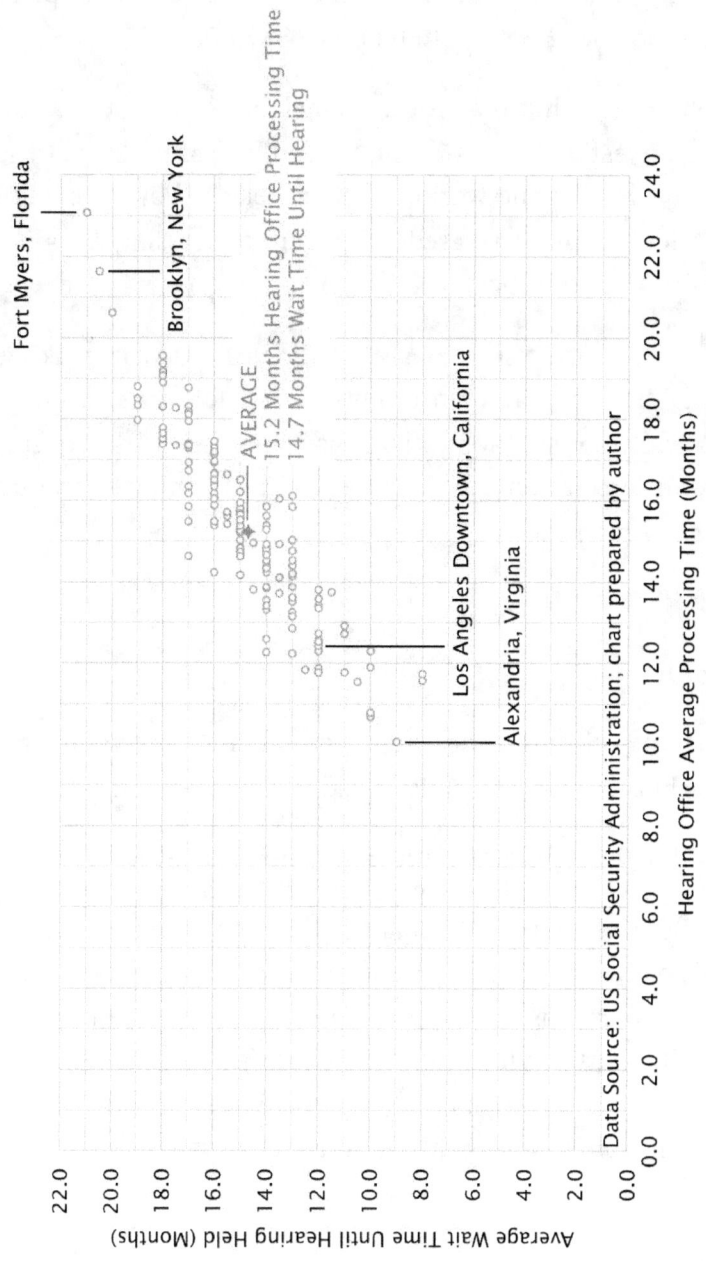

Data Source: US Social Security Administration; chart prepared by author

The US court system also struggles to keep up with the number of cases filed. While the US population grew by only 13% between 2001 and 2014, from 281 million to 318 million, the number of pending civil cases increased by 35% from 250,000 to 337,000.

It goes without saying that court inefficiency is not limited to the US: India has an estimated 30 million pending cases, by far the largest backlog anywhere in the world. A report released by a New Delhi High Court justice claims that based on current processing rates it will take 466 years to clear the backlog.

An inefficient court system has more downsides than making victims wait for justice. It is not uncommon for defendants to await trial in county jails. As a result, long trial processes often lead to overcrowding, additional incarceration expenses for taxpayers and lost productivity by inmates awaiting trial.

Solutions

A number of reforms have the potential not only to increase court efficiency, but to make the judiciary adhere to the principles of liberty:

1. Apply The Principle of Causation and Market Rules

The principle of causation demands that the court system should be financed solely by those who use it — not the general taxpayer. In particular, this means that all court-related expenses ought to be born by the losing party. While to some extent this is already the case, the practice does not reach far enough to make the judiciary financially independent from government funding.

In order to finance themselves, courts need to adopt a market approach and charge court fees high enough to pay for daily operations. Compared to today, court fees would rise — but this is a good thing. In today's world law-abiding citizens who never enter a court in their lifetime subsidize the trials meant to be paid for by the perpetrators who caused them. This needs to stop.

2. Robo-Judges Based on Supercomputers

Most court cases rely at least to some extent on personal assessments and beliefs of justices. Judges can be bribed, and US Supreme Court justices tend to vote along party lines.

In June 2015, the Supreme Court ruled gay marriage to be constitutional, albeit with only a slight majority in a 5-4 vote. Imagine one of the justices in favor of same-sex marriage had changed his/her mind, or voted the other way because of political pressure. Assume that one of the liberal justices had died and been replaced with a conservative during the Bush administration. In any of these cases, millions of people would have to live drastically altered lives.

How can we allow the personal opinion of one individual to decide over the fate of millions? And to what extent do Western democracies represent peoples' popular opinions, if a single Supreme Court justice has the power to change the law of the land?

The appeals process was created to remedy the subjectivity of judges. When a plaintiff or defendant perceives a ruling to be subjective or biased he or she is usually free to have the case reassessed by a higher court. Nonetheless, rather than addressing the core of the problem —

human subjectivity — the appeals process merely passes the power to make an opinionated ruling on to a higher level of authority.

Case law tries to make this process fairer by consulting previous case outcomes when making a new ruling. While the use of case law is well intended, it just means that similar cases will have similar outcomes. The underlying case law is still mostly based on the judgment of a few judges who simply happened to be the first to deal with a certain type of case. Nor does case law guarantee that a ruling conforms to the principles of liberty.

Illustration 8.2 The Subjectivity of the Supreme Court

Should the 9 justices of the Supreme Court pictured here in Washington D.C. interpret our Constitution? The subjectivity of their votes becomes clear when looking at the numerous rulings which were passed or rejected by a small majority of just 5 justices. Image: own work by author

There is one way to eliminate the "arbitrary injustice" of court rulings — employ robo-judges based on supercomputers. By programming a computer system in a way that makes it understand the Constitution, the legal code and the "Law of Liberty," it will be able to objectively evaluate evidence and make judgments based thereon. Such a system will not only ensure compliance with the law, but always result in identical judgments. As a consequence, robo-judges would eliminate the need for the appeal process (with few exceptions), while ensuring that decisions are made independent of racial- and gender-bias.

By electronically linking all robo-judges in a network, hackers and other intruders trying to manipulate the system could be quickly exposed. When a hacker attack occurs all trials in process would be easily halted in order to prevent the manipulation of rulings. Computers also have the advantage of not accepting bribes, do not favor "friends" and work 24/7. The system would instantly eliminate the backlog of court cases found in most countries.

For simple cases like traffic offenses, trials may even take place online. The plaintiff and defendant submit their evidence on a website, with the computer system subsequently making a ruling. Web-based trials have the potential to significantly reduce trial costs and wait times. Say goodbye to taking a day off from work just to attend a court hearing.

With the current state of technology, robo-judges may only be used as advisors to human judges, or for simple cases such as traffic offenses. However, with accelerating technological progress there is little reason not to replace human judges with computers in the future. Remember, a robo-judge does not have to be perfect or accurate in 100% of cases. As soon as the technology convicts fewer innocent people than a human judge does, it is ready for implementation.

Illustration 8.3 Our Court System Is Outdated

New technology such as IBM's Watson supercomputer will allow us to make the justice system more consistent and equitable. Image: tomloel, Bigstock

3. Privatize the Judiciary

Privatization of the court system is a final step to improve efficiency and foster innovation. In a free society, the court system should not be monopolized by a single institution, even if this is the government. Instead, people should be free to establish their own courts, and run them just like any other business.

"Wait a moment" I hear you say. "Are you serious?"

For most people the thought of privatizing the court system is tied to images of corruption, criminal gangs exploiting the system and possibly even anarchy. Whether these stereotypes hold up, is another question. Let us discuss three major concerns of court privatization:

- **Would private courts be free to rule however they want?**

Certainly not. Private courts would be under the jurisdiction of the legal code just as public courts are today.

- **How can we guarantee that private courts are impartial?**

Guaranteeing court impartiality may require a central (government-led) supervisory body. It is this body through which people could file complaints or report suspicions about court corruption. According to the principle of causation, all operating costs of this supervisory body would have to be born by *offending* courts — and not the taxpayer. For example, a person filing a complaint may be required to pay an upfront filing fee of $100, which would be refunded by the offending court in case corruption is established.

A minimum level of government ensures order while still complying with the principles of liberty, provided that government services are financed solely by the people who voluntarily make use of them or violate other's liberties.

The question of whether a privatized court system could work free from corruption depends on whether the supervisory body is impartial in ensuring courts' compliance with the law. With a government-led supervisory body in place, there is no reason to assume that the privatization of courts would lead to more court corruption. While the government supervisory body can be bribed, so can government judges and courts today.

To the contrary, the market mechanism is likely to lower corruption in a world with private courts. Take the example of two hypothetical private court firms — "CourtPerfect" and "Trial-File." Competition between the two companies means that "CourtPerfect" would be more than happy to investigate "Trial-File" and catch the company for biased rulings. If caught, CourtPerfect would report Trial-File to the supervisory body, which then fines or even closes down the offending company. Trial-File would also be ordered to pay for any expenses relating to the case, including CourtPerfect's investigation expenses and costs incurred by the supervisory body.

Similarly, victims of private court corruption could sue the violating court itself, using a competing court provider. Don't you think CourtPerfect would be keen to accept a case from a victim of a competitor's partiality?

CourtPerfect's incentive to "catch" competitors in the act of defrauding clients lies in the opportunity to eliminate a competitor. In comparison, judges in our current government court system face disincentives to report another judge for fraud or bribery. When a judge exposes or reports a colleague, he or she is likely to face retribution from others at work. As a judge, would you risk your career by exposing a colleague's corruption?

In a privatized court system, the plaintiff would be free to choose among court providers to start a trial. The resulting competition drives down trial costs and wait times — just as is the case with any privatized industry.

In a privatized court system, the plaintiff would be free to choose among court providers to start a trial. The resulting competition drives down trial costs and wait times — just as is the case with any privatized industry.

Even if prices increased, this would be the result of scrapping extensive taxpayer-funded subsidies for courts. In other words, costs are re-distributed from law-abiding taxpayers to offenders, while increased competition between court providers increases efficiency and reduces costs to society as a whole.

- **Won't private courts price out the poor from filing lawsuits?**

A fully privatized court system will have numerous competing court providers, all of which would likely offer different payment plans. One company may require the person filing a lawsuit to pay a deposit, which is returned when the defendant is deemed guilty and ordered to cover all trial costs. Another company may be happy to accept any trial without deposit for the sole prospect of charging the losing party court fees.

It is already common practice for some lawyers to work on trials without charging upfront fees. The same would likely be the case for private court providers.

--- **Learn More** ---

- [Video] How corrupt is America's judicial system? https://www.youtube.com/watch?v=GWXLg_e9Ano

--- **Sources** ---

1. US Population - United States Census. http://www.census.gov/popclock/. Retrieved July 28, 2015.

2. Number of Pending Civil Cases in the US - "In Federal Courts, the Civil Cases Pile Up." Joe Palazzolo. Wall Street Journal. http://www.wsj.com/articles/in-federal-courts-civil-cases-pile-up-1428343746. Retrieved July 28, 2015.

3. India's Inefficient Court System - "Justice Delayed is Justice Denied: India's 30 Million Case Judicial Backlog." Ram Mashru. The Diplomat. http://thediplomat.com/2013/12/justice-delayed-is-justice-denied-indias-30-million-case-judicial-backlog/. Retrieved July 28, 2015.

4. Average Wait Time Until Hearing Held Report - US Social Security Administration. http://www.ssa.gov/appeals/DataSets/01_NetStat_Report.html. Retrieved July 28, 2015.

5. Hearing Office Average Processing Time Ranking Report - US Social Security Administration. http://www.ssa.gov/appeals/DataSets/05_Average_Processing_Time_Report.html. Retrieved July 28, 2015.

Chapter 8 - Section 1: The Court System

CORRECTIONAL FACILITIES

CHAPTER 8 - SECTION 2

Correctional facilities including prisons have the main purpose of punishing, and theoretically, rehabilitating offenders. The system is paid for by the victims — the general taxpayers — not by the criminals themselves. The average US prison inmate costs the state $31,286 per year, with New York City paying the most for every prisoner at $167,731 annually. These expenses include food, provision of shelter, security as well as wages and benefits for prison staff. Staff compensation accounts for the majority of expenses at 83% of total incarceration costs.

Given the fact that the US has 2,267,000 incarcerated adults, this means that taxpayers have to pay an estimated $70 billion annually, or about $580 per US income taxpayer (of which there are 120 million).

The United States has one of the most inefficient incarceration systems in the world, not only because of the country's high per inmate cost, but due to its record incarceration rate. While the US has 5% of the world population, we hold 25% of world prisoners. After the Seychelles (a country of just 90,000 located in the Indian Ocean), the US has the highest incarceration rate in the world at 698 per 100,000 adults.

The following table compares the ten countries with the highest incarceration rates with several other notable countries.

Ranking	Country	Incarceration Rate (per 100,000 Adults)
1	Seychelles	799
2	United States	698
3	St. Kitts and Nevis	607
4	Turkmenistan	583
5	Cuba	510
6	Rwanda	492
7	El Salvador	489
8	Thailand	466
9	Belize	449
10	Russia	446
...	...	...
46	Singapore	220
81	UK (England & Wales)	148
122	France	100
138	Germany	78
147	Norway	71
172	Japan	49
185	India	33

Incarceration Rate by Country - International Centre for Prison Studies. http://www.prisonstudies.org/highest-to-lowest/prison_population_rate?field_region_taxonomy_tid=All. Retrieved July 28, 2015. Rankings were adjusted by author to exclude non-country jurisdictions.

There are three main reasons for the high US incarceration rate:

1. **The war on drugs** - Probably the single most significant cause, the war on drugs was officially started in the 1970s by then President Richard Nixon. Since then, the prison population has risen by 700%, while the US population rose by "only" 36%. Today, about 50% of all prison inmates serve due to drug-related charges, 80% of which are based on mere possession of drugs. As will be discussed in chapter 15.3, personal behaviors that do not adversely affect others should not be restricted in accordance with the "Law of Liberty." It is alarming that a non-violent and non-coercive personal lifestyle choice consumes 40% of our incarceration resources.

2. **Strict law enforcement** - An estimated 2.3-5% of the US prison population is innocent (equivalent to 51,000 to 111,000 people), costing society not only incarceration expenses, but the lost tax revenue and labor of otherwise productive individuals. Furthermore, convicts, when finally deemed innocent, have a right to compensation, leading to even higher costs to taxpayers. Not to forget the personal tragedies of the people who lost their jobs and potentially their families as a result of wrongful convictions.

   Liberty means that lack of concrete evidence, including sole reliance on eyewitness accounts, is not sufficient to fine and incarcerate a potentially innocent human being.

3. **An inefficient court system** - As discussed in chapter 8.1 - The Court System, an average US court case takes a whopping two and a half years — a number which only includes waiting time for a trial to be held and the court's evidence processing time.

   While the terms "jail" and "prison" are often used interchangeably, jails are usually managed by local law enforcement. They are used to hold people awaiting trial and punish misdemeanors (rather than felonies). Prisons are usually managed by the federal- or a state government and hold prisoners over longer times for serious felonies.

Long wait times for court hearings mean that a growing number of people which cannot afford bail are locked up in jail to await trial — some of them being innocent.

Solutions

There are numerous liberty-based reforms for our broken incarceration system:

1. The Foremost Objective of Correctional Facilities Should Be to Restore a Victim's Property

How can justice prevail when instead of being compensated, crime victims have to pay for the incarceration and rehabilitation of their perpetrators through tax dollars?

The "Principle of Causation," one of the cornerstones of liberty, tells us that those responsible for an expense should pay for it.

Once a crime happens and the perpetrator is sentenced, he/she should be required to:

• Pay for all costs relating to his/her persecution, capture and rehabilitation. These costs are to be paid directly to police, the court system and rehabilitation/incarceration facilities, plus a profit margin if these institutions are privately operated.

- Compensate the victim for all costs he/she incurred including the value of the fraud/theft, lost wages from work, loss of leisure time and emotional stress.

- Pay a fine, preferably of an amount multiple times the value of the damage caused, to deter future offenses. For the same reason, fare-dodgers are fined many times the amount of a regular bus or metro fare.

For felonies involving large scale fraud, significant property damage or the taking of life, the compensation and fines to be paid by the perpetrator may easily exceed the criminal's income or net worth. How should we deal with situations where offenders are unable to pay their victims?

1) All persecution and trial costs, compensation for the victim and the corresponding fines should be paid by the offender using his/her private net worth. This may involve the use of his/her income and the liquidation of personal assets. If the funds are sufficient to cover these costs, the case is settled, and the offender is set free.

   As will be shown in a moment, incarceration should only be used as a *last* resort to make an unwilling or unable offender pay for his/her crime. Incarceration is not to be used as a punishment or a way to rehabilitate criminals.

   Nonetheless, it should be kept in mind that prisons continue to serve the purpose of keeping dangerous criminals away from the public. In the minority of cases in which criminals represent a threat to public security it would be tolerable to extend prison terms beyond the time required for an offender to pay his/her debt obligation.

1) In case an offender's net wealth is insufficient to cover the expenses of his crime, he will be required to hand over his personal income to a fiduciary. The fiduciary's task is to appoint a majority of the income to the victim's compensation and trial costs, with a minimum amount left to the offender to live on. In order to avoid abuse of the system, a criminal is required to work full time and to his highest potential.

2) In case the criminal is unwilling to work, lacks a job or earns below a certain threshold, he will be subject to imprisonment and made to work until all "debt" is paid off.

A typical work plan for a prisoner may look as follows: assume an offender "owes" persecution expenses, fines, and compensation obligations totaling $20,000. Due to the offender's inability to find work in the open economy, he is sent to a prison to work. The prison has daily expenses for shelter, food etc. of $40 per inmate, while prison work earns the inmate $60 per day.

In order to encourage the offender to pay his debt, the first $20 of his earnings are redirected to debt service, with the following $40 of income being used for the inmate's living expenses:

Provision for the inmate's basic necessities is tied directly to his earnings of the excess $40. To prevent prisoners from only earning the money needed for their living expenses and not making a surplus to repay their victims, their first $20 of daily income are automatically redirected to debt service. If an inmate is unwilling to earn the money needed for debt service and personal living expenses, he/she will be stripped of all but very basic food and shelter.

The inmate is released as soon as all debt obligations to his/her victim, police, and the judiciary are paid. Given that the offender works seven days a week, based on our estimate of his daily prison income, he would be able to pay off the $20,000 in debt obligations in 2 years and 9 months, after which he is set free.

In a prison system in which prisoners are required to pay for their own incarceration and compensate their victims, efficiently operated, privatized prisons are essential. Our current government-run prisons are simply too inefficient to allow inmates to earn enough to pay for their incarceration. The daily cost per inmate in New York City, for example, totals $460. A prisoner had to earn $167,731 per year just to pay for his "accommodation," before any money could be used for debt obligations. Now add the government's difficulty of finding productive jobs for inmates and one can quickly realize that a complete overhaul of our prison system is needed.

So far we have established that incarceration should only be used when an offender is unable or unwilling to pay for his/her persecution and victim's compensation by working a regular job in the open economy (or represents a danger to public safety). Incarceration is not used to rehabilitate or punish offenders. Prison terms depend solely on the time required for an offender to serve his/her debt obligations, rather than the arbitrary term lengths made up by lawmakers.

As shortly mentioned before, offenders who work a regular job but earn an income below a certain threshold are also imprisoned. The income threshold is determined by the amount of money an inmate can earn through prison work.

In our previously used example, the inmate made $60 a day. Subtracting $40 for living expenses, this leaves him with $20 for debt repayment. If the offender can earn more than $20 a day to be used for debt repayment by working a regular job in the open economy, he is free to do so. If he earns less, he will be sentenced to prison work.

As mentioned before, it should not be forgotten that prisons also serve the purpose of keeping dangerous criminals away from public sight. In the minority of cases in which criminals represent a threat to public security it would be tolerable to extend prison terms beyond the time required for an offender to pay his/her debt obligation. In that case, the inmate would only be required to work enough to cover his/her personal living expenses, while any additional income could be spent on consumption.

Let us discuss some additional concerns people have with a privatized prison system in which term lengths depend on an offender's ability to repay his/her debt:

- If fraudsters are allowed to work in the open economy to compensate their victims, what hinders them to become repeating offenders or escape and flee the state or country?

  An ankle-mounted GPS tracker allows authorities to track the offender and extradite him/her from the place he/she fled to. Tracking information can also be used to significantly improve the probability of solving future crimes he/she might commit.

- Such a system would allow the wealthy to easily compensate a victim and pay for the trial expenses, while a poor unemployed person would have to work in prison. Isn't this unfair?

Provided that a wealthy individual accumulated his wealth through legal means (hard work and innovation), he is in every right to benefit from the fruits of his labor by paying obligations in one go. This is just as fair as a wealthy person being able to buy more cars than a less hard working individual.

Imagine three individuals committing *negligent, but unintentional* murder, one of them is wealthy, the other two are not. The wealthy offender is able to compensate the victim's family right away. The second, less wealthy offender is unable to do so and continues working his regular job to eventually pay the family. The third offender is neither wealthy nor has a job, and as a result, is made to work in prison. The large compensation amount makes it unlikely for the less wealthy offenders to ever serve their obligations. For this reason, the wealthy individual ends up paying multiple times the compensation of the poor offenders. Is this fair? — Certainly not to the victim's family.

In cases such as this one, where murder was unintentional, it is important for the non-dangerous offender to compensate the victim's family — not that he sits in prison for 5 or 10 years.

Making offenders of any sort pay for their crimes is far more beneficial to society than making taxpayers pay for their incarceration or even death penalty.

Irrelevant of whether executing criminals is morally justified, the death penalty costs on average $1.1 million *more* than keeping an individual in prison for life. A study found that California has spent $4 billion on the death penalty since 1978. Since then, the state has only executed 13 people, resulting in an average cost of $300 million per execution. Is it worth to make every Californian — from baby to retiree — pay more than $100 to punish 13 murderers by death? Wouldn't it be more reasonable to make criminals work in prison and have them pay for their food, accommodation and their victims' compensation?

Forcing criminals to literally pay for what they did is more effective than any training, boot camp or other rehabilitation programs. Charging an offender a fee equivalent to multiple times the value of the harm caused may even make it profitable to become a victim. This incentive for victims to report crime, and the disincentive for criminals to commit offenses, can help to drastically reduce crime incidence. Even if victimhood were to become profitable, it is unlikely to result in provocations, as provocateurs are offenders themselves and thus liable to the same treatment.

The added benefits of allowing offenders to work openly in the economy include a large decrease in the prison population, along with increased tax revenues (as offenders now pay income tax) and higher GDP (as offenders produce rather than sitting around).

Not to forget that due to higher paying jobs in the open economy (compared to prison work), allowing non-dangerous offenders work a regular job significantly shortens the time until a victim is fully compensated.

2. Privatize Prisons and Jails

As mentioned before, our government-run prisons are far too inefficient to be paid for by inmates, let alone allow offenders to earn enough money to compensate victims. We learned that "living expenses" for a New York City inmate total $460 per day, or $14,000 per month and

$167,731 per year. While the national average is lower at $86 per day ($2,600 per month and $31,286 per year), it is still too high to ever allow an inmate to earn a surplus.

Many US states already contract out management of prisons to private companies. And while some studies have estimated that long run cost savings of privatization can reach 25%, other studies find little to no evidence for improved cost effectiveness. A main reason for the disagreement on how much private prisons actually save is that public expenses for inmates are often hard to estimate. Government expense reports for its prisons usually exclude Social Security benefits for prison staff and other "hidden" expenses such as subsidized land and utilities.

States decide on whether to privatize prison management based on government estimates on current costs and bids made by private companies. As an increasing number of prisons gets privatized, privatization appears to be more efficient at least based on these government estimates.

Today's privately managed prisons are far from being fully privately operated, as the wording falsely implies. Prison providers have little to no say in food choice, accommodation standards, and prison facilities.

A fully privatized incarceration industry would allow private companies to design, build and run prisons as they wish, without government standards on facilities or room size. While this policy may sound alarming to those fearing deteriorating living standards for inmates, it is likely that prisoners will actually see their lifestyles improve.

Victims should be free to choose which prison the perpetrator should be locked in. Reducing an inmate's standard of living to a degree which reduces his/her productivity would be counterproductive to the victim, who is keen for compensation payments.

The competition between prison providers to offer the best-paying opportunities for inmates, in the shortest times, improves efficiency — and shortens incarceration terms.

It should also be allowed for victims to request the relocation of perpetrators to prisons in states with lower incarceration costs. Kentucky and Indiana, for instance, incur costs of only around $40 per inmate per day (around $1200 per month and $15,000 per year) — in line with our previous estimate. These states have lower incarceration costs because of lower land, construction and labor expenses.

Private prisons — as part of the free market — will much more easily find productive work for inmates than government-run prisons could ever do. A building material manufacturer, for example, may partner with a prison to produce cement and concrete.

The advantage of private prisons requiring inmates to pay their debt is that an offender's and victim's objectives align. The inmate wants to quickly repay his/her debt in order to get released, while the victim wants to get compensated.

3. End the War on Drugs (and Any Other Personal Behavioral Choices)

As discussed in chapter 15.3, it is none of the government's business to regulate how we choose to live our personal lives, as long as our lifestyle choices do not adversely impact others.

The war on drugs, including personal possession of and use of drugs is part of the government's intrusion in our natural "right to be left alone." Just as voluntaryism protects everyone's right to opt-out of health care or social security programs, so does it protect the right to personal drug use.

Drug legalization should help to significantly reduce the prison population, save tax dollars spent on law enforcement and the judiciary as well as boost GDP — as previously incarcerated inmates become productive members of the economy. Lax drug laws are also likely to reduce gang violence on the US-Mexican border, as there would simply be no need for complex and dangerous drug smuggling operations — saving thousands of lives in the process. Based on current incarceration rates, legalizing simple, non-violent personal drug possession would free about 870,000 individuals, or 40% of all current inmates.

As will be elaborated in chapter 15.3, drug legalization is only fair to everyone in society if it involves the end of mandatory health care to prevent health-conscious, disciplined individuals from being forced to subsidize the treatment of others' addictions.

Summary

The reforms proposed here are sweeping, and will without question cause resistance from people on both the right and left. For this reason let me summarize my arguments and hopefully make them even more clear:

- The current incarceration system has the purpose to "punish" and "rehabilitate" offenders. In serious cases, the objective is to protect public safety by locking criminals away.

- Holding an inmate is expensive, with the US spending on average $2,600 per month per inmate, or $31,286 per year.

- In many cases, instead of being compensated, victims along with law-abiding taxpayers are forced to pay for criminals' year-long incarceration.

- Some states have already privatized the management of some of their prisons. While a good starting point, we need a complete overhaul of our prison system to make it comply with the principle of causation.

- I propose a system whose main purpose it is to restore victims' property and make criminals pay for their own persecution. Under this system, criminals are required to pay for these expenses from their personal wealth. If this is not sufficient, they have to use their regular income to pay off their victims and the authorities.

- Offenders are incarcerated in only two cases:

  1. When the criminal is unable or unwilling to earn more disposable income in the open economy than is possible through prison work.

  2. When the criminal represents a danger to public safety.

- High fines, along with the requirement of criminals to compensate victims and pay for their own persecution relieves law-abiding citizens from having to subsidize criminals.

- We should emulate the low-cost structure of prisons in Kentucky and Indiana. Privatization and deregulation of prisons are essential to further reducing incarceration costs.

- By legalizing personal drug possession, the prison population could be reduced by up to 40%. Ending the war on drugs would require an end to mandatory health care and other social programs in order to prevent drug users from adversely affecting people with healthier lifestyles.

* By allowing non-dangerous offenders to work in the open economy, we reduce costs, increase the chance of victims being compensated, and boost GDP.

--- Sources ---

1. US Prison Population - US Department of Justice. http://www.bjs.gov/content/pub/pdf/cpus10.pdf. Retrieved July 28, 2015.

2. Cost Per Prison Inmate - "City's Annual Cost Per Inmate Is $168,000, Study Finds." Marc Santora. The New York Times. http://www.nytimes.com/2013/08/24/nyregion/citys-annual-cost-per-inmate-is-nearly-168000-study-says.html?_r=0. Retrieved July 28, 2015.

3. Cost Per Prison Inmate by US State - Vera, Institute of Justice. http://www.vera.org/sites/default/files/resources/downloads/the-price-of-prisons-40-fact-sheets-updated-072012.pdf. Retrieved July 28, 2015.

4. Statistics on the Extent of the US Prison Population - "Watch How Quickly The War On Drugs Changed America's Prison Population." Pamela Engel. Business Insider. http://www.businessinsider.com/how-the-war-on-drugs-changed-americas-prison-population-2014-4. Retrieved July 28, 2015.

5. Increase in the US prison Population Since 1970 - American Civil Liberties Union. https://www.aclu.org/files/assets/massincarceration_problems.pdf. Retrieved July 28, 2015.

6. Incarceration Rate by Country - International Centre for Prison Studies. http://www.prisonstudies.org/highest-to-lowest/prison_population_rate?field_region_taxonomy_tid=All. Retrieved July 28, 2015.

7. Number of Innocent Inmates - Innocence Project. http://www.innocenceproject.org/about-innocence-project/faqs/how-many-innocent-people-are-there-in-prison. Retrieved July 28, 2015.

8. Cost Comparison Between Private and Government Prisons - "Study Finds Private Prisons Offer Massive Cost Savings." The Daily Caller. Peter Fricke. http://dailycaller.com/2014/07/02/study-finds-private-prisons-offer-massive-cost-savings/. Retrieved July 28, 2015.

9. "The Cost of the Death Penalty in Maryland." John Roman et al. Urban Institute, 2008. http://www.urban.org/research/publication/cost-death-penalty-maryland. Retrieved July 28, 2015.

10. Cost of the Death Penalty in California - "Executing the Will of the Voters?: A roadmap to mend or end the California legislature's multi-billion dollar death penalty debacle." Judge Arthur et al. Death Penalty Information Center. http://www.deathpenaltyinfo.org/california-cost-study-2011. Retrieved July 28, 2015.

DOMESTIC SECURITY

CHAPTER 9

Chapter 9: Domestic Security

We will use the term "domestic security" to group public services meant to ensure people's protection from crime (through police) as well as accidents, natural disasters and fires (fire services). Both the police and fire services are paid for mainly through property taxes.

In the upcoming two sections, we will discuss the extent to which the use of these services correlates with property taxes. What is the best way to make the financing of police and fire services comply with the principle of causation? Let us find out!

POLICE FORCE

CHAPTER 9 - SECTION 1

While property values and thus property taxes appear to be correlated with the use of police services, this is not necessarily the case. The most expensive properties in the United States are usually found in gated communities, which often employ private security contractors. Even lower priced properties such as a $200,000 apartment are often protected through private security, especially when located in high-end apartment complexes in large cities.

Even if there was a correlation between property value and a property owner's use of police services, it would not apply to all properties found in the country.

Anyway, property value is not the underlying cause of why we need police in the first place — the cause is crime. Thus, according to the principle of causation those responsible for crime should pay for crime-related expenses, not the victims — property owners.

A Tragedy

An example is best suited to explain everything that is wrong with how we finance police:

Imagine one evening, when leaving the office and returning to your car you realize that someone has broken in and stolen your navigation system. You call the police, which quickly arrive. They agree to file a report. Several hours later you receive a much-anticipated call from the police chief. The perpetrator was filmed by a surveillance camera and subsequently arrested. You are told he was on his way from Canada to Mexico and stopped in your hometown of New York City for a couple of days. Police also found him in the possession of a small dose of heroin intended for personal use, a crime for which they plan to imprison him. Content that they bring him behind bars, you visit the next Best Buy store and purchase a new navigation system.

While catching the criminal sounds like a success, we should be asking whether it was a "financially worthwhile" idea for you to call the police. New York City has the highest cost per prison inmate in the country, topping an almost unbelievable $168,000 per person per year (the US average is $31,386). The people who are going to pay for this are you and your neighbors. Was it really worth to pay that much for a criminal who was planning to arrive in Mexico just a few days later? Is it reasonable for the local community to pay $168,000 a year just to take revenge on a $200 theft and a person's personal drug use?

In our unfortunate example, we have to add another expense to the astronomical incarceration costs. Your police report of the theft pushed the local crime statistic to a new threshold, requiring the police department to hire another officer and acquire a new police car.

While everyone agrees that we need some form of police or security protection, the question is at what cost. In many cases, reporting minor offenses, ranging from drug abuse to small altercations between neighbors can result in unreasonably high expenses. While in theory everyone shares this cost burden, in reality, those individuals who happen to own the most expensive house or apartment, and thus pay the highest property taxes, have to bear the majority of police expenses.

Our current system reminds me of mafia extortion: either you pay for police and/or private security, or you will be the victim of crime.

What can we do about this?

Solutions

There are multiple options to make the way we finance police comply with the principles of liberty:

1. **Apply The Principle of Causation**

   The principle of causation tells us that those responsible for a crime should be responsible for the expenses related to it. In other words: let the perpetrator pay for his/her offense.

   While at the moment government fines paid by offenders contribute to the financing of police, they are far from covering police expenses. Not to forget that any fines paid rarely benefit the victims.

   In order to comply with the principle of causation, a perpetrator would be required to pay administration fees (hereafter called "crime fees") going directly to the coverage of police expenses such as salaries, office rent and police car expenses. The offender would also be required to pay a fine multiple times the value of the damage to the victim — deterring future offenses.

High fines and the prospect of having to pay for police expenses will without question reduce the incidence of crime. However, even if this was not the case, high compensation of victims and the independently financed police system will neutralize any negative effects of criminal behavior.

Under such a system you would think twice about playing loud music next to your neighbor. Even if you are not made to pay a fine, you would have to pay for police visiting you at your door.

There is also the added benefit that people with minor, non-violent altercations will be more reluctant to call police. The associated police cost for the individual knowingly in the wrong encourages independent conflict resolution. This not only frees officers for more important tasks, but makes our economy more efficient, as a lower need for policemen results in more people becoming available for productive tasks.

2. **Apply Market Principles**

In order to ensure that law-abiding citizens are not left to cover billions in police budget holes, police forces should operate based on market principles. To ensure this, we need to eliminate the portion of property taxes usually reserved for police, while denying police departments access to other public funds or bailouts. If the local police are unable to cover their costs they should increase the "crime" fees they charge to offenders. If this income still does not suffice to cover expenses, cut down costs, for example, by laying off a police officer. If, after all, there is not enough crime to finance police through "crime fees," the current police force apparently exceeds local security needs and potentially deprives society of more resources than the criminals they are supposed to fight.

3. **Privatize the Security Industry**

As a final step, one could allow the operation of private "police firms" possessing the same powers as current "public" police. In such a free market system, we would have competing police providers, with hypothetical names such as "PoliceForce" or "CrimeFighters." These companies would challenge one another to catch the most criminals with the highest benefits to the victims.

A concern that has probably come to your mind is that police privatization is open to abuse. Let us see whether this is really the case:

• **Who oversees security providers?**

The short answer is the free market and the court system. The long answer is that competing security firms would be free to investigate (and arrest) each other for potential fraud or corruption. Any serious crimes (such as infiltration of a security provider by criminals) may first be investigated by competing firms, which then forward the case to the court system which deals with complaints in an objective manner. There will always be a security firm happy to expose another firm's wrongdoings as this (1) allows them to charge a "crime" fee from the offending, competing security provider, where the fee is based on the investigating firm's discretion and (2) leads a court to potentially order the offending security provider to cease operations, eliminating a competitor of the investigating firm.

- **Are private security firms free to choose the "crime" fees charged to criminals?**

As in any true free market, security providers should be free to choose a revenue model of their liking. This can involve charging criminals the aforementioned "crime" fees, or even demanding victims to pay an upfront fee. Such an "upfront fee" sounds scary, but do not forget that privatization involves the axing of any taxes currently used to finance public police forces. Furthermore, competition between firms will lead to the most efficient system of catching criminals, while maximizing the benefit to victims. After all, the company promising a victim the highest success rate of solving a crime and offering the lowest upfront fees, if any, along with the highest compensation once a criminal is caught will flourish in the market. Crime victims are the clients of security and police firms, meaning that they are the ones the market caters to.

- **Is it wise for private police services to have the power to arrest people?**

Well, they would need this power to be effective. However, this does not mean that private firms can arrest people at will and get away with it. If somebody is wrongfully arrested, the police firm itself can be investigated for a "crime," by a competing police firm hired by the victim.

In this context, private police are more beneficial to society than public police. If you are innocently arrested by public police, you are left with no right to compensation for your lost time. Not to forget that in numerous countries — such as Russia — public police are used by the elites as a tool to bring dissidents behind bars on the basis of phony crimes. Our current "public police"

217

are de facto immune to persecution when it comes to charging innocent individuals, private police are not — this is what makes the difference.

- **Who defines criminal- and civil law?**

Certainly not private security firms. Privatization of police involves the executive, not the judiciary. Criminal- and civil law would either remain the same as today, or adjusted to be more in accordance with the law of liberty.

However, I should mention that some libertarians have even suggested that law should be made up by the free market, with people being free to do business or marry according to a privately established set of laws and regulations of their choosing.

Nonetheless, any debate on whether law should be privatized is irrelevant in this context. You will likely agree that private law is a highly hypothetical concept, de facto unrealizable in today's world — be it for political or technical reasons. This book is called "Roadmap to Liberty" and has the intention of providing somewhat realistic and achievable ways to make government more liberty-friendly. Having a single, strong set of liberty-conforming laws in place should be sufficient for that.

--- Sources ---

1. Cost Per Prison Inmate - "City's Annual Cost Per Inmate Is $168,000, Study Finds." Marc Santora. The New York Times. http://www.nytimes.com/2013/08/24/nyregion/citys-annual-cost-per-inmate-is-nearly-168000-study-says.html?_r=0. Retrieved July 28, 2015.

FIRE SERVICES

CHAPTER 9 - SECTION 2

Just as police, fire services are usually paid for through property taxes.

Similarly, property-values and taxes are not necessarily correlated to a property owner's use of fire services. Careless people cause fires, not higher property values, yet we still make those with the most expensive properties pay the most. How can we finance fire services in a way that complies with the principle of causation?

The Privatization of Fire Services

Abolish property taxes and finance fire services through other means. This is how it can be done:

1. **Privatize Fire Services and Allow Competition**

   Privatization ensures that fire stations are financed solely on a voluntary basis and not through forced contributions by property owners. People who want to be protected in case of a fire need to purchase a "fire protection" plan from a private fire service provider.

As in any industry, competition allows new firms to enter, improves service and drives down prices.

2. **Free Markets Offer Variable Pricing**

In a free market, fire service providers are free to choose the types of service they want to offer as well as the prices they want to charge. Here are some ideas of the types of service plans private fire service companies may offer:

- A basic insurance plan may charge $20 per 1000 square feet per month and guarantees free firefighting in case of a house or apartment fire. The rate is high enough to keep a fire company financially afloat. The house fire rate in the US is "only" 1 in 320 households per year. Assuming that every property has just 1000 square feet, this means that a company could collect 320households*12months*$20=$76,800 for every house fire it has to fight. At the same time, a fire insurance of $20 per month would translate to just $240 per year, which is easily affordable especially considering that they in part replace thousands of dollars of property taxes.

- Another plan may not demand monthly payments, but a prior deposit of a few thousand dollars in a fiduciary account in order for firefighters to come to your house in an emergency. The deposit is refundable when you move to another area or decide not to fire protect your home anymore. Under this plan, you would only be charged in case of an actual fire.

3. **Do Not Live in Fear**

Many people assume that the free market provides them with less protection. However, private businesses can protect us just as much as governments, and usually at a lower price and better service quality.

For example, in case you are uncomfortable living in a neighborhood where a neighbor may not have fire service protection (putting your house at risk), you may move to an area with a homeowner association (HOA) which requires everyone to be protected. The HOA may even decide to sign up all residents for fire service insurance and include the costs in the monthly HOA fees. Just like many apartment complexes already have private security (which, by the way, is not required by government regulations), in a world with voluntary fire service provision, management of an apartment complex would likely sign up all units for a fire service.

In the rare case you lived in a neighborhood in which the HOA would not insure everyone, *and* a fire of an uninsured neighbor's house threatened your home, you would still be protected by your own "fire protection" plan. Not to forget that you or your insurance company could sue your uninsured neighbor for damages.

A direct benefit of a privatized system is that fire service providers would likely charge higher rates for homes located in areas threatened by frequent wildfires, while people with a history of carelessly causing home fires will be required to pay higher premiums than everyone else.

Let's end the practice of forced purchases — where every house owner in the country has to pay for fire service coverage. Some people prefer not to be insured or protected — and they have every right to it. All mandatory government provisions, including fire services, violate an individual's "right to be left alone" and should be replaced through voluntary opt-in solutions or be privatized altogether.

We need to end the current property tax system where the one who owns the most expensive property pays the most for fire services, rather than the person deliberately moving to a wildfire prone area or the individual placing fire hazards inside his/her home.

A Moral Hazard

Privatization of fire services helps to make people more responsible for their own actions.

It is well known that houses in many parts of Florida and the South are affordable, but also prone to hurricanes. People are moving there because they want to save and the threat of a 2005-like hurricane season seems far away.

On the other hand, there are people who are fully aware of the hurricane risk and move to less risky places like Colorado instead — a state with significantly higher home prices.

When the "penny-pinchers" are eventually hit by a hurricane, the federal government is quick to launch a disaster relief program. This happened after Hurricane Sandy in 2012 and Hurricane Katrina in 2005. In 2005, Congress approved $10.5 billion of relief spending on September 1 and an additional $51.1 billion on September 7. This is more than $510 per income taxpayer — of course, to be paid by everyone including those who decided to move to Colorado.

In a fully privatized, free market world those who moved to hurricane-prone areas have to live with the consequences.

Saving by moving to risky areas and then requiring others to pay for disaster relief is theft.

--- Sources ---

1. "Home Structure Fires" Marty Ahrens. April 2013. National Fire Protection Association. http://bit.ly/1SGq77N. Retrieved July 28, 2015.

2. "After Katrina: Redwood City Soldiers to the Rescue." Dale McKee. The Spectrum Magazine. http://spectrummagazine.net/pdfs/2005_10_SpectrumArchive.pdf. Retrieved July 28, 2015.

INTERNATIONAL SECURITY

CHAPTER 10

Chapter 10: International Security

International security involves protecting a country against foreign aggressors, be it foreign governments or insurgent groups.

Most countries employ military forces along with domestic security apparatuses to do this. The US, China, Russia, India, Pakistan, and Iran spend roughly 20% of their annual government budgets on national defense. European countries tend to spend significantly less, or about 5% of their budgets. The UK and France spend slightly more at 6.3% and 5.4%, respectively, while Germany spends slightly less at 3.3%.

Military and security spending is a huge contribution to US debt. The US defense spending for 2013 alone amounted to $610 billion, or more than the entire GDP of Nigeria, the world's 21st, and Africa's largest economy. In comparison, the second largest military spender, China, had a budget of just $150 billion in 2015, and Russia spent $60 billion.

The United States has around 900 foreign military bases in 130 countries (or 148 jurisdictions, including overseas territories). In stark contrast, all the world's other countries operate a *combined* total of just 30 foreign military bases. This includes the bases owned by Russia, China, the UK, France, and India.

Like all other government provisions, military and security services depend on taxation to remain afloat. According to voluntaryism, forcing people to pay for military actions with which they disagree is nothing else than theft.

Not to forget that many countries, though fortunately fewer than in the past, conscript their citizens to fight. The thousands of years old practice of drafting soldiers has much resemblance to temporary slavery, violating the notions of liberty in every imaginable way.

Conscripted soldiers are essentially treated as property of the state, in so far that anyone who denies service is fined or sent to jail. Just as slaves in the classical sense, soldiers are deprived of their right to leave, refuse to work or demand higher compensation beyond their master's (i.e., government's) set minimum payments.

While almost all Western countries have abolished conscription, at least for the time being, Austria, Estonia, Finland, and Greece still conscript. Outside of the West, around half of all countries in South and Central America, Africa and Asia conscript. This includes Russia, Iran, Israel and South Korea, but not China and most Gulf countries.

Worse than conscription is male-only conscription. Most countries that still practice conscription only require men to serve, either in the military or in other social service positions. However, soldiers fighting at the front only constitute a minority of military personnel. And there is little reason to assume that women are any less suited to support military operations compared to men, especially when considering that many tasks involve non-combative roles. While conscription itself is immoral, we should at least stop discriminating based on gender when determining who has to provide for a country's security — something both men and women benefit from at the end. While Israel is exemplary for conscripting both men and women, the country continues to require men to serve 3 years and women for "only" 2 years.

Illustration 10.1 Countries That Conscript

No Conscription
Conscription

Austria, Estonia, Finland, Greece, and Switzerland are the only Western countries that still practice conscription. Image: own work by author

What often amuses me is that while conservative Republicans object to excessive government spending on welfare, almost every one of them wants to "strengthen" the military.

Ironically, military spending is just another form of socialism, similar to welfare programs and corporate bailouts. It is an example of one portion of the population forcing the other portion to contribute to the financing of their pet projects. Whether the government *forces* (i.e., steals from) you to pay for Social Security or some military bases in the Indian Ocean makes no difference.

For that reason it would be appropriate to consider anyone expanding the military as just another type of socialist — along with a slave driver. Ron Paul is one of the only Republicans correctly pointing out that the military is just another form of a dictatorial government overreach. Yet ironically, it is he who is branded as being left of Obama, not the "socialists" who want to spend your money on Iraq and the Taliban.

Making military, an institution historically opposed to voluntary interactions, comply with the principles of liberty is tough. However, with each of the 120 million US income taxpayers being *forced* to contribute on average $5,000 to military spending every year, it should be obvious that the military-industrialist complex needs a major overhaul.

Reducing the US Military Budget

There is little reason why a gradual reduction of our military should hurt the US or any other country in that matter. A 60% cut in the US' annual military budget from $600 billion to $240 billion would still make it larger than that of China ($150 billion) and Russia ($60 billion) *combined*. Do you really think a reduction in the number of foreign US military bases by 60% from around 900 to 360 would hurt the U.S. of A.? With 360 military bases, the United States would still have 12 times the number of all foreign military bases of all other countries *combined*.

Ironically, our strong military and numerous interventions in the Middle East may have caused the rise in terrorism over the last decade. Between 1993 and 2003 there were a recorded 20,451 terror attacks worldwide. The period between 2003 and 2013, on the other hand, saw this number more than double, rising to 49,478.

Middle Eastern wars result in poverty, death and *terrorism*. US military support for the Taliban and Syrian insurgent groups fueled their rise, while poverty and death resulting from wars led to the radicalization of their followers. The Islamic State has been especially successful in northern Iraq due to the area's Sunni-Moslem majority, which ironically seeks a return to a Sunni-led government similar to that of Saddam Hussein.

After the Second World War, the US military has seen mixed outcomes from its military operations. While the US was defeated in Vietnam, military interventions in Somalia, Afghanistan, Iraq, Libya and Syria have either failed to improve local security or outright transformed the nations into failed states. On the other hand, victories include the US tie in the Korean War, the invasions of Grenada and Panama, the defeat of Saddam Hussein in the first Gulf War and Kosovo's independence from Serbia.

Illustration 10.2 Drone Use Has Not Helped to Reduce Terrorism

The US has used or still uses drones in Afghanistan, Algeria, Libya, Iraq, Syria, Somalia, Pakistan and Yemen. Drone use for surveillance purposes has also been speculated in Iran (remember when they captured a US drone?). For more read http://bit.ly/1INoSOs. Image: Estteban, Bigstock

The claim that "terrorists hate our freedom" and, therefore, attack the US as stated by George W. Bush in 2001 is ridiculous. The Netherlands, for example, are ranked second in terms of press freedom by the NGO "Reporters Without Borders," while the United States finds itself on place 46. In the eye of Islamists, the northernmost of the BeNeLux countries also condones *far more* sinful behaviors than the US. The Netherlands have introduced partial bans of the Islamic veil and Burqa, have a lower drinking age of just 18 years (16 years prior to January 1, 2014) and more promiscuous attitudes towards revealing dress than the US.

Similarly in 2009, Switzerland amended its constitution to outright ban the construction of new minarets. If the Netherlands and Switzerland are far more hostile towards Islamic values, why are they not attacked? Is it because Islamists hate the American freedom of a mandatory 39.6% (top) income tax, while Saudis are punished with an excessive 0% tax rate?

When it comes to economic freedom, the Arab gulf countries are beacons of liberty — not the US as George W. Bush and virtually every other American politician like to claim. The Gulf countries, namely Bahrain, Kuwait, Oman, Qatar, Saudi Arabia, and the UAE, have some of the lowest tax rates and least-regulated business environments in the world. These are the countries that have *economic freedom*, not the West.

Similarly, while many Gulf countries have banned alcohol consumption in public, you will have no problems drinking as much as you want at hotel resorts in Dubai, where drinking is legal. Bahrain, a small island nation connected to Saudi Arabia by a causeway, has arguably less stringent regulations on alcohol consumption than the United States. The country allows Muslims from the age of 18 to purchase alcohol. In fact, Bahrain has become a popular weekend get-away for Saudis wanting to visit nightclubs and to drink.

If the region had no freedoms, as is often claimed, Dubai would not be the 4th most visited city in the world — ahead of New York. Or rank as the second largest shopping capital on the planet, only behind London, but ahead of Paris and the Big Apple.

War hawks won't realize that the real reason the US and other Western countries are occasionally attacked is because the West attacks first. Even the New York Times admits that almost 600,000 Iraqi children perished due to economic sanctions in the five year period following the First Gulf War. These were UN sanction spearheaded by Western and foremost US interests.

When Arabs retaliated for this and other Western atrocities in the Middle East by killing "just" 0.5% the number of people (~3,000) on 9/11, they are the "evil ones." By no means does this mean we should condone terror, however, we should try to understand where their hatred comes from.

Similarly, people are "shocked" when Islamists kill 130 people in Paris after Western military involvement in Libya and Syria exacerbated the local civil wars that so far have killed around 500,000.

Instead of acknowledging the root of Islamic terrorist attacks in the West - deadly Western interventions in the Middle East - we increase military operations after every Islamic "retaliation," perpetuating the cycle of endless wars and terror attacks.

Not only would the US with a smaller military be just as safe, but every of the 120 million income tax payers could save thousands in taxes — *every year*. A 60% cut in the US' annual military budget would still make it larger than that of China and Russia *combined*, but save the average income taxpayer $3,000 a year. How about spending that money on a two week overseas vacation in Paris and London — every 12 months — instead of literally blowing it up in a desert in Iraq or Yemen?

Whether you decide to spend that money on a foreign vacation or not, most of the saved billions will be:

1. spent on domestic causes, rather than 900 foreign military bases, stimulating our economy and

2. re-invested in actual capital stock such as infrastructure, cars and schools, improving our standard of living, rather than wasting the money on otherwise useless landing strips in the Pacific Ocean.

Furthermore, America's image would improve with people not only in Islamic countries, but around the world, potentially leading to better political and economic relations.

Costa Rica and the Military

More than 10% of the world's countries, 21 to be exact, do not have their own military. And while it is true that some of them have signed mutual defense pacts with larger neighbors (such as Liechtenstein's agreement with Switzerland), others have not. Costa Rica, for instance, does not have military forces, nor has it signed a mutual defense agreement with another country.

Did the lack of a military endanger the Central American country? — Probably not. Costa Rica has not been attacked since its Constitution forbid the nation to operate a standing army in 1949. It saved taxpayers billions of dollars in defense spending, which instead was invested in constructive (rather than destructive) projects such as infrastructure or left to citizens in the form of lower taxes. Not to forget the productivity gain of letting young men join the workforce instead of conscripting them into military service.

Remarkable is that Costa Rica is safe, despite its lack of a military, a small population of 5 million mostly unarmed civilians and a geographical location next to politically volatile and crime-ridden nations such as Honduras — the murder "capital" of the world (read chapter 10.1 - Guns for more on that).

Now that the Cold War is over, does this mean the United States could be safe without operating a military altogether? — Maybe yes, maybe no.

How likely would it be for a foreign aggressor, whether it be Russia, China or Iran, to attack a country located thousands of miles and enormous oceans away, with a vast, armed population hostile to the invader? With close to one firearm per US resident (there are about 270 to 310 million guns), it is unlikely for a foreign army to attack and permanently occupy even a single state of the Union.

The US failed to win the Afghanistan and Iraq wars, countries with a combined population just 20% the size of the US — despite spending around $6 trillion. Part of Northern Iraq is controlled by the Islamic State — an organization arguably worse than the Hussein regime, while the Taliban continues to control, and actually advances in parts of Afghanistan. And contrary to the US, civilians in both countries are mostly unarmed, with armed guerrilla fighters (i.e., the Islamic State and the Taliban) representing a small minority of the population. According to the Small Arms Survey, Afghanistan's gun ownership rate is just 4.6 per 100 citizens, about 5% of the US' 88.8 gun ownership rate, and we still failed to entirely free the country of 30 million from Taliban rule. Iraq's gun penetration is also significantly lower than the US' at 34.2 guns per 100 citizens.

How can pro-war politicians persuade us that a few thousand relatively poorly funded insurgents, for example, Taliban or Islamic State fighters (both groups that ironically came to rise *because* of US foreign interventions), have the power to overtake the United States, a country with an enormous, non-compliant and largely armed populace?

On the other hand, it is important to emphasize the US military's impact on the security of countries other than the United States. Most obviously, were it not for US military intervention in the Second World War, today, Nazi Germany and Imperial Japan would probably rule most, if not all of the planet. South Koreans would most likely live under the tyrannical rule of the Kims, and the Soviet Union might have advanced more aggressively into European and Asian countries.

However, the cold war is over, and a cut in America's military budget to $240billion, an end to Middle Eastern wars and a reduction in the number of military bases from 900 to 360 would still leave the US as the most powerful nation on earth by a large margin.

Alternative Ways of Funding Military Action

Even after cutting US military spending by 60%, the average income tax payer would end up paying $2,000 annually for military operations. Are there other ways to finance the military in a *voluntary* fashion?

1. Private Armies

The US already uses private contractors to supply soldiers and intelligence personnel in war zones. However, the use of the term "Private Armies" in the libertarian sense is different. Private individuals and institutions seeking security beyond that provided by a limited government-led army would be free to hire private military-grade security contractors. Such contractors would work similarly to private security firms already used today to secure office buildings, factories, and other private property. In fact, private military contractors such as Academi (formerly known as Blackwater) have operated in the Iraq and Afghanistan Wars, protect shipping lines from piracy off the coast of

Somalia, secure mines in remote areas of Africa and safeguard NGOs and US diplomats around the world. In this context, they can work similarly to private police firms as discussed in chapter 9.1 - Police Force.

2. Voluntary Donations

A military supported by donations provided by industry, commerce and private individuals complies with voluntaryism, however, will most likely have substantially reduced and more volatile financial resources. Still, from a theoretical standpoint, if a nation's economic participants see a higher need to invest and consume in other areas, why should they be *forced* to contribute a higher share of their hard-earned income to the military-industrial complex? Low levels of voluntary donations are a sign that people regard military protection as less valuable than consumption and investment in the domestic economy.

Wars Are Socialist

As highlighted before, defense spending financed through taxation is just another form of socialism. Unfortunately, many anti-war activists portray war as inherently capitalist. Nothing could be further from the truth. The arguments supporting the view that war is the result of socialism, not free market capitalism, are overwhelming. They include:

1. The countries with the most economic freedom are the ones which rarely fight wars. Just take the top 10 countries in the index of Economic Freedom by the Heritage Foundation. The 10 best ranking countries, in order from best to worse, are Hong Kong, Singapore, New Zealand, Australia, Switzerland, Canada, Chile, Estonia, Ireland, and Mauritius. None of the listed countries has

led a war since the Second World War. Australia and Canada are the only countries which have supplied ground forces during wars, namely for the US-led coalition in Afghanistan and against the Islamic State. And contrary to popular belief, the USA is a mixed economy — half-socialist/capitalist — with more taxes and regulations than even former Soviet countries like Estonia.

2. All major aggressor countries in the last century have been socialist and communist, including National **Socialist** Germany, the **Communist** USSR, and **Communist** North Vietnam.

    Wars are made possible by government control of large portions of the economy, the media and the population. On the other hand, by definition free markets are the opposite of statism, requiring 100% private ownership of property and people's right to self-determination.

    Governments have murdered 262 million people in the 20th century alone, in what has been called *"democide."* On the other hand, few to none have been *directly* killed by private businesses. If at all, businesses supported governments in their quest to kill, for example, IBM's development of a registration system for Nazi concentration camps. Or IG Farben, the predecessor to today's chemical giants BASF and Bayer, which supplied Zyklon B poison gas.

3. Do you know of any war started by a corporation? Every single war in history has been initiated by a *statist* government, though admittedly often in collaboration with a small number of companies with strong ties to politics and the military-industrial complex. Take Halliburton, and Dick Cheney, the company's CEO and Chairman between 1995 and 2000 and the 46th vice president of the United States under George W. Bush as example. At the start

of the second Iraq War, Halliburton was the only company invited to bid on a related government tender, and won the $7 billion contract. Thanks in part to the War, the company saw its revenue increase from $12.5 billion in 2002 to $20.5 billion in 2004 — a 65% increase in 2 years.

4. The military-industrial complex — the only party benefitting from war along with governments — is not capitalist. A small group of government officials and cronies taking from the population for their own benefit depends on government control over, and regulation and taxation of the economy. The de facto merger between defense companies and the government is fascism. If you read Hitler's "Mein Kampf" or the Nazi Party's political program you would soon realize that fascists are opposed to free markets. For more on fascism read chapter 3.2 - Special Interests.

5. The overwhelming number of businesses lose out in war - having their offices and shops destroyed, their supplies of goods cut off and seeing their customers lose the financial means to continue buying from them. I challenge you to find a business that is not part of the military-industrialist complex and supports a domestic or foreign war for profit. Corporations ranging from Coca Cola to GM and Microsoft lose out when Iraq, Syria or Libya are devastated, and local populations become unable to buy from them. The few firms that benefit from war are those that collaborate with governments in a fascistic - not capitalistic - fashion.

6. A common argument dubbed the "broken window fallacy" claims that destruction of property leads to increased future demand, and thus economic and business growth. The reason why it is called a "fallacy" is that just because you have your car or house destroyed, you won't necessarily have the money to replace it. To the contrary,

any money spent on a new car has to be taken from somewhere else - maybe requiring you to quit your vacations or cut down on other living expenses. Destruction never increases wealth. Consumer demand depends on income, not the level of destruction. Because wars reduce people's net disposable income, military action always reduces total consumer spending - hurting businesses.

Conclusion

The military is a huge violator of liberty. It lives off of money stolen from the public and "enslaves" (conscripts) citizens, while being responsible for incalculable economic and human losses.

No one should be forced to co-finance the invasion of another country.

If we absolutely have to intervene in other countries' affairs, please stop toppling the governments of relatively well-off and peaceful nations such as those formerly found in Egypt and Libya. Contrary to the negative image portrayed about Gadaffi in Western media, his country offered free electricity to its citizens, gas at $0.14/liter ($0.53/gallon), awarded $5,000 to every newborn child and operated a state bank that provided loans with a zero percent interest rate to everyone who applied. The government even provided housing, farm land and seeds for free to individuals wanting to establish their own farm business.

Instead look at countries such as North Korea, where 1 in 4 children suffer from malnutrition, people are executed for owning a bible and three generations of a family are sent to concentration camps for an "offense" committed by a single individual. It is heart-braking to know that the largest group of North Korea's 200,000 strong prisoner population (almost 1% of the country's 24.5 million people) consists of the children and grandchildren of the original "wrong-doers" and were born inside the camps. Compared to the non-stop coverage about Iran, how often do you hear the media lament about North Korean labor camp conditions, where prisoners fight over picking kernels of corn out of cow dung to survive?

Ask yourself the question why it is not one of the last two remaining Communist countries that we invade, but Libya, which boasted Africa's highest GDP per capita and highest life expectancy just before Western military intervention. Nato forces have transformed Africa's formerly wealthiest country into a failed state partly controlled by the Islamic State as of Summer 2015.

--- **Learn More** ---

- [Video] US military bases around the world - https://www.youtube.com/watch?v=gU8rQWh_qtc

- [Video] Does the US create terrorists? - https://www.youtube.com/watch?v=Tul7qkUbGdg

- Index of Economic Freedom by the Heritage Foundation - http://www.heritage.org/index/

- Democide and the mass murder of 262 million people by governments in the 20th century alone - https://www.hawaii.edu/powerkills/MURDER.HTM

- [Video] What Is Life Really Like In North Korea? - https://www.youtube.com/watch?v=d2SEDagk4YE

--- Sources ---

1. [Video] US Military Bases around the world. Vox News. https://www.youtube.com/watch?v=gU8rQWh_qtc. Retrieved July 28, 2015.

2. Ron Paul says U.S. has military personnel in 130 nations and 900 overseas bases. Politifact. http://www.politifact.com/truth-o-meter/statements/2011/sep/14/ron-paul/ron-paul-says-us-has-military-personnel-130-nation/. Retrieved July 28, 2015.

3. Defense Budgets by Country. Visual Economics. http://visualeconomics.creditloan.com/how-countries-spend-their-money/. Retrieved July 28, 2015.

4. 2013 US Defense Spending. US Government Publishing Office. http://www.gpo.gov/fdsys/search/pagedetails.action?granuleId=BUDGET-2015-TAB-5-1&packageId=BUDGET-2015-TAB&fromBrowse=true. Retrieved July 28, 2015.

5. 2015 Defense Spending of China and Russia. GFP - Global Fire Power. http://www.globalfirepower.com/defense-spending-budget.asp. Retrieved July 28, 2015.

6. Definition of Slavery - "The Politics of Property: Labour, Freedom and Belonging. ." Laura Brace (2004). Edinburgh University Press. pp. 162–. ISBN 978-0-7486-1535-3.

7. "US Wars in Afghanistan, Iraq to Cost $6 trillion." Sabir Shah. GlobalResearch.Ca. http://www.globalresearch.ca/us-wars-in-afghanistan-iraq-to-cost-6-trillion/5350789. Retrieved July 28, 2015.

8. [Video] Does the US create terrorists? - https://www.youtube.com/watch?v=Tul7qkUbGdg

9. US National Debt Clock - US Debt Clock. http://www.usdebtclock.org. Retrieved July 28, 2015.

10. Number of Guns in the US - "A minority of Americans own guns, but just how many is unclear." Drew Desilver. Pew Research Center. http://

www.pewresearch.org/fact-tank/2013/06/04/a-minority-of-americans-own-guns-but-just-how-many-is-unclear/. Retrieved July 28, 2015

11. Nigeria GDP - "GDP by Country." CIA World Factbook. https://www.cia.gov/library/publications/the-world-factbook/fields/2195.html. Retrieved July 28, 2015.

12. Afghanistan's and Iraq's Population - "Population by Country." CIA World Factbook. https://www.cia.gov/library/publications/the-world-factbook/rankorder/2119rank.html. Retrieved July 28, 2015.

13. "2014 World Press Freedom Index." Reporters Without Borders. http://rsf.org/index2014/en-index2014.php. Retrieved July 28, 2015.

14. "The 10 Most Visited Cities in the World." Sarah Schmalbruch. Business Insider. http://www.businessinsider.com/the-10-most-visited-cities-in-the-world-2015-6. Retrieved July 28, 2015.

15. Most Popular Shopping Destinations - "New York, Paris ... Dubai. Why the desert mall is the height of couture." Melanie Rickey. The Guardian. http://www.theguardian.com/world/2014/nov/01/dubai-tops-paris-new-york-luxury-fashion-mecca. Retrieved July 28, 2015.

16. Deaths in Iraq - "Iraq Sanctions Kill Children, U.N. Reports". Barbara Crossette. New York Times. http://www.nytimes.com/1995/12/01/world/iraq-sanctions-kill-children-un-reports.html. Retrieved June 28, 2016.

16. Deaths in Syria - "Death Toll From War in Syria Now 470,000, Group Finds". Anne Barnard. New York Times. http://www.nytimes.com/2016/02/12/world/middleeast/death-toll-from-war-in-syria-now-470000-group-finds.html?_r=0. Retrieved June 28, 2016.

16. "Is Private Security Taking Over Africa?" African Business Magazine. http://africanbusinessmagazine.com/uncategorised/is-private-security-taking-over-africa/. Retrieved July 28, 2015.

17. $7 Billion Contract Awarded to Halliburton - "BBC uncovers lost Iraq billions." Jane Corbin. BBC. http://news.bbc.co.uk/1/hi/world/middle_east/7444083.stm. Retrieved July 28, 2015.

18. "Halliburton Annual Report - 2004." Get Filings. http://www.getfilings.com/o0000045012-05-000055.html. Retrieved July 28, 2015.

19. "10 Things You Didn't Know About Libya Under Gaddafi's So-called Dictatorship." Top Info Post - News Aggregate. http://topinfopost.com/2014/11/16/10-things-you-didnt-know-about-libya-under-gaddafis-so-called-dictatorship. Retrieved July 28, 2015.

20. "North Korea Child Malnutrition: 1 In 4 Kids Suffer From Chronic Food Insecurity And Hunger, UN Says. Peter James Spielmann." The World Post by the Huffington Post. http://www.huffingtonpost.com/2013/03/15/north-korea-malnutrition-un-children_n_2884831.html. Retrieved July 28, 2015.

21. "How a voice from a North Korean gulag affected human rights discourse." Madison Park. CNN. http://edition.cnn.com/2013/05/10/world/asia/north-korea-gulag/. Retrieved July 28, 2015.

22. "North Korean Prisoner Escaped After 23 Brutal Years." Shin Dong-hyuk. CBS News. http://www.cbsnews.com/news/north-korean-prisoner-escaped-after-23-brutal-years-15-05-2013/. Retrieved July 28, 2015.

23. North Korea publicly executes 80, some for videos or Bibles, report says." JoongAng Ilbo. Fox News. http://www.foxnews.com/world/2013/11/12/north-korea-publicly-executes-80-for-crimes-like-watching-films-owning-bible/. Retrieved July 28, 2015.

24. "Libya: From Africa's Richest State Under Gaddafi, to Failed State After NATO Intervention." Garikai Chengu. Centre for Research on Globalization. http://www.globalresearch.ca/libya-from-africas-richest-state-under-gaddafi-to-failed-state-after-nato-intervention/5408740. Retrieved July 28, 2015.

GUNS

Based on the "Law of Liberty," an individual has the right to own and use firearms, as long as he/she does not infringe on the same right of others or harm people.

Gun rights are also an important part of everyone's natural right "to be left alone." In essence, you are free to own firearms and be left alone by regulators, provided that you respect the same right of others.

Besides being a cornerstone to liberty, the ownership of firearms is also protected through the Second Amendment which reads:

"A well regulated Militia, being necessary to the security of a free State, the right of the people to keep and bear Arms, shall not be infringed."

The Fourteenth Amendment, passed in 1868, offers further support by prohibiting states from passing legislation in conflict with the Constitution, including the Second Amendment:

"No State shall make or enforce any law which shall abridge the privileges or immunities of citizens of the United States."

The US Constitution's stance on gun rights is especially significant considering the unique relationship between the US government and the US Constitution. In the United States, government is a product of the Constitution, not the other way around. The Constitution was drafted by the Founding Fathers and written by James Madison — not by a government committee. Delegates from the states subsequently ratified the document on June 21, 1787. This effectively created the country's first modern government with George Washington becoming the first president around 10 months later on April 30, 1789.

In France, the UK, and most other countries, constitutions are products of the respective governments, not vice versa. In these places, it was the ruling party that implemented the constitution, not the constitution that implemented the presidential rule of law, like in the United States.

Because the US Constitution existed before the current US government, it will continue to stand above it. On the contrary, in France (and other countries) the notion persists that government is the grantor of constitutional rights, and can take them away.

Despite the right of Congress to amend the US Constitution through a 2/3 majority in the House of Representatives and Senate, our history emphasizes that people's rights *do not* come from government, but a higher being.

Our rights are god-given (or for atheists, inherent to human morale). The US Constitution is there to protect these rights, and it is the government's duty to protect them in accordance with the Constitution.

This view is very different to that of socialists who see government and the politicians which make it up as the ones who grant rights. Socialists assume that "rights" are a social construct, not inherently god-given or a universal truth.

Even if you reside outside the US and your country's constitution denies you the right to bear firearms, you should, according to the "Law of Liberty" have the right to own and use guns.

A Fact-Based View on Guns

Gun rights are an integral part of liberty. Nonetheless, we shall now consider a number of gun-related myths many believe in.

One common assumption is that high gun ownership rates are related to higher homicide rates. Let us compare global gun ownership with homicides. As shown in following table, the 15 countries with the highest gun ownership rates are mostly the US, countries in Northern-, Western- and Central Europe and on the Arabian Peninsula. These include Finland, Sweden, Norway, France and Germany.

In most cases, the countries with the highest gun ownership rates also enjoy some of the lowest homicide rates. The US has the highest private gun ownership rate in the world, yet only ranks 111th worldwide in homicides. Numerous European countries ranking in the top 15 by personal gun ownership are among the countries with the world's lowest homicide rates. Iceland, for example, ranks 15th in terms of gun ownership with 30.3 firearms per 100 people. At the same time, the small nordic country enjoys the 4th lowest homicide rate in the world, only outshined by Singapore, Liechtenstein and Monaco.

The most violent countries — mostly located in central America — only have a tenth of the US gun ownership rate. Honduras boasts the highest homicide rate in the world at 90.4 homicides per 100,000

Gun Ownership Ranking	Country	Gun Ownership Rate/100 People	Homicide Ranking (out of 218 Territories)	All Types of Homicides /100,000 People	All Types of Homicides /100,000 Guns
1	USA	88.8	111	4.7	5.3
2	Yemen	54.8	109	4.8	8.8
3	Switzerl.	45.7	209	0.6	1.3
4	Finland	45.3	172	2.0	4.4
5	Serbia	37.8	184	1.2	3.2
6	Cyprus	36.4	158	2	5.5
7	Saudi A.	35	198	0.8	2.3
8	Iraq	34.2	79	8	23.4
9	Uruguay	31.8	81	7.9	24.8
10	Sweden	31.6	205	0.7	2.2
11	Norway	31.3	155	2.2	7.0
12	France	31.2	191	1	3.2
13	Canada	30.8	170	1.6	5.2
14	Austria	30.4	195	0.9	3.0
=15	Iceland	30.3	215	0.3	1.0
=15	Germany	30.3	205	0.6	2
...	...	...	...	...	...
49	Guatemala	13.1	6	39.9	304.6
59	Venezuela	10.7	2	53.7	501.9
62	Belize	10	4	44.7	447.0
88	Honduras	6.2	1	90.4	1458.1
92	El Salvador	5.8	5	41.2	710.3

Source: United Nations Office on Drugs and Crime. http://www.unodc.org/documents/gsh/pdfs/2014_GLOBAL_HOMICIDE_BOOK_web.pdf. Retrieved July 28, 2015.

people, while only having 6.2 guns per 100 citizens. This compares to the US homicide rate of 4.7 and a gun ownership rate of 88.8.

The global imbalance between personal gun ownership and homicide rates is reflected in the homicides per 100,000 privately owned guns rate. The US has 5.3 homicides per 100,000 guns while Honduras experiences 1458 homicides — more than 270 times the US rate.

Norway is by many accounts one of the most progressive countries in the world. The Northern-European nation has also some of the world's strictest gun laws. Yet it has 7.0 homicides per 100,000 guns — more than the US at 5.3.

The global disconnection between gun ownership and homicide rates is probably best shown by comparing heat maps displaying the incidence of both. As can be seen in illustration 10.4, gun ownership is highest in the US, Canada, Europe, and parts of the Middle East, while homicide rates are highest in Central- and South America as well as Sub-Saharan Africa.

--- Note on Data Sources ---

On a side note it should be mentioned that due to lack of data on homicides caused by firearms, the numbers used here show the overall rates of intentional homicides. The homicide rates were taken directly from the United Nations Office on Drugs and Crime for which the source can be found at the end of this chapter.

It should also be noted that the gun ownership rates are based on private possession. In a few countries, including Switzerland and Israel, citizens keep government registered firearms at home, all of which have been excluded from the statistics. The exclusion of these firearms has the effect of artificially deflating gun ownership rates in these countries, while inflating the homicides per gun ownership rate. Gun ownership rates are based on the Small Arms Survey conducted by the Graduate Institute of International and Development Studies in Geneva, Switzerland, the link to which can also be found at the end of this chapter.

Illustration 10.4 Comparison Between Private Gun Ownership and Homicide Rates

Private Gun Ownership per 100 People

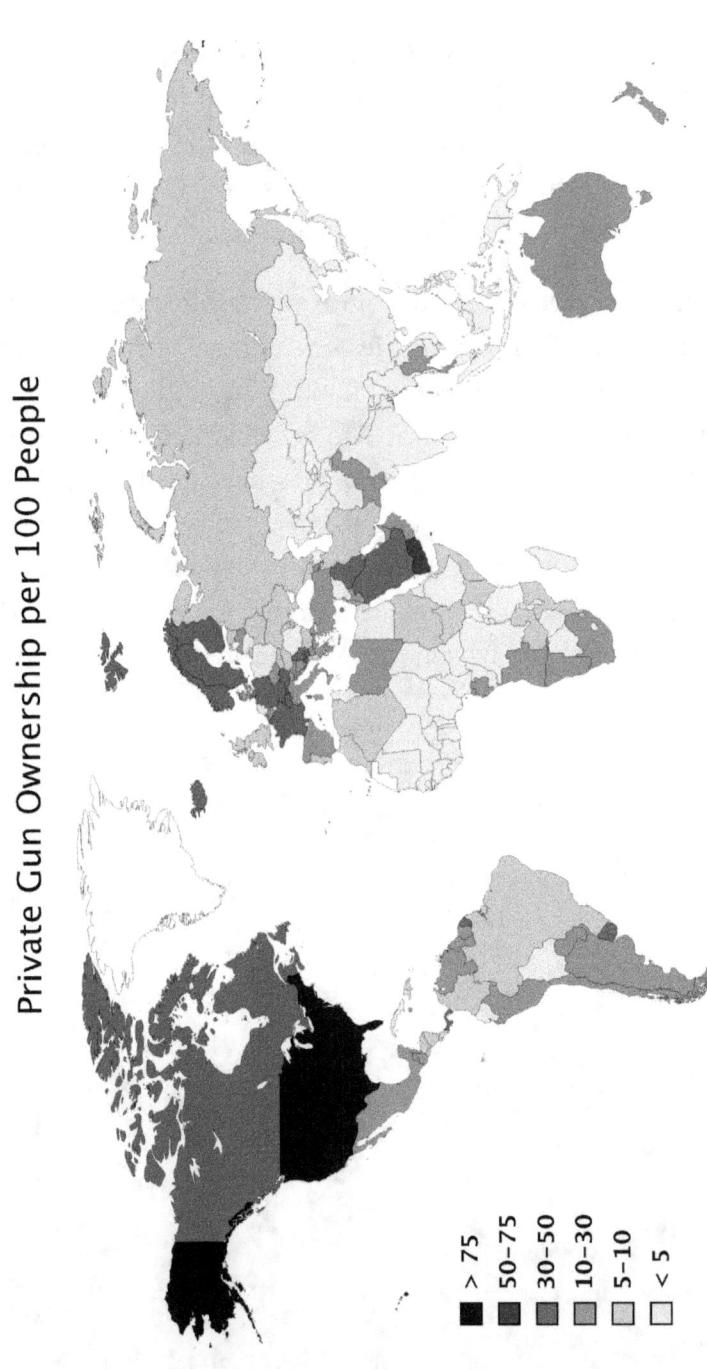

> 75
50–75
30–50
10–30
5–10
< 5

Private gun ownership rates are highest in the US, Canada, Europe and parts of the Middle East. Image: own work by author; data from the 2007 Small Arms Survey

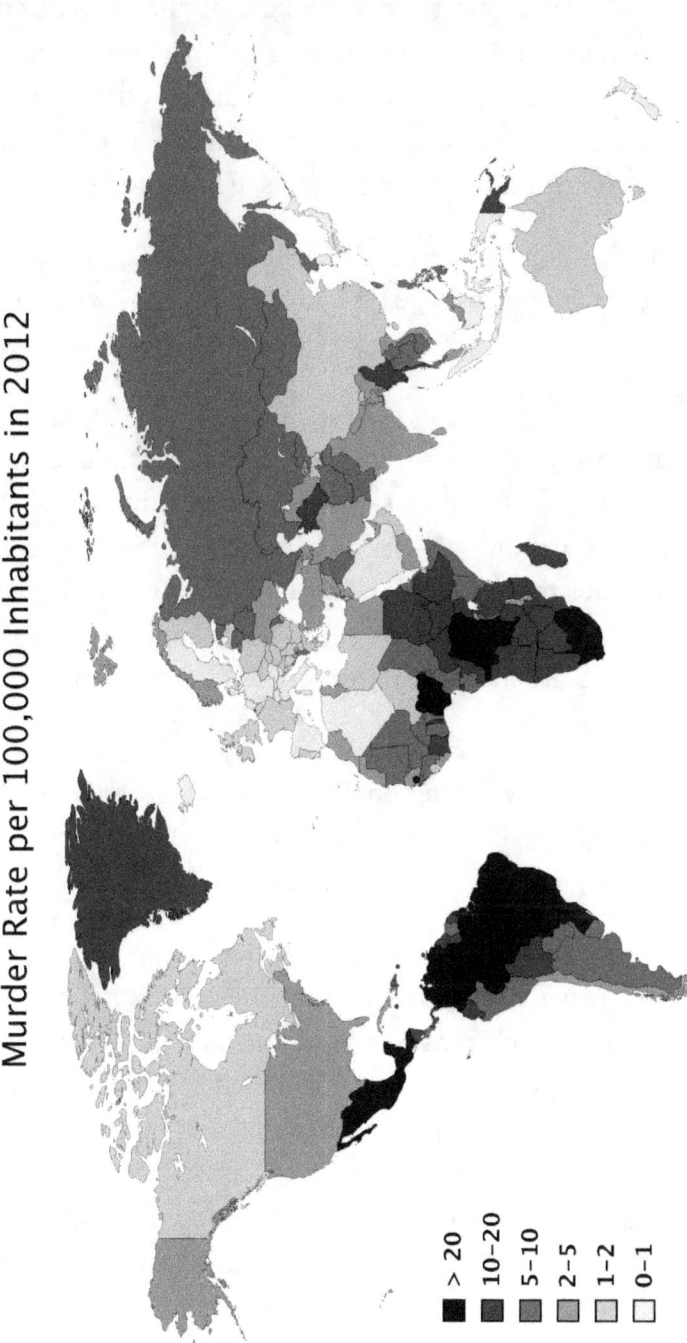

Murder Rate per 100,000 Inhabitants in 2012

> 20
10–20
5–10
2–5
1–2
0–1

Murder rates are highest in Central- and South America as well as Sub-Saharan Africa. Image: own work by author; data from UNODC statistics

There is a similar disconnect when looking at the proportion of US households owning firearms by state, and the corresponding gun murder rates. The computer-generated trendlines on following chart show the inverse relationship between gun ownership and gun homicide rates. As gun ownership increases, gun murders decrease.

Washington D.C.'s gun murder rate of 16.5 per 100,000 people is more than 3 times the national average of 4.7, while its gun ownership rate is the lowest in the entire US. The district's gun murder rate is too high to be displayed in scale.

There are dozens if not hundreds of factors affecting crime rates, including poverty, ethnic diversity, and population density. These outside factors are among the reasons why Honduras suffers a 19 times higher murder rate than the US, while having only a 16th of the gun ownership rate. It is these places which show that people's values and approaches to life are the most important factor determining crime rates.

Similarly, Hawaii and Washington D.C. have two of the lowest gun ownership rates in the US. However, while Hawaii enjoys below-average gun crime, D.C. suffers the highest.

The inverse relationship between gun ownership and gun crime suggests that private gun ownership helps deter crime, while permitting law-abiding citizens to defend themselves. Wherever you go, whether it be Chicago, Ireland or Jamaica, cities and countries which imposed stricter gun laws experienced significant upticks in homicides shortly thereafter. When the UK introduced a complete handgun ban in 1997, its homicide rate skyrocketed by 50% in the following five years. Banning guns does not disarm criminals, nor does it prevent people from using other objects such as knives to murder. What gun bans do, however, is turning law-abiding citizens into defenseless victims.

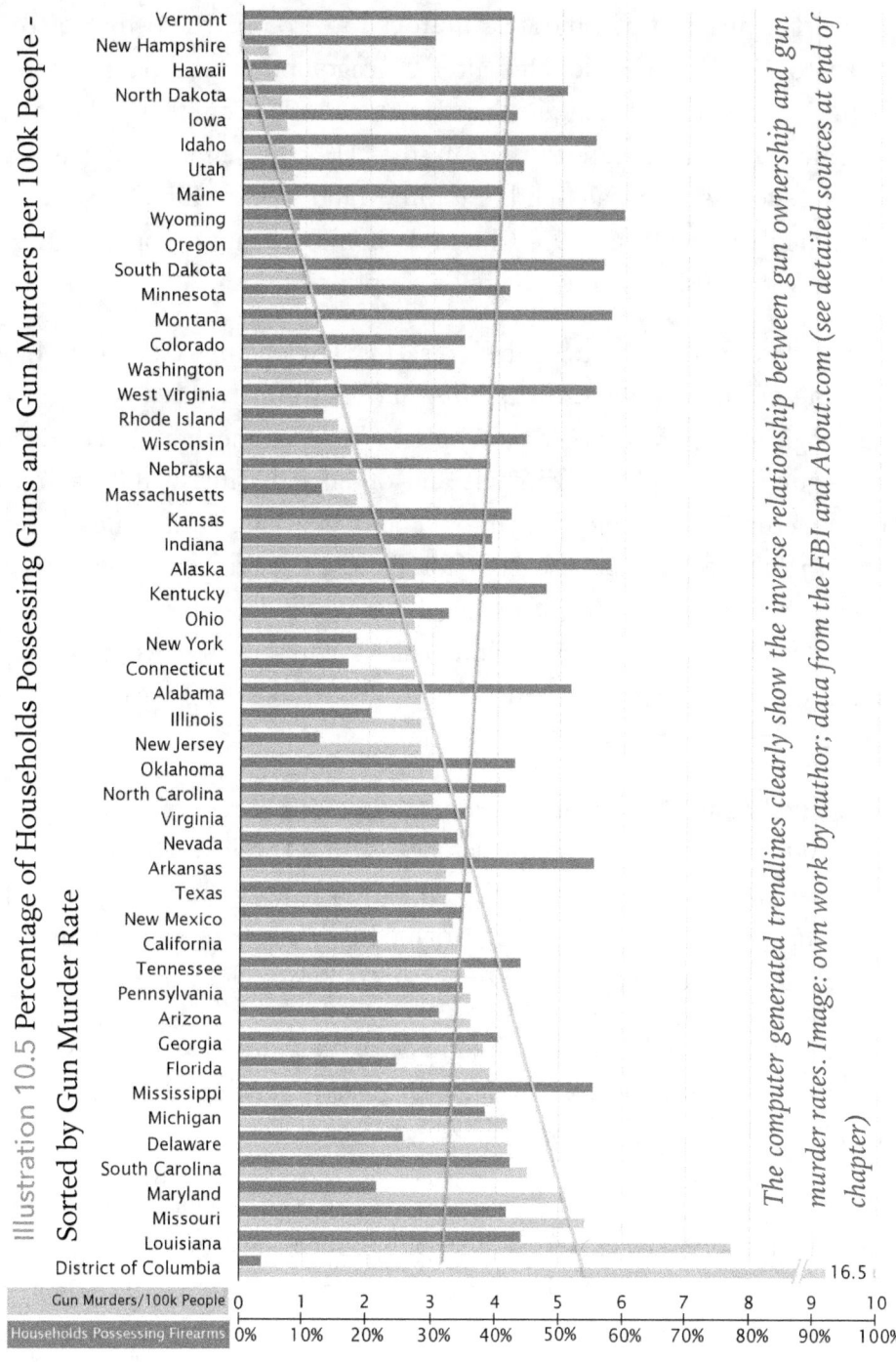

Illustration 10.5 Percentage of Households Possessing Guns and Gun Murders per 100k People - Sorted by Gun Murder Rate

The computer generated trendlines clearly show the inverse relationship between gun ownership and gun murder rates. Image: own work by author; data from the FBI and About.com (see detailed sources at end of chapter)

Similarly, the ratio of Chicago's murder rate compared to that of the other top 10 US cities doubled after Chicago and several other Illinois municipalities introduced gun bans in the 1980s. Comparing the ratio of Chicago's murder rate to that of other US cities eliminates external factors such as national trends in crime rates. When Illinois passed a concealed carry bill in 2013, Chicago's homicide rate dropped to a 56 year low — within a year of the bill's adoption.

Generally speaking, gun control disarms law-abiding citizens, while keeping criminals fully armed. After all, if criminals cared about new gun legislation, they would not be criminals in the first place. Even with gun bans in place, criminals and organized crime will be able to manufacture or smuggle guns into a country or city. For example, even though France bans guns except for licensed sport use and hunting, there are at least twice as many illegal guns in the country — 15 million — as legal firearms — 7.5 million. This is why France, despite having some of the strictest gun laws in the world, also ranks 11th in gun ownership.

The Small Arms Survey reports France's ownership rate to be 31,2 guns per 100 people. This closely matches a rough calculation using the reported number of illegal and legal firearms. The 22.5 million guns (15 million illegal and 7.5 legally owned) divided by the country's population of 64 million results in about 35 guns per 100 people.

In France, possessing illegal firearms like the fully automatic AK-47s used by the Charlie Hebdo shooters in Paris in January 2015 can result in a fine and up to 7 years in prison.

With the government failing to prevent the illegal import and distribution of Marijuana and other drugs into the United States, how do you think it could possibly succeed in doing the same for firearms?

Allowing criminals (along with the government) to monopolize firearm ownership practically removes any deterrent robbers face when attacking citizens or breaking into a home. This is why New York mafia boss Sammy "the Bull" Gravano admitted in a 1999 interview with Vanity Fair that:

"It (gun control) is the best thing you can do for crooks and gangsters. I want you to have nothing. If I'm a bad guy, I'm always gonna have a gun. Safety locks? You pull the trigger with a lock on, and I'll pull the trigger. We'll see who wins."

Take Mexico as an example. The country has a homicide rate of 21.5 — four times that of the US — yet also some of the toughest gun regulations in the world.

Similarly, in the US *all major* mass shootings, including those in Aurora, Blacksburg, Charleston, Columbine, Newtown and Tucson took place in gun free zones, were victims were disarmed. We are yet to hear about a rampage killing at a gun show, gun shop, or other area with high gun concentration. In fact, for every case of gun-related death (including accidents and suicides), there are more than 80 cases in which citizens use guns to protect life (see "Learn More" section at end of chapter).

Our Founding Fathers regarded the right to keep and bear firearms as essential to protect the people from tyrannical government overreach. As Adolf Hitler, a vehement gun control advocate said:

"The most foolish mistake we could possibly make would be to allow the subject races to possess arms. History shows that all conquerors who have allowed their subject races to carry arms have prepared their own downfall by so doing."

When criminals and tyrants tell you that they exploit gun control in their favor — take them for their word.

--- **Learn More** ---

- A factual look at guns in America. http://americangunfacts.com/#action.

--- **Sources** ---

1. US Constitution - Archives.gov. http://www.archives.gov/exhibits/charters/constitution_transcript.html. Retrieved July 28, 2015.

2. Civilian Gun Ownership Rates by Country - "Small Arms Survey 2007." Graduate Institute of International and Development Studies in Geneva, Switzerland. http://www.smallarmssurvey.org/fileadmin/docs/A-Yearbook/2007/en/Small-Arms-Survey-2007-Chapter-02-annexe-4-EN.pdf. Retrieved July 28, 2015.

3. Countries by Intentional Homicide Rate - United Nations Office on Drugs and Crime. http://www.unodc.org/documents/gsh/pdfs/2014_GLOBAL_HOMICIDE_BOOK_web.pdf. Retrieved July 28, 2015.

4. Table 20: Murder by State, Types of Weapons, 2010 - Uniform Crime Reports. Crime in the U.S. 2010. FBI. https://www.fbi.gov/about-us/cjis/ucr/crime-in-the-u.s/2010/crime-in-the-u.s.-2010/tables/10tbl20.xls. Retrieved July 28, 2015.

5. "Gun Owners as a Percentage of Each State's Population." Deborah White. About.com. http://usliberals.about.com/od/Election2012Factors/a/Gun-Owners-As-Percentage-Of-Each-States-Population.htm. Retrieved July 28, 2015.

6. Chicago Crime Rate at Historic Low - "Chicago crime rate drops as concealed carry applications surge." Kelly Riddell. Washington Times. http://www.washingtontimes.com/news/2014/aug/24/chicago-crime-rate-drops-as-concealed-carry-gun-pe/?page=all/. Retrieved July 28, 2015.

7. "Murder and Homicide Rates Before and After Gun Bans" - In the UK, Chicago, Ireland and Jamaica - Crime Prevention Research Center. http://

crimepreventionresearchcenter.org/2013/12/murder-and-homicide-rates-before-and-after-gun-bans/. Retrieved July 28, 2015.

8. Illegal Guns in France - "France has strict gun laws. Why didn't that save Charlie Hebdo victims?" Adam Taylor. Washington Post. https://www.washingtonpost.com/blogs/worldviews/wp/2015/01/09/france-has-strict-gun-laws-why-didnt-that-save-charlie-hebdo-victims/. Retrieved July 28, 2015.

9. Mafia Support of Gun Control - "The Reluctant Don." Howard Blum. Vanity Fair. http://www.vanityfair.com/news/1999/09/The-Reluctant-Don/. Retrieved July 28, 2015.

10. Guns Used for Protection - "A Factual Look at Guns in America." Vici Media. http://americangunfacts.com. Retrieved July 28, 2015.

11. "Fake Quote Files: Adolf Hitler on Gun Registration, Conquest and Disarmament." Daniel Bier. The Skeptical Libertarian. http://blog.skepticallibertarian.com/2013/03/19/fake-quote-files-adolf-hitler-on-gun-registration-conquest-and-disarmament/. Retrieved July 28, 2015.

MARRIAGE AND RELIGION

CHAPTER 11

The First Amendment of the US Constitution protects our freedom of religion:

"Congress shall make no law respecting an establishment of religion, or prohibiting the free exercise thereof..."

Freedom of religion is taken for granted and rarely challenged — at least in the Western world. While being protected by the Constitution, freedom of religion is also guaranteed by the law and principles of liberty.

In this chapter we will mostly discuss the place of marriage in government. Historically speaking, marriage has been a mainly religious concept — bonding a male and female partner for life in order to ensure a safe upbringing of offspring. The practice is deeply anchored in all major world religions and has been the norm for thousands of years. Marriage was already practiced when people lived mostly in nomadic tribes while countries and today's major world religions did not exist.

The institution of marriage is a social construct and deeply entrenched in the belief system of most people. Even agnostic atheists, who claim to know that there is no god usually believe in marriage between two individuals. For reference, following illustration outlines the difference between theists, atheists, gnostics and agnostics.

Illustration 11.1 Definition of Theists, Atheists, Gnostics and Agnostics

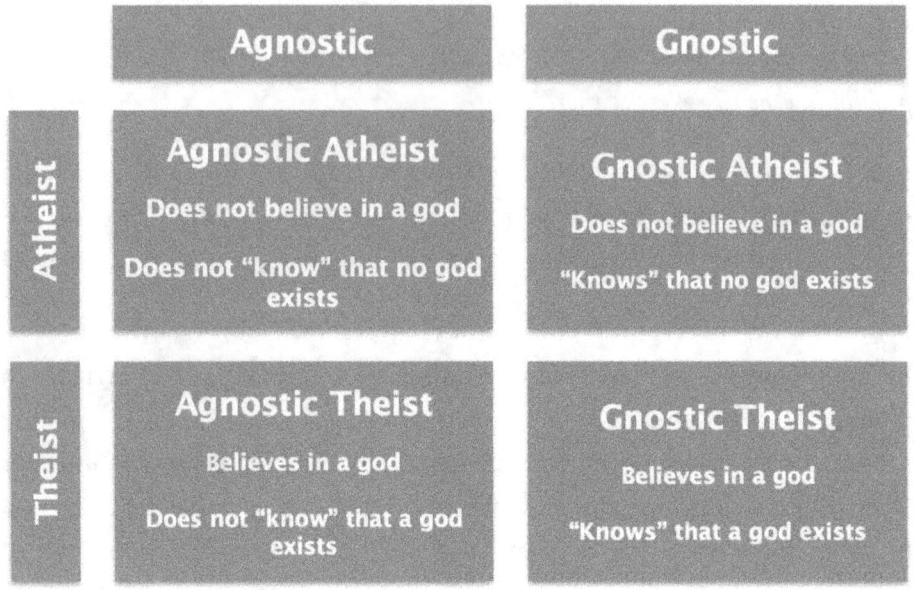

Devout Christians would consider themselves "gnostic theists." Image: own work by author

On first look, this appears to be a paradox. How can a traditionally religious concept like marriage continue to exist if the number of the unaffiliated increases in the US and Europe? The answer may lie in the fact that although unaffiliated, every individual is part of a "religion." Let me explain.

Religion is commonly described as an *"organized collection of beliefs, cultural systems, and world views that relate humanity to an order of existence"* (Clifford Geertz, 1973).

Geertz' definition suggests that even someone who is unaffiliated and does not believe in god can be considered religious. How, you ask?

Chapter 11: Marriage and Religion

Because every individual has a set of beliefs and values, concerning everything from how the universe came into existence to how one should behave in society. Each of these *unique* belief- and value systems corresponds to a form of "religion."

Even members of a world religion will not adhere exactly to the same values and cultural norms advocated by the local clergyman, Pope, Ayatollah or Dalai Lama. At best, members of a religion will share most of their beliefs and values with fellow members.

Realizing that it is normal to have a unique world view enabled me to free myself from the shackles of an "official" religion. While I am officially unaffiliated, I do believe in God and follow Christianity's Ten Commandments.

It may be none of my business, but I encourage you to at least question the practices of the religious institution you belong to (if any). I personally regard it as morally questionable to accept Pope Francis' Marxist views on free markets and social justice as synonymous with the word of God. If you believe in God, build a direct connection with him and do not let a corrupt clergyman or Marxist Pope get in between you and the Creator (these are Forbes Magazine's words, not mine; see "Learn More" section at end of chapter). There is no reason why your own "religion" should be considered any less valid than Roman Catholicism, Islam or Buddhism.

We have now established that the institution of marriage, with all its variations, represents a cultural and religious concept. Naturally, individual opinions on marriage, whether it be on gay marriage or polygamy, differ. And because the various views on marriage are nothing more than a part of everyone's personal world view or religion, there is a case to be made that beliefs about marriage, too, should be protected under the US Constitution.

In practice, this means that the government's authority to define and grant marriages violates the First Amendment's protection of personal religions.

How is it justified for the government to have a monopoly on the right to define marriage? Instead of being government controlled, the institution of marriage should be privatized. In order to protect liberty and personal freedoms, marriage should be privately defined and authorized by citizens — not a central body of authority.

Individuals desiring to form a bond in whatever configuration they prefer may seek a marriage certificate issued by a private religious institution. If no existing church is willing to issue a marriage certificate to a gay or polygamous couple, the partners may start their very own "religion" along with their own church. This solution guarantees the preservation of every individual's belief system, as long as it does not interfere with those of others and the principle of voluntaryism. Privatization of marriage also solves the ongoing debates on gay marriage and any other potentially upcoming marriage controversies as there is no central body which decides what constitutes marriage and what does not.

If marrying partners desire more than a "symbolic" bonding ceremony performed by a private church, they should draft a "marriage" contract, setting out the terms on how to dissolve the marriage, domestic duties and child custody. The government, however, has effectively pre-written a marriage contract valid for all marriages. This makes it difficult for partners to change conditions of "marriage" even when they draft their own custom marriage contract — as government legislation usually trumps private agreements.

It is none of the government's business to define how marriages are supposed to work, nor who can marry whom — provided the involved parties fully consent. All of these decisions are to be made by the affected individuals on a private case-by-case basis.

When marriage is privatized, how can the government assess which partnerships qualify for marriage-related tax benefits? The solution is simple. As will be discussed in chapter 13 - Discrimination: while private individuals have every right to discriminate, government has not. The current practice of offering tax benefits to married partners discriminates against those who do not want to marry, be it because of financial reasons, a personal belief system, asexuality, or simply because they cannot find the right partner.

But doesn't marriage encourage offspring, ensuring future tax revenue? — Yes and No.

1. Non-married, childless individuals usually have more time to work and advance their career, generating more income and thus tax revenue than their child-bearing peers.

2. A small, but steadily increasing percentage of marriages do not produce children (6% as of 2010). Why should a childless married couple pay less in taxes than two childless singles? Should singles be financially punished for their bad luck of not being able to find the right partner?

3. As of 2013, 39% of children below the age of 18 either live with an unmarried single- or no parent. These people have children, but receive less tax benefits than childless married couples.

4. About a fifth of those aged 25 and above have never been married, which is equivalent to 42 million US adults. Should they all be obliged to pay higher taxes because of their personal lifestyle choices?

5. In a sustainable system of governance, the taxes paid in by each individual should approximately equal the government handouts one receives. In this context, a shrinking population (due to lower birth rates) should not be a problem, assuming that reduced government revenues are accompanied by lower expenditures. However, as we all know, this is not the case for Western governments. Ever more people are needed to pay for older generations as discussed in chapter 5 - Social Welfare. Nonetheless, the government should not encourage the immoral continuation of this pyramid scheme through tax benefits for married couples. As unpleasant as it sounds, older generations have to start to live within their means instead of taking from their children and grand-children.

The US Constitution prohibits the government to discriminate based on religion. In order to comply, the government has to stop regulating marriage. Let people define marriage, issue marriage certificates and decide what it means to be married on their own, personal terms. The government has no right to define who can marry whom or discriminate against singles tax-wise.

--- Learn More ---

- A TED post on why science is a religion http://www.ted.com/conversations/9998/science_is_a_religion.html.

- An article by the CATO Institute on the privatization of marriage - http://www.cato.org/publications/commentary/privatize-marriage.

- Fraud Thriving In U.S. Churches, But You Wouldn't Know It - http://www.forbes.com/sites/walterpavlo/2013/11/18/fraud-thriving-in-u-s-churches-but-you-wouldnt-know-it/.

- Top Ten Reasons Why Rush Limbaugh Is Right: The Pope's Statement IS Marxist - http://www.forbes.com/sites/harrybinswanger/2013/12/19/top-ten-reasons-why-rush-limbaugh-is-right-the-popes-statement-is-marxist/.

--- Sources ---

1. US Constitution - Archives.gov. http://www.archives.gov/exhibits/charters/constitution_transcript.html. Retrieved July 28, 2015.

2. Definition of Religion - "Religion as a Cultural System." Clifford Geertz. 1973.

3. Proportion of Childless Marriages - "More married women in U.S. aren't having children." Emily Alpert Reyes. L.A. Times. http://articles.latimes.com/2013/dec/08/nation/la-na-childless-couples-20131208. Retrieved July 28, 2015.

4. Proportion of Children Living With Single Parent or Alone - "Less than half of U.S. kids today live in a 'traditional' family." Gretchen Livingston. Pew Research Center. http://www.pewresearch.org/fact-tank/2014/12/22/less-than-half-of-u-s-kids-today-live-in-a-traditional-family/. Retrieved July 28, 2015.

5. Proportion of People Who Were Never Married - "Record Share of Americans Have Never Married." Wendy Wang and Kim Parker. Pew Research Center. http://www.pewsocialtrends.org/2014/09/24/record-share-of-americans-have-never-married/. Retrieved July 28, 2015.

ABORTION

CHAPTER 12

Chapter 12: Abortion

The abortion debate mainly centers on an unborn's right to live and a woman's right to control her body.

In essence, abortion violates the "Law of Liberty." The law states that one has the right to do whatever one likes to do; unless one infringes on the same right of others or *harms people*. Abortion *harms* unborn children.

If at all, abortion may be a "positive" liberty, in that it is a woman's *freedom to* have a child removed from her womb. As discussed in chapter 1 - Principles of Liberty, the "positive liberty" to abort is in direct violation with the "negative liberty" of an unborn to remain untouched. As a short recap, the terms "positive" and "negative" are not indicative of "good" or "bad." "Positive liberties" simply refer to *freedoms to,* e.g., abort or get free education, while "negative liberties" are *freedoms from,* e.g., abortion/murder, taxes and excessive regulations.

Both sides in the abortion debate claim to advance "freedom," yet only **"negative liberties"** such as the *freedom from* abortion/murder can be reconciled with the law and principles of liberty.

As part of this chapter, we will look at various pro-choice arguments and analyze their validity — in a moral and libertarian context.

1. **Abortions Taking Place in the First 3 Months of Pregnancy, When the Fetus Cannot Live on Its Own, Are Acceptable**

   A fetus' ability to survive outside the womb increases from 40% in the 24th week of pregnancy (around 5.5 months) to 80% in the 28th week (around 6.5 months).

   However, just because an individual including an unborn baby is unable to survive on his/her own *does not* justify his or her death.

269

Otherwise, shutting down life-supporting medical equipment for a patient who was just accepted into an emergency room would be equally justifiable.

2. **A Fetus Is Connected to the Placenta and Thus Part of the Woman's Body. This Gives Her the Right to Have the Fetus Removed**

This common claim oversees the fact that a fetus has its own DNA, different to that of the mother. A unique string of DNA clearly identifies a fetus as a separate living organism.

Conjoint twins have the same DNA, but different phenotypes. Phenotypes define the ways in which DNA is expressed. This is why conjoint twins do not look identical.

Hopefully, everyone agrees that a conjoint twin has no moral right to murder his/her other half. So how can a mother be permitted to murder her unborn baby which actually differs by DNA and not merely by phenotype?

3. **A Baby Born into an Unloving Relationship or Household with Lack of Financial Means Is Better off Being Aborted**

According to this argument, it would make just as much sense to kill a three-year-old child who grows up with an abusive, unemployed single parent in an inner city neighborhood. Yet killing a three-year-old, in any situation, is rightly considered murder.

Unwanted children should be made available for adoption or church-funded foster care. There is no shortage of foster parents wanting to adopt children. In fact, the shortage of children is so large that wait times for prospective foster parents reach 12 months and more. Even if a child does not find adoptive parents it can be taken care of by churches and other charitable organizations — as was the case in the past. An abundance of unwanted children has never been a problem, even not before abortion was legalized and birth rates were significantly higher.

One reason for long wait times is extensive government regulations and screenings concerning the adoption process. People wanting to adopt a child need to pass lengthy assessments, while bearing and raising a biological child remains unregulated. Let us deregulate the adoption process and help unwanted children find a home.

4. **A Woman Has the Right to Live Without Obligations and Restrictions Caused by a 9-Month Pregnancy**

This rather shallow argument bears two moral hazards:

1. A woman is almost always jointly responsible (along with the father) for a pregnancy, and as a result, should face the responsibility for carrying out a baby.

2. Is the concern of parents to have a 9 month pregnancy, career and financial disadvantages, and loss of individual freedom *more important* than a human's right to live an average of 80 years? Wouldn't it be more humane for society and immediate family and friends to accept parents' decision to give a baby up for adoption than ending a child's life?

5. **A Pregnancy Caused by Rape Makes the Victim Suffer**

While this argument is likely valid for any rape victim, it does not justify another far more substantive crime — murder. A rapist should be prosecuted for both, the act of rape itself and the potentially stressful pregnancy which follows.

However, how is it justifiable to punish a third party, the baby, for a crime he or she did not commit? Abortion of an unborn baby makes the rape victim herself a perpetrator.

Furthermore, allowing abortion in cases of rape would incentivize women to lie about regular pregnancy. This moral hazard not only causes the loss of life, but may very well lead to the persecution of innocent men. Bloomberg, for instance, reports that up to 41% of rape accusations are false, and this is despite abortion being legal in the United States. Imagine how high this number would be if abortion was only legal in cases of rape.

It is also worth mentioning that only 5% of rapes result in pregnancy.

6. **Abortion Should Be Legal in Cases of Incest or Serious Disability**

Incest or serious disability of the unborn child may permit abortion — if properly executed. A decision to abort would depend on an objective assessment on whether the child's disability significantly reduces his or her ability to live a satisfying life. The optimal litmus test for this decision would be to ask the unborn whether he or she would prefer euthanasia to life. As consulting the unborn is obviously not possible, at least for now, decisions on aborting a disabled child remain subjective.

In contrast to an unloving and/or a financially deprived environment, as discussed in point 3, the effects of serious disability cannot be improved through adoption.

7. **An Undeveloped Fetus Has Not Developed Personhood Until Several Months After Inception**

The discussion on whether any life should be protected or only life with a developed personhood ignores the fact that we are still unsure when personhood begins. To be on the safe side, shouldn't we refrain from abortion at least until we are 100% certain on when both life and personhood begin? After all, we still try to rescue accident victims in a plane crash even when we are not 100% certain that they have survived.

Even if personhood was not developed until a certain pregnancy stage, as long as an unborn infant can be considered "life," it should remain protected under the proclamation of the US declaration of independence that "*Life*, Liberty and the pursuit of Happiness" represent inalienable rights.

8. **An Unborn Baby's Physical Reactions to Outside Stimuli (Such as Sound and Touch) Can Be Detected Starting from Week 20 of Pregnancy. What Speaks Against Aborting a Fetus Before He/She Is Sensible to Stimuli and Pain?**

Just because a fetus is not reacting to stimuli does not mean it cannot feel pain. We do not know for sure from which week a fetus starts being pain-sensitive. Anyway, this argument is irrelevant as the criterium of whether a human organism can feel pain should not decide on whether he/she has a right to live. Just because someone fell into a coma (and, as a result, is pain-insensitive) does not mean we have a right to kill that person.

Chapter 12: Abortion

It seems harsh, but in the vast majority of cases abortion is the practice of having another human (the unborn infant) pay with his/her life for a man and woman's careless sexual relations.

How pro-abortion activists can permit parents to murder a child just because they do not want to live with the consequences of their actions is beyond me.

Interestingly, socialists are anti-free-choice when it comes to almost any issue ranging from voluntary exchanges to one's decision not to get health insurance. Sadly, one of the only issues where socialists permit choice is when it comes to murdering your own child.

--- Learn More ---

- [Video] on the Sixth Commandment - Do not Murder. https://www.youtube.com/watch?v=0RENPaY043o.

--- Sources ---

1. Survival Rate of Infants outside the Womb by Week of Pregnancy - "Risks of Early Labor." Healthline.com. http://www.healthline.com/health/pregnancy/preterm-labor-prolonged. Retrieved July 28, 2015.

2. Waiting Times for Adoptions - "Longer wait times, higher costs for U.S. adoptions." Kathleen Kingsbury http://www.reuters.com/article/2013/01/15/us-adoption-domestic-waits-idUSBRE90E15Y20130115. Retrieved July 28, 2015

3. Proportion of False Rape Accusations. Bloomberg View - "How Many Rape Reports Are False?" Megan McArdle. http://www.bloombergview.com/articles/2014-09-19/how-many-rape-reports-are-false. Retrieved July 28, 2015.

4. 5% of Rapes Result in Pregnancy - "The claim that the incidence of rape resulting in pregnancy is 'very low.'" Glenn Kessler. Washington Post. http://www.washingtonpost.com/blogs/fact-checker/post/the-claim-that-the-incidence-of-rape-resulting-in-pregnancy-is-very-low/2013/06/12/936bc45e-d3ad-11e2-8cbe-1bcbee06f8f8_blog.html. Retrieved July 28, 2015.

5. US Declaration of Independence - Archives.gov. http://www.archives.gov/exhibits/charters/declaration_transcript.html. Retrieved July 28, 2015.

6. Time From Which Unborn Infants Can Feel Pain - "Unborn babies can feel pain." Minnesota Citizens Concerned for Life. http://www.mccl.org/unborn-babies-can-feel-pain.html. Retrieved July 28, 2015.

DISCRIMINATION

CHAPTER 13

Chapter 13: Discrimination

Discrimination can be defined as:

"Making a distinction in favor of or against a person based on the group, class, or category to which that individual belongs rather than on individual merit."

Discrimination has different implications for governments compared to private individuals and businesses.

Governments oversee the legal framework of a country, and are responsible for the implementation and protection of laws and regulations. Because government is meant to represent all citizens, and, in essence, is owned by all of its citizens, it is obligated to treat them equally. This notion is ingrained in the second paragraph of the US Declaration of Independence, which reads:

*"We hold these truths to be self-evident, that **all men are created equal**, that they are endowed by their Creator with certain unalienable Rights, that among these are Life, Liberty and the Pursuit of Happiness."*

According to the Declaration's author, Thomas Jefferson, and the 56 delegates of the Continental Congress who ratified the document July 4, 1776, humans are given their rights by their Creator. It is the government's task to ensure their protection.

Assuming that our Creator does not discriminate among humans, the government — protector of those rights — is not meant to discriminate among people.

Positive and Negative Discrimination

There is "positive" and "negative" discrimination. "Positive discrimination" refers to the practice of *advancing* the interests of one group of people on a non-merit basis, while leaving others behind.

"Negative discrimination" involves the *disadvantaging* of certain people based on a non-merit basis.

Waving women's requirement to serve in war, while men are conscripted, is a classic example of positive discrimination favoring women. Refusing to hire a black person, on the other hand, is an example of negative discrimination.

In this context, the terms "positive" and "negative" do not imply that some forms of discrimination are good and others are bad. They merely refer to the way discrimination is implemented — by favoring or disadvantaging someone.

Discrimination Against (White) Men

Today's Western governments "positively" discriminate virtually all groups of people — from women, to Blacks, to Aborigines and other minorities. The countless government programs and laws advancing their interests leave out just one group of people — White men. Ironically, it is those who mostly pay for these schemes and implement them in Congress, who do not qualify for them.

Government is owned by all — and should not discriminate among its owners.

The countless programs supporting everyone but White men are not only examples of "institutionalized discrimination," but have severely disadvantaged men. Contrary to popular opinion, it is minorities and especially women who are the winners in today's society.

Blacks and Other Minorities: Affirmative action is a prime example of "positive" discrimination. It lowers university entry requirements for

Blacks and other minorities, while Whites from similarly poor backgrounds are left behind.

While affirmative action is used in the US, many other Western countries have similar programs. In the UK it is called "positive action," while in India it is known under the term "reservation."

The US incarceration system is often labeled "racist." Activists claim courts are largely biased as 4.7% of adult Blacks are in jail or prison, while this is the case for only 0.7% of Whites. However, we are not allowed to mention the fact that according to the FBI, Blacks account for 28.1% of offenses, are responsible for 49.4% of murders and 54.9% of robberies, all while accounting for just 12% of the US population.

At the same time, the media almost completely ignore the widespread and worsening discrimination of Whites in places like Zimbabwe, where White farmers are prohibited from filing court cases. Denying Whites access to the court system has made them defenseless to Zimbabwe's 2005 declaration to turn all *White-owned* land into state property.

Women: It is a myth that women are disadvantaged in the workplace. Feminists keep repeating that women earn 77 cents for every dollar earned by men. However, this number entirely ignores occupation, tenure and education levels. When adjusted for these factors, the pay gap disappears. In fact, in 147 out of the 150 largest US cities median income of young, childless single women working full-time is 8% higher than that of similar young men. In Atlanta and Memphis, young women earn around 20% more than men. It is only when females start prioritizing child raising to their careers that their wage advantage diminishes.

Chapter 13: Discrimination

The simple notion that a woman earns less than a man *doing the same work* is absurd. If this were the case, a business could simply lay off all men and replace them with female employees that perform to the same level — but at a lower cost — saving the company thousands. Do we see this happening? — No, because there is no pay gap.

Despite already enjoying an advantage in the labor market, women now benefit from ever more countries introducing quotas for women on corporate boards. Countries including France, Germany, the Netherlands, Norway, and Spain have already done so. In these countries, women are promoted to higher positions not because they are qualified but because they are female.

If a woman earns less than a man, it is because of her career choice — not due to discrimination. The free market determines wages based on society's need for different professions. Men usually follow those incentives, working in positions where they are most needed. In many cases this means that they trade high salaries for wellbeing. Women, on the other hand, value work they enjoy more than a high income. As a result, women earn less than men, not adjusted for occupation. They are free to do the good-paying, unpleasant work that society values. If women prefer to do something else than serving the market it is their responsibility when they earn less.

There is a government agency just for women, the "United States Women's Bureau" (WB). Most other Western countries have similar institutions. Have you ever heard of a government agency just for men? — Probably not, as there are none.

This is a form of "institutionalized government discrimination" against men, and especially White men as men from minorities have their own agencies. Ironically, it is probably (White) men who could need such an institution the most:

Chapter 13: Discrimination

Men are 20 times more likely than women to suffer from fatal injuries at work as they occupy more accident-prone jobs. They are also more likely to be laid off and less likely to be re-employed than females.

Ever since the late 1970s, more women are attending university than men. As of 2012, 56.4% of students at public US universities are female, with 43.6% being men. For private schools this gender gap increases to 59.3% for women and just 40.7% for men. This is the case despite 51% of people in the 18-24 year age group — the majority — being men.

Activists complain about female genital mutilation which is estimated to affect 100-140 million women worldwide. Yet nobody talks about male genital mutilation — circumcision — which affects around 30% of men around the world or more than 1 billion in total. Male circumcision is universally practiced for Muslims and Jews as well as in many African countries, with 95% of Nigerian men being circumcised.

Just compare the almost non-existence of female genital mutilation in the US with the fact that more than 75% of American men are circumcised. Circumcision is just as intrusive, and especially in Africa often done without anesthetics.

Despite the public notion to the contrary, in the UK, for which data was available, the same percentage of married men, 3.4%, report domestic abuse as married women — and this despite the fact that men are *less* likely to report domestic abuse.

Similarly, we are constantly bombarded with news about women being raped. What many do not know is that in the United States more men are raped than women, mainly due to prison rape.

Have you ever wondered why most homeless people you see on the street are men? It is because 80-90% of all homeless are male. While women have their own government agencies, and illegal immigrants and refugees are provided with free housing — sometimes in re-configured luxury hotels — homeless middle-aged men who paid taxes for most of their lives are left on the streets. In fact, it was reported that the US government spends $231 per illegal immigrant *per night* at the South Texas Family Residential Center in Dilley, more than the cost of a double room in a nearby San Antonio Hilton Hotel (see "Learn More" section at end of chapter).

Our justice system favors women when it comes to assigning child custody in a divorce. And of the 400,000 people in the US receiving post-divorce spousal maintenance — or alimony — just 3% were men, despite the top-earner in 40% of households being female. In a recent case a man was sent to jail for 6 months for overpaying child support and seeing his son "too often" (see "Learn More" section at end of chapter).

Allow Private Individuals and Businesses to Discriminate

Most readers will intuitively agree that government should not discriminate among its citizens for the aforementioned reasons. The main controversy in the discrimination debate is whether private individuals and businesses share the same obligation.

Due to their inherent differences to governments, private individuals and businesses are not obligated to be non-discriminatory in their actions. Here are 6 reasons why this is the case:

1. Private Individuals and Businesses Are Not Governments

Private institutions, be it individuals, businesses or any other associations do not represent the nation. Nor are they "owned" by all citizens as government is. Private institutions have the sole objective of advancing their own interests, not those of others.

2. Discrimination Complies With "God Given Rights"

Libertarianism assumes that the "god-given rights" referred to in the US Declaration of Independence come down to the "Law of Liberty." The law of liberty states that one has the right to do whatever one likes to do; unless one infringes on the same right of others or harms people.

People should be free to engage in any type of exchange, as long as it does not infringe on the same right of a third party. Based on voluntaryism, anyone may freely opt-out of an exchange.

Your reason for not engaging in an exchange with someone else is irrelevant, be it that you have differing interests, limited time or simply do not like the other person because of his/her gender or ethnicity. Your "right to discriminate," or only engage in transactions with those you like, is protected by the law of liberty and voluntaryism.

Banning discrimination violates your right to do whatever you like to do, as long as you do not infringe on the same right of others or harm people.

3. Discrimination Does Not Harm People

Another misconception is that discrimination harms its "victims." Let us make this clearer through following example. Imagine two friends are living in the wilderness, being entirely self-dependent. One of them is Hispanic, one is Asian. On an unusual day, a hiker happens to cross their path and greets both of them. He carries some food and bottled water which he offers to share. The problem: the hiker personally distrusts Hispanics and limits his offer to the Asian. The Asian, out of courtesy and gratitude accepts the hiker's supplies, leaving his friend barehanded. Soon after, the hiker leaves, never to be seen again.

In this obvious case of discrimination, was the hiker right in offering food only to the Asian? Most people would regard the hiker's action as unfair, potentially racist. However, we should recognize the hiker's right to share with whomever he chooses.

Did the hiker's choice harm the Hispanic? Maybe from an emotional standpoint, but not when looking at it from a financial or material perspective. All the hiker did is improve the Asian's relative "net worth." The Hispanic is neither better nor worse off due to the hiker's visit.

Accordingly, discriminating against people when sharing or doing business fully conforms to the law of liberty.

Shouldn't the hiker be held liable for "emotionally harming" the Hispanic? — Not necessarily. Whether the Hispanic is offended or not depends on his personality — whether he is sensitive to other people's behaviors. If the visiting hiker was held liable for emotional harm, millions of people could seek "compensation" for being emotionally upset after a co-worker got a raise or their neighbor got a better offer on a car he purchased.

It is the harm-free nature of discrimination that makes it an acceptable practice by individuals and businesses alike — and fully conform to the law of liberty.

4. Private Property Rights Are More Important Than Discrimination

If you are an owner of property, you have full authority over its use. Private property rights are essential to liberty. Damaging or stealing someone's property infringes on the victim's right to be left alone, voluntaryism and the law of liberty, which states that one person's actions should not harm another party.

As a property owner, you have the authority to decide who may enter it. Making this decision requires discrimination. By only allowing family members to enter your home, for instance, you discriminate against anyone who is not your relative. The same is the case when you only let people you know personally, or like the personality of, to enter your property.

The point is that banning discrimination is equivalent to the abolishment of property rights. Once anti-discrimination legislation tells you to treat everyone equally when it comes to letting people enter your home, you are stripped of your ownership rights.

While it seems far-fetched that the government would prohibit you from deciding who can enter your house or apartment, this is already the case for businesses. Good luck with trying to ban a certain gender or ethnic group from buying your service or entering your store.

A Toronto barbershop I went to several times while living in Canada, for example, refused to cut the hair of a woman entering the shop. While the hairdresser is men-only, the barber's officially cited reason for refusing the service was his religion — which bars Moslems from touching women. The disgruntled customer went so far as to file a complaint with the Ontario Human Rights Tribunal. Luckily, the case was resolved shortly thereafter through mediation.

Why are house owners free to choose who can enter their houses, while business owners have been stripped of that right?

If everyone is truly equal before the law, then please respect the property rights of business owners just as much as those of private homeowners.

5. Discrimination Is Human and Cannot Be Avoided

Everyone discriminates against others, whether we admit it or not. Imagine following situation: you are planning to hire a new employee for your business. There are two candidates. The first applicant has had a similar job for the last 2 years and is slightly more educated than the second candidate. The second candidate is completely new to the industry and less experienced overall. Both candidates demand the same salary. On a merit basis, the choice is obvious — the first candidate offers better value.

However, the second candidate happens to share your gender, is interested in the same sport and was born in the same town as you. As a result of your mutual interests, you decide to hire the second applicant.

Cases of discrimination like this one are common. This has not changed with the fact that we are told that discrimination is "bad."

Our government tries to prevent this type of discrimination in large companies, requiring diversity studies and other workforce assessments to encourage employee diversity. However, it is much more difficult to control the millions of small businesses which fall below the employee thresholds which require diversity initiatives.

Even if you do not own a business you might have discriminated against others in the past. Did you ever buy from a certain store because the shop owner reminded you of one of your relatives, or because you share a personal interest? If so, you probably discriminated against a shop which offers better service or prices due to your preference to buy from someone you are similar to.

I am focusing on the ways people discriminate against others not because I want to reprimand them, but because I want to show that discrimination is normal and nothing to be ashamed of. Discrimination is part of human nature.

I sometimes wonder about the hypocrisy of anti-discrimination activists which complain about Chick-fil-A (a US fast food chain) donating money to "discriminatory" anti-gay organizations. The same activists are then leading well-publicized boycotts of franchisee-owned stores, many of them either having nothing to do with the controversy or whose owners may even support same-sex marriage. As always happens in situations like this one, the media labels Chick-fil-A "discriminatory," while the activists discriminating against innocent franchisee-owned stores are seen as "defenders of freedom."

Let us go further and make the entirely hypothetical assumption that a Chick-fil-A restaurant bans same-sex partners from entering its stores. Such a move would not only cause public outcry but almost certainly result in legal action against the company. Chick-fil-A is not permitted to discriminate against same-sex couples, but same-sex couples are allowed to discriminate against Chick-fil-A.

How is it justifiable that one party to an economic exchange, namely the customer, is free to discriminate against businesses and their owners whose political opinions or even race he/she is objected to? While the other party to the exchange, the business owner, is forced to serve whatever customer enters his store?

Society not only accepts the double-standards applied to customers and businesses in this regard, but essentially proclaims that discrimination practiced by some people is tolerable, while for others it is not.

This all too common double standard applied to customers and businesses is similar to the dichotomy of consumer and business rights discussed in the upcoming chapter 15.1 - Consumer Protection.

6. Discrimination, Even If Publicly Accepted, Will Not Become Prevalent

Market forces mean that a business that discriminates against a portion of society, be it a certain gender or race, will be punished through lower profits. This happens because:

1. The business loses out on some of its potential customers, which will be happily served by its competitors.

2. Activists and parts of the public will boycott the business in solidarity with the people who are discriminated against.

The reason why discrimination was widespread in the American South is not because businesses did not follow their profit incentive, but rather because government institutionalized discrimination in its laws. And as we have discussed before, government, which is owned by and meant to represent all citizens is the only institution not allowed to discriminate against portions of the populace.

We will now look at how the free market tackles discrimination in the following mini-case.

Marketing to Blacks

After Coca-Cola largely ignored marketing its soft drinks to Blacks in the 1920's and 1930's, its main competitor Pepsi Cola realized the potential of this largely untapped market. In order to benefit from this niche, Pepsi started hiring entirely Black marketing teams in the 1940s. The company employed Black sales representatives to sell Pepsi to Blacks in the rural South and urban areas in the North. The company also used Black ad models, displayed ads in magazines catering mostly to Blacks and hired Black composer and pianist Duke Ellington as the company's spokesperson.

Illustration 13.1 Pepsi Ad Focusing on a Black Family

Image: PZR Services

pzrservices.typepad.com/vintageadvertising/2007/06/vintage-pepsi-c.html

Conclusion

As shown by the systematic discrimination against (White) men, governments discriminate, something they are constitutionally prohibited from doing. However, businesses and private individuals have every right to take discriminatory actions — which are protected by the law and principles of liberty.

Discrimination may cause emotional pain, but it is naturally human. It is a side effect of making the protection of every individual's personal liberty the number one priority.

--- Learn More ---

* An overview of race, Coke and Pepsi can be found here http://www.thewire.com/national/2013/01/brief-history-racist-soft-drinks/61515/.

* Luxury Hotel to Be Converted Into Immigrant Housing. http://www.newsmax.com/Newsfront/luxury-hotel-immigration-housing-Texas/2014/07/16/id/583065/.

* How housing an illegal immigrant for a night in the United States' biggest detention center costs more than a stay at the nearest four-star Hilton Hotel. http://www.dailymail.co.uk/news/article-3154389/More-ammo-Trump-housing-illegal-immigrant-night-United-States-biggest-detention-center-costs-stay-nearest-four-star-Hilton-Hotel.html.

* Clerical Error In Child Support Payments Leads To Six-Month Jail Sentence For Clifford Hal. http://www.huffingtonpost.com/2014/01/21/child-support-error_n_4637465.html.

--- Sources ---

1. "Mugabe Strips Whites of Rights." Ben Freeth. Zimbabwe Independent. http://www.theindependent.co.zw/2014/07/18/land-mugabe-strips-whites-rights/. Retrieved July 28, 2015.

2. "Zimbabwe's white farmers targeted for new Mugabe land grabs." Peta Thornycroft and Aislinn Laing. The Telegraph. http://www.telegraph.co.uk/active/11442408/Zimbabwes-white-farmers-targeted-for-new-Mugabe-land-grabs.html. Retrieved July 28, 2015.

3. FBI Crime Statistics - FBI. https://www.fbi.gov/about-us/cjis/ucr/crime-in-the-u.s/2012/crime-in-the-u.s.-2012/tables/43tabledatadecoverviewpdf. Retrieved July 28, 2015.

4. Young Women Earn More than Men - "Workplace Salaries: At Last, Women on Top." Belinda Luscombe. Time Magazine. http://content.time.com/time/business/article/0,8599,2015274,00.html. Retrieved July 28, 2015.

5. More Women Attend University than Men - "The Male-Female Ratio in College." Daniel Borzelleca. Forbes. http://www.forbes.com/sites/ccap/2012/02/16/the-male-female-ratio-in-college/. Retrieved July 28, 2015.

6. "What is female genital mutilation and where does it happen?" Sarah Boseley. The Guardian. http://www.theguardian.com/society/2014/feb/06/what-is-female-genital-mutilation-where-happen. Retrieved July 28, 2015.

7. Global Incidence of Circumcision - "Circumcision, the ultimate parenting dilemma." Cordelia Hebblethwaite. The BBC. http://www.bbc.co.uk/news/magazine-19072761. Retrieved July 28, 2015.

8. "The Other Gender Divide: Where Men Are Losing." Mona Chalabi. The Guardian. www.theguardian.com/news/datablog/2013/may/07/men-gender-divide-feminism. Retrieved July 28, 2015.

9. More Men Are Raped than Women - "More men are raped in the US than women, figures on prison assaults reveal." The Daily Mail. http://www.dailymail.co.uk/news/article-2449454/More-men-raped-US-women-including-prison-sexual-abuse.html. Retrieved July 28, 2015.

10. "Why Do So Few Men Get Alimony?" Emma Johnson. Forbes. http://www.forbes.com/sites/emmajohnson/2014/11/20/why-do-so-few-men-get-alimony/. Retrieved July 28, 2015.

11. "Rights complaint against Muslim barber who refused to give woman haircut quietly resolved." Sarah Boesveld. National Post. http://news.nationalpost.com/toronto/rights-complaint-against-muslim-barber-who-refused-to-give-woman-haircut-quietly-resolved. Retrieved July 28, 2015.

Chapter 13: Discrimination

RACISM

CHAPTER 13 - SECTION 1

There are various definitions of racism. Depending which dictionary you consult, or what newspaper column you read, you will be left with a different impression on what the term "racism" refers to.

In its most general form, racism alludes to the belief that "some races share different *inherent* physical and cognitive characteristics. These render some races as inferior, and others as superior."

Before digging deeper into this controversial topic, it is important to point out that racism can, but does not have to lead to discrimination. I urge you to keep this in mind while reading on.

Try to think about the following questions from an objective viewpoint: does the average Asian possess different mental and physical capabilities than a Caucasian or Black individual? Are differences between ethnic groups a result of variations in their DNA?

If you answered both of these questions with a yes, does this make you a racist? If so, is racism inherently bad or scientific? And is it possible to be a "racist" in a non-derogatory way?

Let us look at a paper titled "Thirty Years of Research on Race Differences in Cognitive Ability" by Rushton and Jensen. The paper makes a holistic assessment of 30 years of research on the racial differences in mental ability. It concludes that overall, the studies ranging from the 3-decade long period indicate inherent biological differences between races, which are reflected through variations in cognitive skills and physical traits.

The cumulative research suggests that, on one hand, cognitive abilities are correlated to environmental factors such as economic position. Yet after adjusting for environmental factors, there was still a significant variation in mental ability based solely on race. The same is true for differences in physical traits, such as body mass and bone strength.

In the admittedly controversial book "The Bell Curve," authors Herrnstein and Murray present average IQs for various ethnic groups in the US. Jewish Americans on average were found to have an IQ 7 points higher than Asians and 10 points higher than Whites.

Ethnic Group	Intelligence Quotient
Jewish Americans	113
Asians	106
Whites	103
Latino	89
African Americans	85

According to the research paper "Natural History of Ashkenazi Intelligence" (Gregory Cochran et al., 2006), numerous studies have indicated the average IQ of Ashkenazi Jews to be ranging between 112 and 115, or 0.75-1.00 standard deviations above the European average. Ashkenazi Jews are from German and Eastern European origin and include personalities ranging from Albert Einstein to Sigmund Freud and the Rothschild banking family.

Referencing Professor J. Philippe Rushton in his book "Race, Evolution and Behavior, A Life History Perspective," the differences in IQ scores between races are supported by variations in the number of cortical neurons in the brain. According to him, a Black person, on average, has 13,185 million neurons, a White person (including Jews) has 13,665 million and what he refers to as "Orientals" have on average 13,767 million neurons.

While Ashkenazi Jews and Asians triumph in cognitive ability, Blacks have been shown to possess a genetic advantage when it comes to physical strength and development. Blacks, on average, have less body fat, more muscle mass, higher bone density, wider shoulders and narrower hips than both Caucasians and Asians, giving them a significant edge in physical endurance and performance.

Similarly, Black children develop much faster than children from other races. While "Oriental" children start to walk at around 13 months of age, White children start at 12 months, and Blacks at 11 months. Black children also start growing their first permanent set of teeth at a younger age of 5.8 years, with Whites and Orientals lagging behind at 6.1 years. Not to forget that while 51% of Black babies are born at 39 weeks of pregnancy, this is the case for only 33% of White babies — with White babies on average being born later. Despite spending less time in the womb, Black babies are more developed at time of birth.

It is a scientific fact that people from different ethnic origins, on average, feature different mental and physical characteristics. Even if saying so out loud is a no-go. We can see the effects of these racial differences wherever we look:

The cognitive superiority of Ashkenazi Jews, for instance, has meant that in 1933 Germany, despite just representing 0.76% of the population, Jews made up 16.3% of all lawyers, 10.9% of doctors, 8.6% of dentists, 5.6% of directors and producers, 5.1% of editors and writers, 2.8% of judges as well as 2.6% of university professors. The Jewish overrepresentation in high ranking professions was even higher in large cities, with Jews accounting for 48.5% of lawyers in Berlin and 45.3% of lawyers in Frankfurt.

In spite of the apparent discrimination they face, on average, Asians in the US earn higher median incomes at $67,065 than non-Hispanic Whites at $58,270. Illustration 13.2 shows this gap over time.

Similarly, it is no coincidence that Blacks are overrepresented in sports. Although accounting for just 12% of the US population, Blacks make up 75% of all NBA basketball players.

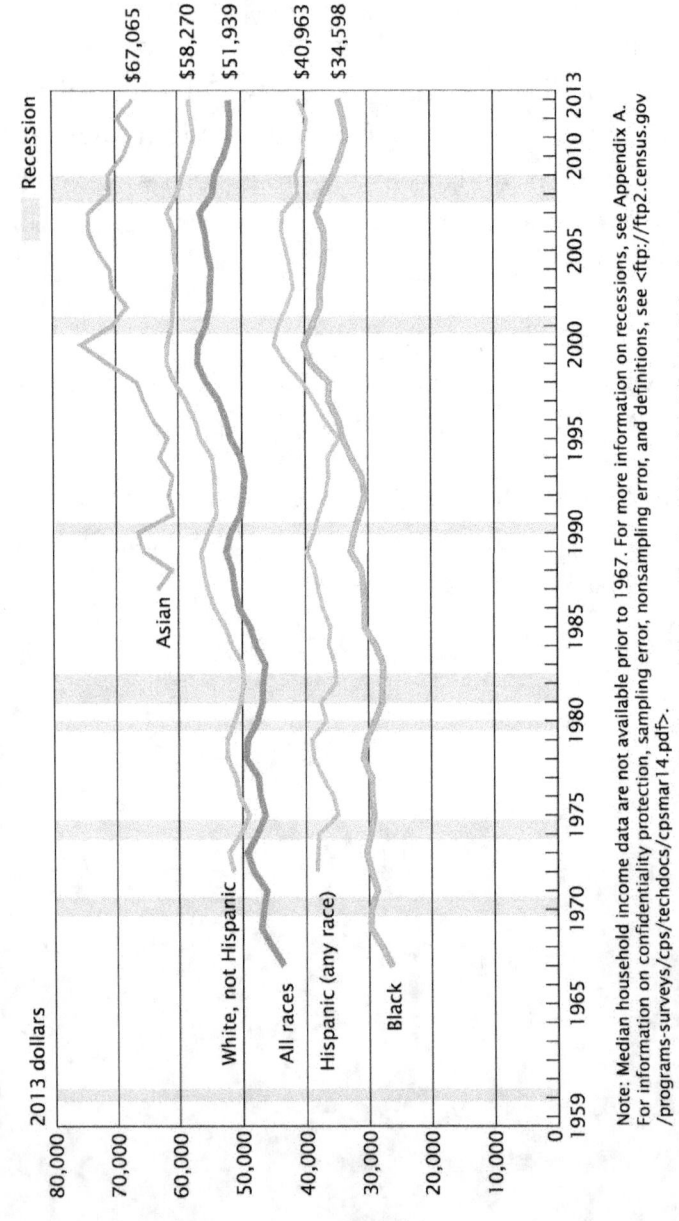

Illustration 13.2 Real Median Household Income by Race

Asians enjoy the highest median income of any race in the US. Image: "Income and Poverty in the United States: 2013" report. Census.gov. https://www.census.gov/content/dam/Census/library/publications/2014/demo/p60-249.pdf

It should be obvious to anyone that there are biological differences between ethnic groups. Depending on the definition of racism you use, accepting these scientific facts — technically speaking — may render you a racist.

Racial differences in mental and physical characteristics, by definition, leave one race superior in some characteristics, and another race superior in other characteristics. Whether a race is "superior" to another depends on the weight you assign to different traits.

When it is the number one priority to have an enduring military with high physical fitness, Blacks might be considered the superior race. However, when one deems the development of advanced aeronautical systems more important, Jews and Asians may be considered "superior."

It should be mentioned that while on average some ethnic groups have certain superior characteristics to others, there are always exceptions to the norm. IQ scores are normally distributed among a race, meaning that a physically fit Asian may very well be in better shape than an average Black.

Racism and Discrimination

Racism and discrimination are related, but nonetheless different concepts. As discussed in the previous chapter, discrimination refers to the different treatment of someone based on that person's traits on a non-merit basis. Reasons for discrimination can vary widely, ranging from religious beliefs to the way one dresses. Discrimination can also be positive, i.e., favoring someone, or negative, i.e., disadvantaging someone.

And yes, one of the reasons for discrimination can be racism.

However, while racism, just as your political leanings, may lead to discrimination, this does *not have* to be the case. You can recognize, for example, other people's racially defined differences, and still treat them with respect and in the same way as anyone else.

Are there Races?

There is this popular argument that races are merely a social construct, and that there is only one "human race."

As a result of natural selection, ethnic groups have developed significant genetic differences. Over time, human DNA mutates. And while most of these natural mutations remain without effect, others change our physical endurance or the way we look. As harsh as it sounds, nature "eliminates" individuals with gene combinations unfit for survival. For example, individuals unfit for extreme heat perish in desert environments, leaving men and women with more suitable DNA to reproduce.

Because of the differences in climates, terrains, flora, and fauna found around the world, natural selection has, over tens of thousands of years, led to genetic differences between peoples. We use the term "race" to refer to these genetically different groups of people.

Humans as a whole are a species, not a race. Similarly, we use the term "race" to refer to subgroups of plant and animal species.

Even if you should stick with your view that there is just one "human race," you should accept that there are people with different ethnic characteristics. If you do not want to call them "races," simply use the more politically correct term — ethnic groups. It does not change the fact that peoples have inherent cognitive and physical differences.

Does accepting science make us "racists?" - You decide.

Due to our obsession with political correctness, merely mentioning that there are racial differences can land you in trouble. Keep this in mind when pondering with the thought of discussing racism in public.

On a final note, I want to make clear that on a topic as controversial as racism you may want to do your own research. I was not associated with any of the research presented in this chapter and do not guarantee its accuracy. Feel free to look at my sources and make your own conclusions.

--- Learn More ---

- [BOOK] Taboo: Why Black Athletes Dominate Sports And Why We're Afraid To Talk About It. http://www.amazon.com/Taboo-Athletes-Dominate-Sports-Afraid/dp/158648026X

--- Sources ---

1. "Thirty Years of Research on Race Differences in Cognitive Ability." J. Philippe Rushton and Arthur R. Jensen. 2005. Psychology, Journal of Public Policy, and Law. The American Psychological Association. http://www.udel.edu/educ/gottfredson/30years/Rushton-Jensen30years.pdf. Retrieved July 28, 2015.

2. "The Bell Curve: Intelligence and Class Structure in American Life." Richard J. Herrnstein and Charles Murray. 1994. Free Press. ISBN: 0-02-914673-9.

3. "Natural History of Ashkenazi Intelligence." Gregory Cochran, Jason Hardy, Henry Harpending. 2006. J Biosoc Sci. http://www.ncbi.nlm.nih.gov/pubmed/16867211. Retrieved July 28, 2015.

4. "The Jewish Enemy: Nazi Propaganda During World War II and the Holocaust." Jeffrey Herf. Harvard University Press. Pages 35 and 36. http://bit.ly/1DsADbv. Retrieved July 28, 2015.

5. Median Household Income by Ethnicity - "Income and Poverty in the United States: 2013." US Census. https://www.census.gov/content/dam/Census/library/publications/2014/demo/p60-249.pdf. Retrieved July 28, 2015.

6. "Race, Evolution and Behavior, A Life History Perspective - Physical Differences Between People From Different Ethnicity." Professor J. Philippe Rushton. http://www.harbornet.com/folks/theedrich/JP_Rushton/Race.htm. Retrieved July 28, 2015.

Chapter 13 - Section 1: Racism

IMMIGRATION

CHAPTER 14

Around 232 million people are currently considered by the United Nations to be international migrants. The US' entire non-Indian population is a result of immigration. As of 2010, the US' five largest ancestry groups are, in order, Germans (accounting for 49 million Americans), Blacks and African-Americans (41 million), the Irish (35.5 million), Mexicans (32 million) and the English (27 million).

Immigration is the direct result of a number of pull- and push factors which include:

Pull-Factors (pulling migrants into a country)

- Political stability

- Higher standard of living

- Available jobs

- Social benefits

- Relatives already living in the country of destination

- Attractive culture, same spoken language

Push Factors (factors pushing migrants out of their country of origin)

- Political instability, war and conflict

- Discrimination and religious or political persecution

- Low standard of living, or even poverty and famine

- Unemployment

- Low prospect of achieving one's dreams and visions

Pull- and push factors mean that international migrants are mostly comprised of people with low incomes and low levels of education, searching for jobs in high-wage countries.

Immigration is a significant problem in the US, the country with the largest immigrant population in the world. As of 2013, 41.3 million US residents were born outside of the country's borders, including an estimated 11.6 million illegal immigrants. Similarly, as of 2010, Europe had a total immigrant population of 47.3 million, including 31.4 million immigrants born outside the EU. The other 15.9 million migrated between EU member countries.

Should there be unrestrained migration of people between countries? From a purely libertarian viewpoint and under consideration of the "Law of Liberty," the answer is yes. Though this assumption depends on three major immigration-related problems we first have to address. These include:

1. Immigrants Take Advantage of Generous Welfare Systems

This is probably the most significant problem faced by countries with a large influx of migrants. Generous welfare systems not only attract immigrants but cause resentment in the local population — potentially resulting in xenophobia and jingoism. There are two simple solutions to deal with this threat:

1. Prevent immigrants from receiving benefits before having worked and continuously paid taxes, for example, for 5 years.

2. Abolish our current mandatory welfare system and replace it with an optional opt-in welfare scheme. Or even better, privatize welfare entirely. As discussed in chapter 5 - Social Welfare, a privatized welfare and social security system is

voluntary and only pays benefits to those who paid in. This eliminates the problem of unemployed immigrants exploiting the system.

Furthermore, as illegal immigrants often work illicitly and, as a result, do not pay taxes, they use public infrastructure without paying for it. However, there is a simple solution for that, too. As discussed in chapter 4.3 - Consumption Tax, we can make everyone, including illegals and foreign tourists, pay for infrastructure and utilities by replacing all current taxes with consumption taxes.

Alternatively, we could finance all public resources through a market-based model. Under such a model, as discussed in the respective chapters 5-10, public resources would be paid for on a pay-as-you-go basis rather than through taxes. For example, mileage based road tolls would replace fuel taxes. An even more far-reaching step would be to privatize public services entirely. With all resources in private hands, immigrants would find it harder to profit from other people's property or receive free handouts.

Eliminating the options for immigrants to exploit public infrastructure and existing welfare programs discourages mass-immigration, while allowing us to benefit from the up-sides of immigration such as an increased labor force and an influx of people who arrive because they want to contribute to society, rather than exploit it.

2. **Immigrants Take Jobs**

While there are studies suggesting that immigrants tend to take jobs locals do not want to do, other commentators disagree. Nonetheless, whether this is actually the case or not should be irrelevant.

Cheap immigrants allow local businesses to significantly reduce their labor costs, for example, in the low-skill agricultural sector. This is because:

1. Immigrants are prepared to accept lower wages than locals along with longer working hours and harsher working conditions. Even the lowest wages paid in the US are likely higher than what low-skill migrants could earn in their home countries.

2. Based on the law of supply and demand, an influx of immigrant workers increases the supply of labor and, as a result, reduces the market wage.

As part of voluntaryism, farmers (and any other business owners) should be allowed to freely associate and initiate exchanges with whomever they want. If they prefer to use machines for milking cows rather than employing workers — so be it. And if they rather employ immigrant workers than locals — why not?

According to the law of liberty, a business does not have any obligation to favor hiring people who, out of pure luck, were born in the same area compared to those who were raised thousands of miles away.

Employing immigrants benefits:

1. businesses through lower wages

2. immigrant workers through incomes that are higher than in their respective home countries, and

3. consumers through lower prices

Businesses should be free to hire the person who does the best job at the lowest price, independent of ethnic origin, family connections or where a person happened to be born. Again, this does not mean that companies should be discouraged from hiring locals demanding higher wages. Voluntaryism states that business owners are free to do business with whomever and however they please.

3. **Immigrants Bring Crime**

When looking at the numbers, this favorite anti-immigration argument appears to hold up. More than 25% of the US prison population represents foreigners, of which 68% are from Mexico. It is estimated that every year foreign prisoners cost US taxpayers at least $1.6 billion.

Foreigners, which make up around 12% of the US population (41.3 million out of 320 million), account for twice the proportion of incarcerations, the aforementioned 25% of the US prison population.

It is true that under the current system immigration increases crime per capita and represents a significant cost to taxpayers. However, the best solution to this particular immigration problem is not necessarily to reduce immigration, but to fully privatize both the prison and court system as discussed in chapter 8 - The Judiciary.

A Last Note

While discussing immigration, we should not forget to differentiate between low-skill immigrants which barely speak the local language and highly educated professionals. Unfortunately, the US has often made it easier for low-skilled workers who pay little to no taxes to enter the country, while childless foreign professionals are left with little chance of moving to the United States. As is widely known, Mexicans like to obtain US citizenship for their children by bearing them on US soil. These "anchor-babies" then allow parents and other relatives to enter the country.

The immigration debate can easily be resolved by allowing free migration in accordance with the "Law of Liberty," while simultaneously preventing immigrants to exploit government services.

Furthermore, unrestrained international migration will only be beneficial to a receiving country if the legislative is reformed in a way that prevents immigrants to vote for benefits coming their way. As discussed in chapter 3.1 - Passing Laws, this can be done by basing policy decisions not on popular opinion, but the Constitution and the law and principles of liberty.

--- Sources ---

1. Number of International Immigrants - "On the move: 232 million migrants in the world." Mona Chalabi. The Guardian. http://www.theguardian.com/news/datablog/2013/sep/11/on-the-move-232-million-migrants-in-the-world. Retrieved July 28, 2015.

2. "The Largest Ancestry Groups In The United States" Liz O'Connor et al. Business Insider. http://www.businessinsider.com/largest-ethnic-groups-in-america-2013-8. Retrieved July 28, 2015.

3. "U.S. Immigrant Population Record 41.3 Million in 2013." Karen Zeigler and Steven A. Camarota. Center For Immigration studies. http://cis.org/immigrant-population-record-2013. Retrieved July 28, 2015.

4. Number of Immigrant Population in the EU - MoveEurope. http://www.artiszelmenis.lv/moveeurope/. Retrieved July 28, 2015.

5. US Prisoner Population - "Most foreign prisoners in US are Mexicans - report." Valeria Perasso. BBC. http://www.bbc.com/news/world-us-canada-13201212. Retrieved July 28, 2015.

REGULATIONS

CHAPTER 15

Government regulations, which are "rules or directives made and maintained by an authority (i.e. the government)" have continuously grown in number without a sign of slowing. Just look at the growth of the number of U.S. regulatory restrictions between 1997 and 2012 in following illustration. "Regulatory restrictions" are counted as statements containing terms such as "shall" and "must."

Illustration 15.1 Increase in Number of Regulatory Restrictions

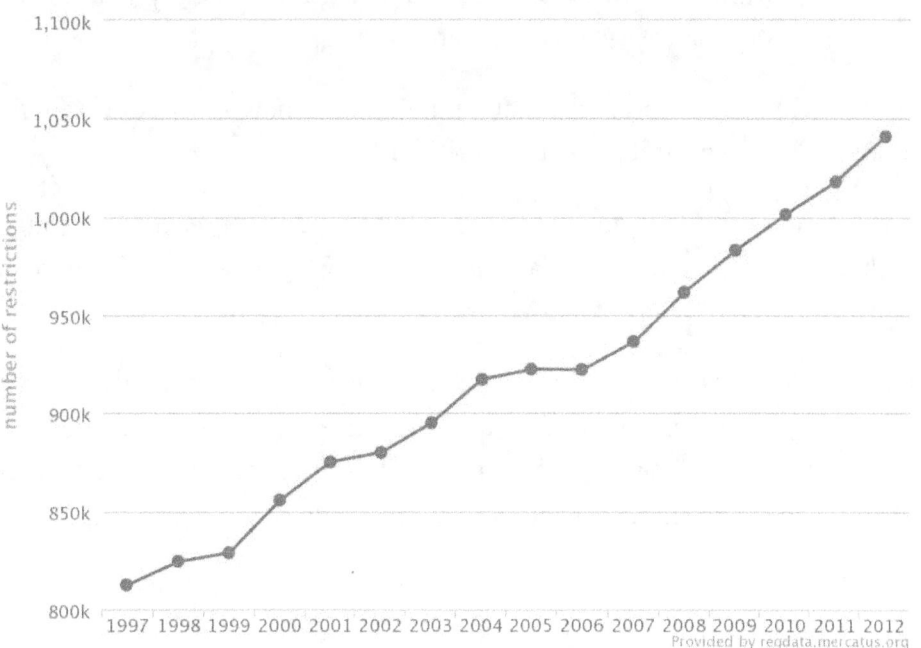

The number of U.S. regulatory restrictions increased by more than 28% between 1997 and 2012. Image: regdata.mercatus.org

In the year 2010, the number of US regulatory restrictions exceeded 1,000,000 for the first time, and comprised around 100 million words. Alone in the 15 year period between 1997 and 2012 the total regulatory word count saw an increase by a whopping 40%.

In effect, regulations represent the majority opinion of several hundred congressmen on how "we the people" should live. By definition, regulations — along with their supervisory agencies such as the EPA — violate the "Law of Liberty." Regulations prevent people from "doing as they please, as long as such behavior does not harm others."

Voluntaryism, too, is violated by regulations which either ban certain behaviors or prohibit voluntary interactions between individuals. These can range from activities such as driving without a safety belt to the setting of wages and prices by a business.

The notion of liberty is that individual behavior should remain unregulated — even if it results in *self*-harm.

In a world without regulations, civic order would be preserved through regular tort law, not regulations. Tort law is sufficient to punish individual behaviors that cause harm to *others*.

Let us now look at concrete examples of situations usually deemed to require government regulation and how the free market can resolve them. We will look at these in the three following sections - Consumer Protection, Environmental Protection, and Individual Lifestyles.

--- Learn More ---

* An interactive website on the number of US federal regulations by RegData.org http://regdata.org.

--- Sources ---

1. Bills Passed by Congress by Year - https://www.govtrack.us/congress/bills/statistics. Retrieved July 28, 2015.

CONSUMER PROTECTION

CHAPTER 15 - SECTION 1

Consumer protection is widely perceived as essential, specifically in the food and healthcare industries, to protect the public from harmful substances. The Food and Drug Administration (FDA) regulates the labeling requirements of food products, the testing of medications and authorizes food and medicine for mass consumption.

In a truly free market, food and drug security as well as labeling are ensured through a number of market-based mechanisms. In this section we will look at how these market mechanisms work to protect consumers — no regulations needed. While the following arguments are based primarily on the food and drug industries, where safety is arguably of the greatest concern, they apply just as much to other industries ranging from real estate to the automobile sector.

It Is in the Producer's Interest to Adhere to High (Voluntary) Safety Standards

Many people erroneously believe that without government regulations companies would do whatever they want, to the disadvantage of unprotected consumers. Just the thought of consuming food and medications which have not been government-approved alarms many.

However, free markets and standard tort law are arguably better in overseeing producers than government regulators could ever be. The food industry is a great example:

Under tort law, supplying mislabeled or spoilt meat to consumers represents "fraudulent misrepresentation." The individuals and businesses responsible would be fined accordingly. Fraudulent misrepresentation is a century-old concept that can apply to virtually all human interactions. We do not need lawmakers to make up regulations — our existing law is sufficient.

Even without government regulations, restaurant- and supermarket chains are quick to terminate suppliers which violate their promise to deliver safe food. Large chains depending on suppliers have a lot to lose when a tainted food scandal breaks — from loyal customers to profits. There is a strong threat suppliers face from chains and other consumers who may cancel contracts at their will, and sue them for "fraudulent misrepresentation" and breach of contract when food quality is not delivered. This is the free market at work. If you are still not convinced, consider these following real-world cases:

The US saw a large scale peanut-salmonella contamination in 2009. The company responsible, the Peanut Corporation of America, was quickly sued for misrepresentation by consumers and competitors alike. In combination with lost consumer trust, the scandal resulted in the company's chapter 7 bankruptcy filing.

The scandal came to light as hundreds of consumers suffered from salmonella poisoning in late 2008. Government inspections only started in January 2009, when the scandal had already broken.

Similarly, in 2014, Husi Food Co., the Shanghai meat supplier to McDonald's and KFC in Mainland China, was found to have produced large quantities of tainted and expired meat. In this case, the conditions were brought to light by a disgruntled employee. The company's production facility was soon closed and its contracts were immediately canceled by the fast food giants.

While government agencies do uncover food scandals in some cases, most are brought to light by whistleblowers as shown by the Peanut Corporation and Husi Food Co. Whistleblowers usually include underpaid and disgruntled employees, independent testers contracted by restaurant- and supermarket chains as well as harmed consumers.

The reason for the ineffectiveness of government inspectors is simple. The number of food processing facilities is simply too large to be inspected at regular intervals. Even though the FDA inspected 15,900 facilities in 2009, this covered a mere 4-5% of operating processing plants. Statistically speaking, this means that the average plant may only be inspected every 20-25 years.

Then let us hire more inspectors!

The problem with food security is not that there are too few inspectors or a lack of regulations (there are too many for reasons lined out later in this chapter). The issue is that it is impossible to control all types of behavior.

Let us go back to the Shanghai meat producer. One of the main complaints was that Husi Food Co. employees put meat which overflowed to the floor back into the production line. How do government inspectors want to prevent this? During the few hours an inspector is on site employees can simply refrain from their usually careless behavior and instead discard any overflowing meat.

Furthermore, it is not unheard of that producers bribe investigators who managed to spot a violation.

Another challenge is that of underground factories. Especially in emerging markets, factories producing everything from electronics to clothing and food may remain unregistered with the authorities. In some cases, such illegal factories use the address and "store-front" of officially registered businesses to sell their produce. How are governments supposed to investigate them?

The most effective supervision depends on the diligence of people and companies closely related to violators. Shortly after KFC had discovered high levels of antibiotics in its meat products several years ago, it ended relations with more than 1,000 small-scale poultry farms across China. This decision alone made the company's food safer than any regulation or team of inspectors could have ever done. It is virtually impossible for the state to oversee 1,000 meat suppliers. The market mechanism always trumps government oversight.

The same logic also applies to other industries. The National Highway Safety Administration admits on its website that many of the recalls that have affected 390 million motor vehicles since its foundation in 1966 have been initiated voluntarily by manufacturers, and were not due to government decree.

Most Exchanges Involve Multiple Parties

Most of the products you buy can be traced back to a lengthy supply chain with numerous suppliers and sub-suppliers. The production and sale of a frozen pizza, for instance, involves a multitude of entities, including:

- Wheat farmers

- Wheat processors

- Dozens of different suppliers delivering ingredients ranging from tomato sauce to cheese and toppings such as tuna

- The packaging supplier

- The firm putting all ingredients together

- The logistics firm

- The wholesaler

- The retailer

All of these entities have an interest in ensuring the pizza's food safety. The farmer will test the wheat for pesticide concentration and other impurities. The pizza producer controls the dough for bacterial contamination. The wholesaler and retailer will follow their own custom procedures to ensure they only sell safe food.

All this is done because every firm along the supply chain has something to lose when a scandal breaks. When a pizza is found to be contaminated with pesticides, the wheat producer, wheat processor, pizza manufacturer and the retailer face repercussions, in the form of fines (resulting from the violation of regular tort law, not regulations) as well as the loss of customer trust and orders.

We do not need frequent inspections or complicated regulations. Regular tort law that punishes lying firms is sufficient. Firms emphasize food security on their own due to their dependence on customer trust and orders. This is why food scandals are so rare despite government

inspections only taking place every 20-25 years for an average plant —
statistically speaking.

The Nature of Food Contamination Makes it Hard for the FDA to Spot

Large food scandals are rare, and those that happen are usually brought
to light by whistleblowers and consumers that are directly affected.
Government regulators are not only mostly ineffective compared to
market players in ensuring food safety, but generate costs that outweigh
the benefits of their inspections.

Illustration 15.2 Government Inspections Do Not Work

*There are not only far too many food production facilities to be efficiently
inspected, but most harmful contaminations only become publicized once people
get sick. Shown here is a dairy processing plant. Image: fotomy, Bigstock*

Think about it: have you ever heard of a case where a government food inspection was the first to break a scandal *and,* as a result, saved lives? The 2013 horse meat scandal in Europe was first exposed by Irish authorities, yet not a single consumer was saved from disease or death. After all, horse meat is a common food in some non-Western cultures.

Inspectors will always have a hard time catching potentially *deadly* contaminations because of the vastness and quick turnaround time of our food supply chain. When a regulatory violation takes place, the contaminated food is usually consumed within weeks, and the scandal breaks once a consumer gets sick. It is virtually impossible for an inspector to catch a contamination in the month-long period between production and consumption — *before the scandal is exposed on its own.*

You May Already Buy Non-FDA-Approved Food Products

If you buy food directly from farms, shop at farmers' markets or eat food made by the Amish, chance is you already consume products whose manufacturing process was not overseen by a federal regulatory agency.

Were these products — manufactured without regulatory oversight — any inferior to those bought from an FDA-approved food producer in a Walmart? Ironically, people buy from non-approved "local" producers because they trust them *more* than heavily regulated and overseen food companies.

The Force of Consumer Demand

If consumers demand extensive product labeling, the market will deliver — no regulations are needed. The forces of supply and demand state that when people prefer extensive labeling, companies that provide extensive product information make more money. For the same reason, we do not need a law requiring manufacturers to display product images on packaging. Producers show product illustrations because consumers demand it, and removing them would hurt sales.

How this works in the real world is probably best shown by Whole Foods Market, the US supermarket chain that specializes in natural food. There is no national requirement to label GMO products. Yet due to consumer demand, the company labels all of its GMO-free and organic products, while working to provide full GMO transparency for everything it sells by 2018.

Amazon's customer product review feature is another example of how consumer demand and the profit motive generate more relevant product information than government regulation would ever require.

In fact, there have been cases where the authorities actively prevent consumers from accessing product information. For example, the FDA bans dietary supplement manufacturers from displaying information on their packaging that suggests that a product prevents, cures, or mitigates a disease or condition — *even* when the claims have been proven through extensive laboratory testing and independent studies.

How can the government ban companies from communicating confirmed information if it allows customers to make more informed purchase decisions? Is it because the FDA wants to protect politically powerful drug companies from competition by dietary supplement manufacturers?

Despite the fact that the free market provides consumers with more product information than legally required, it still goes against voluntaryism to force companies to show product features.

The law of liberty and voluntaryism imply that individuals and firms should be free to engage in unregulated exchanges, as long as the involved parties voluntarily consent. This includes both parties' right to propose whatever offers they like. A company, for example, should be free to offer chocolate bars that do not feature nutritional information or lists of ingredients. Consumers are free to choose whether to accept and to buy them or not.

If you don't like the lack of labeling, then simply don't purchase the product.

Neither consumers nor the government have the right to force producers to amend their offer — i.e., the product and packaging they sell.

Otherwise, producers had the right to force consumers to amend their offer — namely forcing buyers to submit their names and home addresses when making a purchase. If consumers had the right to know where the ingredients of a chocolate bar came from, then producers had the right to know where consumers got their money from!

Why do we have this double standard when it comes to consumer and producer rights? Shouldn't everyone be treated equally?

According to voluntaryism, exchanges involve voluntary offers — made by both sides. And no party has the right to force the other side to amend its offer. Period. Forcing companies to feature product information not only violates liberty in every imaginable way, but can be considered duress — a tort.

We have a case of duress if:

1. the offending party threatens the victim with violence or imprisonment

2. the threat of violence makes the victim sign a contract that otherwise would not have happened

3. the resulting contract is unfair to the victim.

The requirement to force businesses to follow government-set labeling regulations satisfies all three conditions:

1. The government threatens businesses with fines, and potentially with close down if they do not comply.

2. This threat leads companies to finalize sales contracts with consumers that involve extensive labeling of their products. Without the threat, these contracts would not have happened, or been significantly different — involving products that are not labeled.

3. The resulting contracts harmed the companies as they had to invest time and money to update packaging with product information. New packages have to be designed, and already manufactured packaging material has to be discarded — at the companies' cost.

With all requirements being met, government requiring companies to label their products is technically speaking illegal. Our dear government only gets away with it because it is not subject to the laws that apply to everyone else.

A company's right not to show labeling does by no means imply that firms are free to put harmful substances into food products. If what is sold clearly identifies as bread — even if no information on its ingredients is given — then the producer has to ensure that it is edible. Using harmful, non-edible materials to create a bread look-alike that feels and tastes like the real one represents fraudulent misrepresentation — a tort, that is punishable under existing law.

On a final note, I would like to address the fact that current labeling regulations exclude small food producers. If you visit a mom-and-pop diner, you are unlikely to find a list of ingredients for your dinner, e.g., for the house-made sauce on your steak. Why are large companies such as McDonald's required to display nutritional information, while small businesses aren't? Can we please apply the same play rules to everybody?!

The FDA's Lengthy Testing Process of Drugs Cost Lives

We only ever hear the view that FDA regulations protect us from unsafe drugs. And it is true. There have without question been cases where the FDA prevented harm, for example, by not approving the drug Thalidomide®.

Thalidomide® was originally used against nausea in pregnant women. In countries where the drug was approved it resulted in 10,000 birth defects, including 5-7,000 cases in the medication's country of origin — Germany.

Nonetheless, what most people forget is that the FDA's lengthy approval processes themselves are a reason for thousands of deaths. The FDA's delay of the prostate-cancer drug Provenge® alone is estimated to have caused the loss of 82,000 life-years (note that life-years are not the same as lives!).

Even if we keep the current drug approval process in place — why not allow patients to take non-approved drugs on a voluntary basis? Many of these patients, including those that suffer prostate cancer, have little alternative to waiting in the hospital bed to die. What gives government bureaucrats the right to prevent people from ingesting non-approved drugs? They could be a patient's last chance to recover.

Regulations Cost the US Economy Trillions Every Year

One reason why many medical treatments are so cost prohibitive is the lengthy and complex drug testing process required for final approval. Treatment of one patient with the aforementioned prostate-cancer drug Provenge®, for example, adds up to $93,000. Every year of testing and delayed sales translates into a fallout in revenue, while the pharmaceutical company's facilities, staff, and research have to be paid for. In the end, it is the consumer who ends up paying for these expenses. There are many people out there — me included — who would prefer lower drug costs in exchange for shorter drug approval processes.

A 2014 study by the Small Business Administration (SBA) estimated government regulations to cost the economy a whopping $1.75 trillion every year. The report suggests the cost of *economic regulations* (concerning employer-employee conduct, safety standards, working hour caps, labeling regulations, etc.) to be $1.448 trillion. The cost of *environmental regulations* (regarding pollution, waste disposal, efficiency requirements for appliances and cars etc.) account for $330 billion. Comparing these figures to the US GDP of $17 trillion, we could boost total output by 10% if we were to restructure our regulatory environment.

The Drug Approval Process Is Inaccurate

FDA regulations cost us billions, while providing the public with a false sense of security. Merck's Vioxx® FDA-approved anti-inflammatory drug increased patients' risk of heart disease and was directly related to 40,000-70,000 deaths. Only after the side effects of the drug became public 5 years following the drug's FDA approval did Merck remove Vioxx® from the market.

The FDA is also known to have approved numerous harmful food additives ranging from food colorings to preservatives.

It Is Not You Who Benefits from the FDA

Large food and pharmaceutical firms love the FDA and regulations. Regrettably, the media have made people believe that large corporations support minimal regulations. In reality, large companies are the driver behind many costly and complex regulatory requirements. It is these that help them eliminate smaller competitors. Contrary to industry leaders, startups and small businesses often struggle to keep up with costly drug approval processes or the need to hire lawyers in order to comply with the thousands of pages of regulations passed every year.

Reynolds American is the second-largest tobacco company in the US, selling brands such as Pall Mall and Camel. Interestingly, the company is lobbying for more regulations in the e-cigarette market. As is often the case, the regulations in question only impact smaller competitors which use a slightly different e-cigarette technology than Reynolds American.

All major companies lobby for more regulations as part of their business strategy. McDonald's, Kraft, Nestlé and Walmart, among others, lobby bills requiring increased food safety standards which make it harder for smaller competitors to keep up.

Final Words

Regulations are inefficient in protecting consumer interests, and in some cases cause more harm than they prevent. The market mechanism already provides for food and drug safety, so why not give it a chance? According to voluntaryism, people and businesses should be free to do exchanges with whomever, however they want.

What right does a government agency have to prohibit two consenting parties to exchange a non-FDA-approved food product or drug — as long as they do not harm a third party?

Regulations are a tool used by governments and big businesses alike to control and exert force on average mom-and-pop shops and small businesses. Do not hand that power over to the government.

--- Learn More ---

- Big corporations and big government go hand in hand. http://www.freedomworks.org/content/big-corporations-and-big-government-go-hand-hand.

--- Sources ---

1. "FDA Delay of One Drug Causes 82,000 Lost Life-Years." William Faloon. LifeExtension.com. http://www.lifeextension.com/Magazine/2010/11/FDA-Delay-of-One-Drug-Causes-Lost-Life-Years/Page-01. Retrieved July 28, 2015.

2. "Why a Major E-Cigarette Company Is Lobbying for More Regulation." Ted Cooper. The Motley Fool. http://www.fool.com/investing/general/2014/09/17/why-a-major-e-cigarette-company-is-lobbying-for-mo.aspx. Retrieved July 28, 2015.

3. "Millions Spent Lobbying Food Safety." Laurel Curran. Food Safety News. http://www.foodsafetynews.com/2010/08/millions-spent-lobbying-food-safety-during-second-quarter/#. Retrieved July 28, 2015.

4. "Kentucky Fried Chicken says goodbye to 1,000 Chinese farm suppliers." Cheryl K. Chumley. The Washington Times. http://www.washingtontimes.com/news/2013/feb/26/kentucky-fried-chicken-says-goodbye-1000-chinese-f/. Retrieved July 28, 2015.

5. "The McDonald's Meat Supplier Scandal In China Keeps Escalating." Paul Carsten. Business Insider. http://www.businessinsider.com/mcdonalds-china-food-supplier-scandal-2014-7. Retrieved July 28, 2015.

6. Number of FDA Inspectors and Food Production Facilities - "More problems with FDA's ability to inspect food facilities." Marion Nestle. Food Politics. http://www.foodpolitics.com/2011/12/more-problems-with-fdas-ability-to-inspect-food-facilities/. Retrieved July 28, 2015.

7. "Whole Foods Market History." Whole Foods Market. http://
    www.wholefoodsmarket.com/company-info/whole-foods-market-history.
    Retrieved July 28, 2015.

8. Voluntary Motor Vehicle Manufacturer Recalls - National Highway Traffic
    Safety Administration. http://www.nhtsa.gov/Vehicle+Safety/Recalls+&
    +Defects/ci.Motor+Vehicle+Safety+Defects+and+Recalls
    +Campaigns.print. Retrieved July 28, 2015.

9. "Hairball: The Cost Of Federal Regulation To The U.S. Economy." Clyde
    Wayne Crews Jr. Forbes. http://www.forbes.com/sites/waynecrews/
    2014/09/10/hairball-the-cost-of-federal-regulation-to-the-u-s-economy/.
    Retrieved July 28, 2015.

ENVIRONMENTAL PROTECTION

CHAPTER 15 - SECTION 2

Regulations concerning the environment have the objective to protect "publicly owned goods." Using economic terms, they intend to reduce negative externalities. An externality is a benefit or cost caused by an activity of one party that unintentionally affects another party.

A *positive externality* represents the unintended benefits enjoyed by a third party to an economic activity. A classic example includes the increase in economic activity around a newly opened factory. Nearby shop owners, for example, benefit from increased spending power by workers.

A *negative externality* refers to the unintended costs born by a third party to an economic activity. In the case of a factory, this could be the air pollution unintentionally affecting the health of nearby residents.

Governments try to encourage positive externalities through the payment of subsidies, while discouraging negative externalities through regulations and taxes. By doing so, the government hopes to maximize positive externalities, while making those responsible for negative externalities pay.

The problem is that any economic activity causes *incalculable* positive and negative effects on society, not because they are necessarily large but because they are complicated to compute. This makes it impossible to correctly assess whether subsidies, regulations and/or taxes should be used to encourage or correct a certain behavior.

In this context, government officials often inaccurately reward and punish companies based on their perception on which behavior is good and which is bad. Even worse, government powers to subsidize and tax are often abused to "help out" campaign donors in manipulating the market. Strong relations between congressmen and the tobacco industry, for example, have led to the subsidizing of tobacco farmers in the South. At the same time, politicians wary of the effects of smoking have heavily regulated and taxed tobacco products. The cost of implementing policies that offset each other, along with the ongoing administrative expenses, result in enormous inefficiencies and lost national wealth.

There is a better way to protect the environment and our health — the privatization of public resources. Privatizing public goods has two major advantages:

1. People Take More Care of What They Own

In 1900, the African white rhinoceros species was almost extinct. A mere 20 rhinos of the species remained in a single South African reserve. In stark contrast, as of 2010 there are 20,000 of the animals, mainly thanks to privatization. In fact, white rhinoceros have become the most abundant rhino species in the world.

Illustration 15.3 **Privatization of Wildlife**

Privatization has helped protect dozens of wildlife species from poachers, including Gazelles shown here. Image: Oleg Znamenskiy, Bigstock

The "1991 Theft of Game Act" passed in South Africa institutionalized the private ownership of wildlife, making it worthwhile for locals to domesticate and reproduce rhinos for their own long-term benefits. Legal rhino owners are ever since allowed to carefully "harvest" rhino horn in a non-harmful way, and sell it on the open market. Rhino horn regrows naturally, but in the past poachers had little incentive to carefully catch and anesthetize the animals in order to get the horn — killing the animals was easier. Before 1991, careful harvesting of horn would have cost more time and money, while the animals would have ended up killed by other poachers anyway. With the privatization of wildlife, former poachers became the immediate beneficiaries of an animal's regrowing horn — creating an incentive to keep rhinos alive. Before privatization, all imaginable regulations intended to help the rhino species had failed.

The fact that people care more about what they own than public goods is a main reason for the Soviet Union's failure. Private property rights allow people to reap the rewards of the care they put into a resource.

For example, as long as others are allowed to use your personal car or apartment you will likely be reluctant to invest in mechanical repairs or buy a new couch on your dime. The same reasoning applies to public spaces, wildlife, and environmental resources ranging from fishing rights to groundwater.

Overfishing, for instance, can be easily contained through the extension of property rights to fishing areas. This can be done by selling patches of oceans and lakes along with all associated property rights to private fishermen. Fishermen are only allowed to fish in the areas they own, but in the quantity they want.

Overfishing would directly affect the owner of the area — making people adopt sustainable fishing practices on their own.

You might argue that fish migrate over large distances, likely crossing areas owned by various owners and making it difficult to contain fish populations. And while this is true, there are two solutions, again provided by private enterprise. A large company could take over competing "areas" and establish a private system in which it auctions off rights to fish a given amount of sea life. A second option would be the use of aquacultures. Owners of small ocean- or water areas may transform them into bordered-off aquacultures, where fish are raised and fed in a confined space. Aquacultures already account for about 50% of the world's production of aquatic organisms, including fish, crustaceans, and aquatic plants. Aquaculture production has doubled between 2000 and 2010, from 40 million to 80 million tons annually.

Privatization of natural resources makes their owners care more and, as a result, has the potential to improve the efficiency of the huge areas of publicly owned bodies of water and land. Privatization is far more successful in protecting the environment than regulations can ever be. Telling people how to treat others' property will always be less effective than letting them own and care for what they use.

2. Private Property Damage Can More Easily Be Accounted for

Let us assume you visit a public park, leaving trash from a picnic behind. Most likely, none of the other visitors will reprimand you — simply because the park you pollute is not theirs.

If a police officer happened to be in the area and fined you, where does the revenue from the fine go to? Is it paid to those visitors whose park experience you just diminished? Or is the fine redirected to finance the new police headquarter or a public museum? And who sets the height of the fine — what is the methodology used?

Above questions all point to the arbitrary nature of the management of public resources. If a polluter is fined at all, the fine will likely not be in accordance with the actual damage he or she caused, but with what some bureaucrats thousands of miles away came up with.

Privatizing the park, on the other hand, can resolve these moral dilemmas. Under privatization, the park owner may ask for an entrance fee, charging actual park users rather than every taxpayer. If entrance fees fail to cover the maintenance costs, it is a sign that not enough people value the park enough to justify its upkeep. It should be closed down rather than be forcefully subsidized by taxpayers who never use or even see it.

Charging an entrance fee is not the only way how private owners can finance a park. Parks can become part of housing communities and be paid for through homeowner association fees. And shopping centers may incorporate them into their properties as already done today. In a free market world, if you decide you rather keep your money than have it spent on a park, you can simply move to an area without parks and homeowner associations.

When extending property rights to manage environmental pollution, any property owner is free to use/pollute his or her own property. Only the use/pollution of another unconsenting individual's property is criminally charged. In such a case, compensation equivalent to the damage caused is to be paid — no arbitrary government fines or pollution regulations are needed.

Under a system of extended property rights, a fine to be paid by a polluter equals the harm caused *and* is paid directly to the victim. This is very different to the government's approach to avoiding pollution. Today, polluting companies, such the operator of a coal plant, are required to pay arbitrary fines estimated by bureaucrats. They are paid directly to the government — not those immediately affected by the pollution event.

This results in fines not being aligned with the harm caused, leading to market inefficiencies. Take a coal plant operator producing $100 million in annual economic output, but creating costs of $50 million in pollution. In a free market, harm caused equals compensation to be paid. The pollution cost is determined by the market, for example, by setting compensation amounts for nearby residents on an individual basis in court. It would also be possible to consult residents on their annual compensation demands before building a plant.

The market also decides whether the plant should continue operations. If the profits generated by the plant operator allow for the annual compensation payment, the plant continues operations — still producing a net profit for its owners. If the compensation claims are higher than the profits generated, the plant closes down.

In our regulation-based society, however, the plant is shut down based on arbitrary government regulations on pollution levels — ignoring whether the plant generates more output than it causes harm. As a result, a plant may continue to operate despite causing more harm than economic value, or be shut down although generating a net benefit to society.

Not to forget that in a free market, a plant operator compensates those harmed directly, rather than paying a fine to a government department.

For the same reason, a trading system for pollution permits remains morally questionable. The number of pollution permits the government makes available for purchase is solely based on the judgment of government bureaucrats. Again, the money companies pay for these permits is not used to directly compensate the victims of pollution.

Unsolvable Issues?

It is often argued that certain types of environmental stress — such as air pollution — are too complex to be addressed solely through the extension of property rights. In the case of air pollution, pollutants emitted by one factory can spread worldwide over a period of months or years, making it difficult to attach any one person's respiratory disease to a single polluter.

In special cases like this one, the extension of property rights may not address pollution on its own. Yet even in these cases is it appropriate to abolish regulations, taxes and subsidies to "steer" polluters' behavior — for following reasons:

1. While individual producers contribute to pollution, it is not just them who benefit. Imagine a coal-fired power plant emitting sulfur and other toxins into the nearby environment. The cheap energy produced by its unregulated furnaces drive down electricity prices for everyone. Or take the goods manufactured by factories located in countries with lax environmental regulations. Both consumers in emerging and Western countries benefit from the low-priced products made possible in part by saving on environmental protection.

2. In obvious cases, where an individual air polluter is responsible for the harm of others, the extension of property rights remains effective as a tool to address pollution. For example in the Bhopal incident, where Dow Chemical could be held liable for breaking the property rights of nearby residents. Or take the coal-fired power plant from our previous example. If a nearby farmer can prove that higher levels of sulfur have led to the acidification of his soil, he may sue the power plant for compensation.

   Furthermore, the impact of a single coal plant's emissions on people hundreds of miles away is likely too small to be quantifiable. This makes any approach to calculating the adverse impact of a plant's pollution on far-away residents more expensive than the potentially resulting benefits.

3. Every individual pollutes at least to a small extent, and this type of pollution is almost impossible to track. When you do a barbecue on a weekend you contribute to air pollution. Whether you extend property rights or use regulations, small-scale pollution sources are difficult if not impossible to account for. Simply ignoring small-scale pollution is more practical and cost-effective.

--- Learn More ---

• Saving African Rhinos: A Market Success Story by Perc Case Studies http://www.perc.org/sites/default/files/Saving%20African%20Rhinos%20final.pdf.

--- Sources ---

1. Statistics on Aquacultures - Food and Agriculture Organization of the United Nations. http://faostat.fao.org/site/629/default.aspx. Retrieved July 28, 2015.

INDIVIDUAL LIFESTYLES

CHAPTER 15 - SECTION 3

Just as there are regulations concerning economic transactions and the environment, there is legislation directing people's personal lifestyles. Typical policies regulating behavior include bans on gun possession, criminalization of drug use, mandatory wearing of seat belts and the rather new requirement of all US residents to purchase health insurance.

"The Law of Liberty" clearly lays out that everyone has the right to live his/her life as one pleases, given that one respects the same right of everyone else and does not harm others.

Accordingly, any rules requiring seatbelt use or mandatory health insurance violate liberty. It is irrelevant whether such regulations represent the opinion of a dictator, a government committee or 51% of the population. No one has the right to decide over the personal lifestyle choices of others.

Someone's decision not buy health insurance may bring him- or herself at risk, but does not affect others. And while that individual is not free to force others to remain uninsured, nor are others morally entitled to force him/her to buy health insurance.

Personal lifestyle choices should remain untouched by government regulators as long as they do not harm others or infringe on others' rights.

The unfortunate truth is that the majority often prefers to force its opinion on the minority, rather than respecting liberty and other people's ways of life.

Many of today's regulations, including mandatory health insurance, the banning of drugs and the requirement to wear seat belts, are views shared by the majority. Why do we have to suppress people with minority preferences, if they do not force them onto us or harm others?

Sadly, only when becoming exposed to differing viewpoints do many people realize the effects their bans and regulations have on the minority. For example, parents of increasingly outspoken LGBT children realize the suppression experienced by these individuals, while they might have been indifferent or even anti-gay before. This is what led to the shift to a more open approach to marriage.

Unfortunately, most people do not realize that there are legitimate reasons for differences in people's lifestyle choices. Unless this changes, and more people appreciate the ideals of liberty, suppression of minorities will continue.

Even if we don't understand the motives behind other people's lifestyle choices, should we respect rather than ban them.

I am personally opposed to drugs of any kind, including alcohol. And while I believe that mineral water would do everyone good, it would never come to my mind to ban other beverages or to lecture people on their drink choices. Some people simply prefer the taste of sugary sodas to a healthy lifestyle — and this is fine. People's differing preferences mean that there will never be a beverage that fits all, a religion that everyone likes, or an education system that everyone supports. Contrary to governments, the free market and liberty respect these differences, and work to serve them based on the profit motive.

No personal lifestyle choice is too strange or abnormal, and given that it abides by the principles of liberty (such as voluntaryism), should be equally respected.

Regulations Lead to More Regulations

Assume no drug was banned, and our health care system was entirely voluntary and private. The free market would charge drug-addicts more than those that live healthily, or even deny them health care access entirely. Because insurers are free to do business with individuals of their liking, some people's drug use would not affect or *harm* the general population. In accordance with the law of liberty, everyone is free to consume anything of his/her choice.

Once the government makes health insurance mandatory, and requires premiums to be comparable for everyone, drug users become the society's burden. Because everyone is forced to "subsidize" the drug addicts that are now part of the system, drug use *harms* others.

Yet it is not drug use that violates the law of liberty's requirement not to harm people — it is government regulation. The reason drug addicts now harm the general population is because government forces everyone else to pay for drug-related conditions.

It is the requirement to buy health insurance that violates the law of liberty and voluntaryism. This first regulation results in a chain reaction, leading to drug use infringing on other people's liberty to remain financially unaffected from the consequences of addiction. This makes people want to introduce drug-bans, in turn violating people's right to choose for themselves what to ingest.

In order to finance higher health care costs, the government may subsidize the system through additional taxes, resulting in even more violations of the law and principles of liberty.

A drug ban is also likely to result in illegal gang activity and crime, leading the government to pass another liberty-violating regulation — gun-control.

As you see, one regulation quickly leads to another. And before we know it, the government regulates every aspect of our destiny.

The only way to allow people to fully determine their lives is to abolish most, if not all regulations. The majority of currently regulated personal behaviors do not affect the lives of others anyway. In the few cases that people are actually harmed by someone else's lifestyle, we can use regular civil and criminal law to set things straight. There is simply no need for liberty-violating regulations micro-managing our fates.

TRADE AND PROTECTIONISM

CHAPTER 16

The "Law of Liberty" has a simple answer to trade and protectionism: "One should be allowed to trade freely with whomever one wants, as long as the same right of someone else is not infringed."

While unrestrained free trade makes sense from an ideologically "libertarian" viewpoint, it does, too, from a purely economic perspective. Yes, the US and many other service-based economies in the West have lost millions of manufacturing jobs to emerging markets in the past decades. But in total, this shift in economic activity has not only greatly improved worldwide economic efficiency, but increased global wealth *and* fairness. Here is why:

Trade between Individuals, Cities, States and Countries

We can categorize the tendency of humans to agglomerate into different levels of hierarchical groups as follows:

1. The Individual

2. The Family Unit

3. The Town/City Level

4. The District/County Level

5. The State/Provincial Level

6. The Country Level

7. The Continental Level

8. The Global Level

Chapter 16: Trade and Protectionism

Virtually all countries allow free trade within their own borders (i.e., between different regions such as Texas and California) — encompassing groups 1-6 featured in the list. In some regions, countries have started to form free trade areas. Prominent examples include NAFTA (USA, Canada, Mexico), Mercosur (South America) and the EU.

While technically speaking Mercosur represents a customs union and the EU an economic union, both are also free trade areas. There is often confusion between the functions of free trade areas, economic unions and other stages of economic integration. Illustration 16.1 shows an overview of the stages of economic integration between countries. A more integrated stage always also includes the characteristics of the lower stages. For instance, a customs union is always also a free trade area, and an economic union is always also a customs union and free trade area.

While most people focus on whether free trade is "good" or beneficial to them, any free trade discussion always centers on the border of the free trade area — be it the border of the country itself, or of a larger multi-country region.

Have you ever heard someone advocating for the abolishment of free trade between cities in the US, or families in a town? — I bet not. The idea of introducing protectionist trade barriers between bordering cities in the same country seems absurd. Everyone knows that Detroit specializes in cars, the Los Angeles metro in entertainment, the San Francisco area in high-tech and the internet, Houston in energy and New York in finance and media. This is because people and businesses with similar interests and skills cluster, be it in the form of a small group of shops on main street or numerous financial firms in NYC.

The forces behind this phenomenon are so-called "economies of agglomeration." For example, New York has an existing labor pool of

Illustration 16.1 Stages of Economic Integration

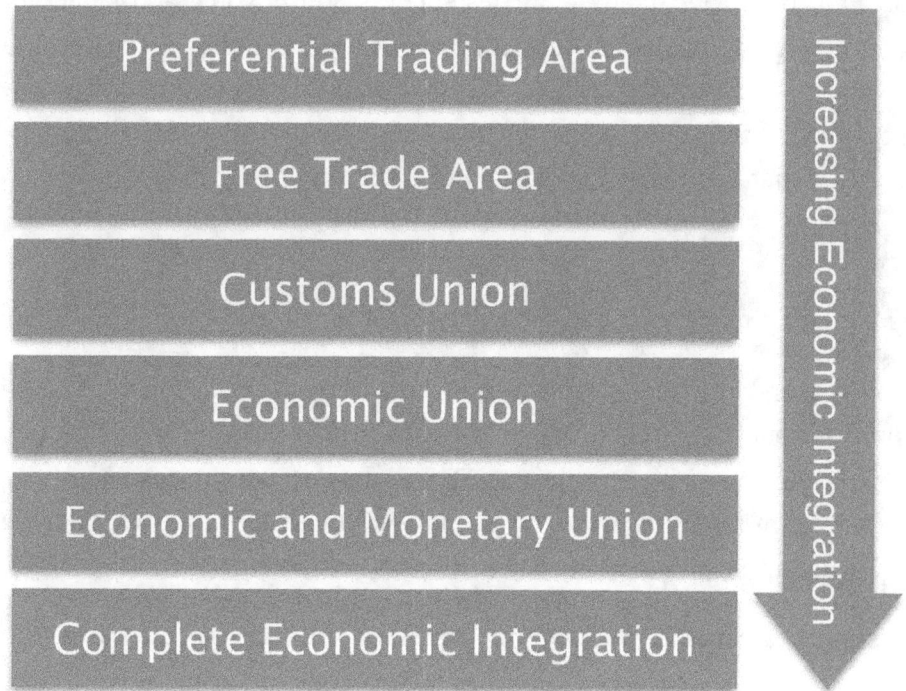

NAFTA represents a free trade area, while the EU is an economic union. The Eurozone, which consists of 19 of the 28 EU countries (as of July 2015) represents an economic and monetary union. Image: own work by author

experienced finance professionals, making the area attractive for upcoming financial firms. Energy firms in Houston benefit from an existing infrastructure for the movement of oil and natural gas, making it less expensive for new energy firms to set up there, compared to Chicago or Phoenix.

These forces do not only exist within national economies. They are also prevalent on a global scale between countries, if not more so. Countries such as Vietnam and Bangladesh have large labor pools of cheap, unskilled labor, making them perfect for rudimentary manufacturing jobs. On the other hand, countries such as South Korea and Japan are specializing in consumer electronics while Germany has a competitive advantage in producing technologically advanced cars and machinery. If individuals, cities and states within a country are able to trade freely, why is it that countries on a global scale should not?

Trade Deficits

One reason why some people are wary of free trade is the fate of countries such as Greece, and to a lesser extent the US, both of which suffer from massive trade deficits. These deficits are the result of both countries' more competitive neighbors — namely Germany in the case of Greece and China and Mexico in the case of the US.

In simple terms, a trade deficit means that a country imports more than it exports. This would be equivalent to you consuming more goods and services (e.g., clothes, cars) than you produce. Because your levels of consumption and production are measured in terms of expenses and income, your "personal trade deficit" is equivalent to how much you spend more than you earn in income. While trade deficits happen when nations spend more than they take in, in the long term, the free market will automatically balance national spending with national income.

Similarly, your "personal trade deficit" will resolve either when you decide to stop spending more money than you take in, or you run out of money. The same is the case for national economies.

On a side note, I should mention that a trade deficit is not to be confused with a budget deficit, which refers to government spending being larger than government revenues.

Greece's trade deficit is due to locals spending more on imported goods than they sell to foreigners in the form of exports. As Greek businesses and consumers get shorter on money, their country's trade deficit shrinks. Thus, in a pure free market, Greece's inability to buy imports would eliminate the trade deficit on its own. The reason why it continues to persist (although at a lower level than just a few years ago) is because the IMF, European Central Bank (ECB) and Eurozone member countries continue to provide the South-East European country with loans to finance new imports. Yes, the free market solution to trade deficits can be painful, but it forces countries to live within their means. Greece has lived above its means ever since it entered the Eurozone. They should be grateful to have enjoyed an unsustainably high living standard for so long, not resent that they return to the standard of living they "earn."

The US, on the other hand, can continue to import more than it spends because it receives money from other sources, namely foreign direct investment (FDI) and other financial investments by foreigners. Common inflows of money originate from foreigners buying US stocks, businesses, and properties. For example, both Japan and China have so far injected $1.2 trillion *each* into the US economy through treasury note purchases. Similarly, Chinese investors have recently paid $2 billion to acquire the Waldorf Astoria Hotel in New York, prompting Obama to end the 80-year long tradition of US Presidents staying at the famed hotel.

The US continues to rank among the top three recipients of FDI, with net FDI inflows topping more than $290 billion in 2013.

We should not forget that US states, too, have trade deficits with each other. For example, Texas exports more to Alabama than vice versa, creating a trade imbalance between the two. Trade deficits between US states are never cited as a reason to introduce protectionist measures between US states, so why are trade deficits a "valid" reason against inter-country trade?

Absolute and Comparative Advantages

Many advocates of trade barriers confuse the concepts of absolute and comparative advantage of a country. If you have never heard about these concepts, do not worry, we will tackle them below. They are essentially a mathematical proof for why trade makes all trading parties better off.

Having an absolute advantage means that using the same amount of resources, a country can produce a larger number of units of a certain good. A comparative advantage, on the other hand, means that a country can produce a good at a lower relative opportunity cost.

I know it sounds complicated, but it is easier than you think. Let us use following example to make both concepts clear.

Hours of Work Required for Production		
Country	Software Program	Mobile Phone
US	70	140
China	60	80

In above example, China has an absolute advantage in the production of both software programs and mobile phones, because both products require fewer resources (i.e., working hours) when produced in China compared to the US.

The US, however, has a comparative advantage in the production of software programs. In order to produce one software program, the US has to give up 70h of working time — which is equivalent to the manufacturing of 0.5 mobile phones (70/140). China, on the other hand, has to give up 60h of working time — equivalent to the production of 0.75 mobile phones (60/80). Essentially, in the US it costs 0.5 mobile phones to produce one piece of software, while in China it costs 0.75 mobile phones.

Therefore, the US has a comparative advantage (i.e., lower opportunity cost) to produce software, despite China overall being more cost effective in the production of both goods.

By definition, this means that China has a comparative advantage in the production of mobile phones, as it costs 1.33 pieces of software to produce one phone in the Middle Kingdom, but 2 pieces of software in the US. To derive these numbers, just take the inverse of the original opportunity cost figures (80/60=1.33, 140/70=2).

Due to differences in skill sets and available resources, every individual, city, state and country has a comparative advantage in the production of a specific service or good, even if overall, they may be a less efficient manufacturer.

In above example, both the US and China would be better off by specializing in the product in which they have a comparative advantage, and trading with each other the respective goods they do not produce/ specialize in.

Let us look at another example. Assume you are a self-employed accountant mainly doing two tasks: preparing financial statements and filing tax returns for your clients. Your friend is also a self-employed accountant doing exactly the same. Here is an overview of how much time both of you take for the two tasks:

Hours of Work Required to Complete a Job		
	Preparing Financial Statements	Filing Tax Returns
You	10h	5h
Your Friend	6h	4h

As shown in the table, your friend takes less time to complete both jobs — in other words, he has an absolute advantage in both. You, on the other hand, have a comparative advantage in filing tax returns. In order to file one tax return, you have to give up working time equivalent to the preparation of 0.5 financial statements (5/10). Your friend, on the other hand, has to give up working time equivalent to the preparation of 0.67 financial statements (4/6).

Assume both of you have a 100h work week. You both try to complete approximately *the same number of both jobs*. On your own, you and your friend are able to complete the following number of jobs:

Number of Jobs Completed Per Week (in 100h)		
Country	# of Financial Statements Prepared	# of Tax Returns Filed
You	6 (6*10h=60h)	8 (8*5h=40h)
Your Friend	10 (10*6h=60h)	10 (10*4h=40h)
TOTAL	16	18

One day, you and your friend talk about the time both of you need to complete the jobs. Due to your different opportunity costs in completing the tasks, you decide to work as partners in a new company you name "Two Friends - Accredited Accountants," and split up the work. You concentrate on filing tax returns while your friend specializes in preparing financial statements. The new output of jobs in your joint company is as follows:

Number of Jobs Completed Per Week (in 100h)		
Country	# of Financial Statements Prepared	# of Tax Returns Filed
You	0	20 (20*5h=100h)
Your Friend	16 (16*6h=96h)	1 (1*4h=4h)
TOTAL	16	21

As a result of specializing, both of you now still prepare the same number of financial statements as before (16), but increased the output of tax filings by more than 14% from 18 to 21.

In total, as both of you specialize in what each of you does best, you end up being better off. Both of you decide to split the productivity gain by 50:50.

A protectionist, on the other hand, would have advised you not to work with your friend, as he is more cost efficient in doing both jobs and may "steal" your work.

While some people may lose their job as a result of free trade, in total, always more people benefit thanks to the mathematically proven efficiency improvement.

Illustration 16.2 Trade Improves the World Economy

Allowing every country to specialize in the production of what they are best at and to trade on a global scale benefits every nation. Image: Amfreedom, Bigstock

An Ethical Question

Another strong argument for free trade is that prohibiting two parties to engage in a mutually beneficial exchange is just *not fair.* Let me use another example:

Assume you own a dry cleaning business. To do your job, you have to buy tens of thousands of disposable coat hangers every year. You can buy them from a local supplier who charges you $0.05 per piece, or a Chinese producer, who charges just $0.01. If you buy 40,000 units per year, the local supplier will cost you $2,000 while the Chinese producer will charge a total of just $400.

Your dry cleaning business hardly breaks even, and switching from the local to the Chinese coat hanger supplier would enable you to use $1,600 for a once-in-a-year visit to your family on the other side of the US.

The only problem: lobbyists hired by the local firm just succeeded in banning the Chinese coat hanger imports due to alleged "unfair competition." As a result, you are forced to cancel this year's family visit.

In a situation like this, any two or more consenting parties should be free to engage in a voluntary exchange — in accordance with voluntaryism. Instead, the local supplier violated the dry cleaner's and Chinese manufacturer's right to engage in a voluntary, mutually beneficial exchange, while indirectly "forcing" the cleaner to buy overpriced coat hangers locally.

While buying from China eliminates some jobs at home, by definition, these losses are more than compensated for by gains enjoyed by others — ranging from customers to workers abroad. Laid off workers in the US or UK are better suited to perform more complex work than doing rudimentary tasks that can be done more efficiently in Vietnam. Just as shown by our accountant example, giving the job to the most efficient producer leads to global economic growth, and in total benefits more people than it hurts.

Global manufacturing and trade can only be viewed negatively if you value the interests of a few comparatively inefficient workers, say, in the US, as more important than the larger net gains enjoyed by customers and other workers worldwide. How can it be justified to artificially impair free trade, and as a result inhibit the creation of global wealth, just to protect a small group of people whose inefficiency makes them fear for their occupations?

If you do not want to discriminate, you should purchase the coat hangers from the business that offers the lowest price and the best quality. If a Chinese manufacturer delivers the best value, why not choose him instead of a local producer? As discussed in chapter 13 - Discrimination, businesses and individuals are free to discriminate. However, wouldn't it be nice if you chose the people you do business with on a merit basis — rather than based on ethnicity, country of origin or friendship and nepotism?

Let us buy from people who deliver a better value product, and not from those who had the luck to be born in a town close to you.

Exploited Workers?

Critics of globalization, and international trade in particular, often argue that manufacturing in developing countries inevitably leads to the exploitation of workers. This is a dangerous fallacy.

Free markets are based on voluntary interactions, which take place solely because both involved parties benefit. This is why you thank the barista at your coffee shop when you get a coffee, and the barista thanks you for the sale.

Nobody is forced to work at foreign-owned factories in China or Bangladesh. People work there voluntarily. Why? — Because factory jobs pay more than operating a food stall or being a farmer. The same is true for working conditions, which are better than 7 days of back-breaking work on a field or the prospect of having to inhale toxic smoke from a street stall all day. This is why the Fair Labor Association (FLA), when doing a survey of hundreds of Chinese Foxconn workers (Foxconn is the company that assembles iPhones and iPads), found that 48% of them regarded their working hours to be reasonable, while 34% wanted to work more. Only 18% thought they worked too much. Again, people do not want to work more hours because they do not earn enough — they earn more than in traditional occupations. Workers want to work longer shifts because it allows them to have a higher standard of living. Ironically, it is Chinese government regulations that limit the work week to 48h that put a hold on people's aspirations.

Even more ironic is the fact that Western labor rights organizations campaign for the closure of foreign-owned factories, essentially advocating to relegate factory workers to the poverty-filled fate of their parents. We have to remember that it was low-skill manufacturing jobs that lifted hundreds of millions of Chinese up into the middle class. In fact, according to the Pew Research Center, 700 million people stepped out of poverty between 2001 and 2011 alone — mostly thanks to increased manufacturing by Western companies in China and South Asia. Had we listened to anti-free-trade activists and unions in the West, today, these people would continue to suffer poverty.

Additional Talking Points

We discussed the absurd logic of allowing free trade between cities and states, but not between countries. We talked about how the market mechanism resolves trade deficits and about the mathematical proof that unrestrained free trade makes all parties better off. We also addressed the ethics of not allowing two consenting parties to engage in a mutually beneficial exchange.

There are also many other benefits of free trade. Some of them are listed below:

- Fewer wars between trading nations because of the potential loss in beneficial trade. Interdependence of economies in terms of resource production and consumption is also a reason why trade reduces the incidence of wars

- More choice for consumers — you may buy Japanese, German and other foreign-manufactured cars instead of only a few locally produced models

- Increase in global GDP, as shown by the accountant example in this chapter

- Lifting up of hundreds of millions of people into the middle class in emerging countries such as China and India

- The fairness of allowing the "most efficient" producer to get a job — independent of his/her ethnic origin

- Improved cultural relations — e.g., the spread of Buddhism to Western countries and of political freedoms such as visa-free travel around the world

On a Last Note

It is important to point out that the free trade policies in place today between many countries are far from "free." Trade agreements that are thousands of pages long tend to advantage businesses with ties to politics. Just look at the planned TPP (Trans-Pacific Partnership) agreement between 12 Pacific rim countries. Why are only the largest of Fortune 500 corporations invited to negotiations, and why are discussions kept secret? As outlined in more detail in chapter 3.2 - Special Interests, free trade agreements should eliminate regulations, not create thousands of pages of new ones. What we need is true, universal and unrestrained free trade between consenting individuals and businesses.

--- Sources ---

1. Net Inflows of Foreign direct investment - World Bank. http://data.worldbank.org/indicator/BX.KLT.DINV.CD.WD?order=wbapi_data_value_2013+wbapi_data_value&sort=desc. Retrieved July 28, 2015.

2. "The Truth About Foxconn Workers: They Want To Work More, Not Less." Henry Blodget. Business Insider. http://www.businessinsider.com/apples-foxconn-workers-want-to-work-more-2012-3?IR=T. Retrieved July 28, 2015.

3. 700 Million People Rose Out of Poverty Between 2001 and 2011. "A Global Middle Class Is More Promise than Reality." Rakesh Kochhar. Pew Research Center. http://www.pewglobal.org/2015/07/08/a-global-middle-class-is-more-promise-than-reality/. Retrieved July 28, 2015.

MONETARY SYSTEM

CHAPTER 17

Commonly, a country's monetary system is overseen by its central bank. The central bank sets the money supply in an economy through three main mechanisms:

1. **Reserve Requirements** - Reserve requirements require commercial banks (such as Citibank) to keep a minimum percentage of customer deposits as reserves. The bank is prohibited from loaning out these reserves to other customers.

   If the central bank wants to increase the money supply, it reduces the reserve requirement from say 10% to 7%. Citibank is now free to use an additional 3% of customer deposits to lend out to other clients. The increase in money lent out by Citibank increases the money supply, as money supply includes both customer deposits and loans. The practice of lending out customer deposits is known as fractional reserve banking.

2. **Discount Rate** - When you need a loan, you go to a commercial bank like Citibank. When a bank needs a loan, it borrows money directly from the central bank.

   The "discount rate" is the interest rate charged by a central bank on loans lent to commercial banks. When the central bank wants to increase the money supply, it reduces the discount rate. At a lower interest rate, commercial banks are more likely to lend from the central bank, and in turn pass the money on as loans to businesses and individuals.

   Any money lent by the central bank to commercial banks is created from scratch and often referred to as "money printing." As a result, lower interest rates increase the money supply.

3. **Open Market Operations** - Through so-called "open market operations," the Fed purchases treasury notes (bonds) on the open market when it wants to increase the money supply. In order to decrease the money supply, it sells these bonds.

   The open market refers to the now digital marketplace in which market participants such as banks trade bonds and other financial assets.

   This is how it works in detail: the Fed "prints" money which allows it to purchase government bonds from banks like Goldman Sachs. This increases the money supply in the economy, because the original bond holder (e.g., Goldman Sachs) is now in the possession of newly printed currency. If the Fed wants to reduce the money stock again, it re-sells the bonds to the market. The money received by the Fed from the bond sale is withdrawn from the economy.

   The same can be done with other types of assets such as mortgage-backed securities. Large-scale asset purchases have been referred to as quantitative easing in the past.

Depending on the country, a central bank may be dependent on, or independent from the government. A central bank is dependent when it is controlled by the government, as is the de facto case in India. It is independent when the central bank controls the money supply without government interference. This is officially the case in the US, the Eurozone and the UK.

There has been a trend towards making central banks independent from governments. The reason for this is that in the past, governments "abused" their control of the money supply by "printing" money to finance budget deficits. The resulting hyperinflation will be discussed in more detail in chapter 17.2 - Fiat Currencies.

Nonetheless, it has been debated whether independent central banks indeed help prevent excessive inflation. The Fed, for example, followed political pressure by Washington and big banks to purchase financial assets worth trillions after the 2008/2009 financial crisis — questioning its autonomy.

Illustration 17.1 The Federal Reserve Building in Washington DC

The Fed's Washington D.C. branch is located between the Lincoln Memorial and the White House. Image: vpp, Bigstock

--- Sources ---

1. US Constitution - Archives.gov. http://www.archives.gov/exhibits/charters/constitution_transcript.html. Retrieved July 28, 2015.

2. "Central Bank Transparency and Independence by Country." N. Nergiz Dincer and Barry Eichengreen. Sept 04, 2013. The Bank of Korea Working Papers. http://www.bok.or.kr/contents/total/eng/boardView.action?menuNaviId=1941&boardBean.brdid=12594&boardBean.menuid=1941&boardBean.rnum=1. Retrieved July 28, 2015.

Chapter 17: Monetary System

THE FEDERAL RESERVE

Paragraph 5, Section 8 of Article 1 of the US Constitution grants Congress the right to coin money. However, the Founding Fathers debated whether *government* should have this responsibility or whether it should be passed on to a central bank. Thomas Jefferson, 3rd President of the United States, was a vehement opponent of central banks. According to his own words:

"If the American people ever allow private banks to control the issue of their currency, first by inflation, then by deflation, the banks [...] will deprive the people of all property until their children wake-up homeless on the continent their fathers conquered [...]. The issuing power should be taken from the banks and restored to the people, to whom it properly belongs."

Despite facing opposition, Alexander Hamilton eventually led the creation of the "First Bank of the United States" — becoming the first central bank after US independence. The bank was founded in 1791 and operated on a 20-year term.

After seven years without a central bank, the "Second Bank of the United States" was founded in 1818, surviving until 1836 when

Andrew Jackson, another strong opponent of central banking, closed it down. Jackson argued that:

"If Congress has the right under the Constitution to issue paper money, it was given them to use themselves, not to be delegated to individuals or corporations."

The third central bank to have come into existence and the one still around today is the Federal Reserve, founded in 1913 under Woodrow Wilson.

The Merits of Having the Fed

Why were various Founding Fathers opposed to central banking? There are many reasons, some of them we will discuss below:

1. The Federal Reserve Is Not "Federal"

Just like Federal Express is not government-owned, nor is the Federal Reserve. The Fed is made up of 12 branches, prominent examples of which include the branches in New York and San Francisco. Shares of these branches are owned by so-called "member banks." About 38% of the US' 8000 commercial banks are members of the Federal Reserve System through their share ownership in the Fed's 12 branches.

The Fed's income is comprised of two sources. The first is the interest its branches receive on treasury notes and other financial assets they hold. The second source is the interest received from the money lent out to member banks such as Citibank.

In 2013, the Fed recorded total income of $90.5 billion, though this number fluctuates widely based on current holdings of interest bearing assets and the current discount rate. Despite being owned by commercial banks, only about 1-2% of the Fed's income is paid out to its bank shareholders. In 2013, such dividend payments made up just $1.6 billion. The vast remainder of the $90.5 billion in income was remitted directly to the US treasury.

2. Is the Fed Needed?

As just discussed, the Fed's income is mostly remitted to the treasury. Ironically, much of that remittance comes from the government in the first place, as it corresponds to the interest paid by the treasury on the government bonds held by the Fed.

Why not let the government mint its own currency just like the coinage act of 1792 envisaged, instead of transferring money back and forth between the treasury and the Federal Reserve?

3. The FED and Its Member Banks Are Corrupt

The Fed's acquisition of treasury notes and other financial assets are enormous. Between 2008 and early 2015 alone, the Fed purchased a total of $3.5 trillion in financial assets. This compares to the US GDP of around $17 trillion. All of these assets, including treasury notes and mortgage-backed securities, were purchased on the open market — usually directly from large banks.

A crucial question to ask is why the Fed purchases treasury notes from banks such as Goldman Sachs, instead of directly from the federal government. Banks selling treasury notes to the Fed charge a premium, the government does not. As a result of these "indirect purchases," the middlemen, mostly large investment banks, are making billions. Isn't it interesting that the same banks profiting from this scheme are also major shareholders in the Federal Reserve System?

4. The Interest Paradox

The interest paradox is popular with people wanting to abolish the Fed, and gets repeated on numerous websites around the web. However, it has a logical fallacy which is often overseen. I included it in this book as even though it is invalid, it is valuable to know.

The theory goes as follows: central banks loan money at the "discount rate" to commercial banks — a main process through which money comes into existence. When repayment of the principal is due, the respective commercial bank has to pay principal plus interest.

However, if all money comes into existence through the Fed's issuance of loans to commercial banks, where does the money to pay for the interest come from?

Assume commercial banks and the government repaid all the principal on their loans and bonds to the Fed. Because all money in circulation originates from this principal, a world without debt would mean a world without money.

It is argued that even if all principal is repaid with all money in existence, there remains the interest component which cannot be paid for — making it impossible to eliminate all debt.

The argument concludes that the only way to prevent the economy from running out of money and commercial banks becoming unable to repay loans, and specifically interest, is for banks to borrow ever more from the Fed, leading to an eternal spiral of ever increasing debt.

The same concept can be applied to open market operations. Over the lifespan of a treasury note, the government pays to the note's bearer (i.e. the Fed) principal and interest. However, if money comes into existence through the Fed's purchase of treasury notes, where does the money for the interest come from?

Only when I started extensive research did I realize the paradox's fallacy. As mentioned before, the Fed's income from interest is in part remitted as dividends to member banks, and in part to the treasury. By definition, the interest to be paid by commercial banks and the treasury on Fed loans and bonds equals the Fed's income. As this income is remitted back to the economy (i.e. to member banks and the treasury), the amount of money extracted by the Fed through interest equals the money remitted back.

As a result, it is indeed *possible* for all central bank debt to be repaid. Even though this means that all money vanishes as the amount of money in circulation equals *exactly* the amount of outstanding central bank debt.

5. Nobody Oversees the Fed

While the Federal Reserve was established through the "Federal Reserve Act" passed in Congress in 1913, it is not part of any of the government's three branches — the executive, the legislative and the judiciary. It is not overseen by the president, the Congress or the Securities and Exchange Commission (SEC). Even its ownership structure remains unknown to the public until this day. Let me repeat this: there is no publicly available information on how much of the Fed is owned by which commercial banks, such as Citibank.

6. The Fed Manufactures Financial Crises

Isn't it interesting that the reason why the Fed was founded is the assumption that it would stabilize financial markets? The Fed's rationale was to smooth out the booms and busts of the business cycle.

Ever since its creation, financial crises have not only continued to occur but have become worse. This is how the Fed creates financial crises:

Over a period of several years, the Fed drastically expands the money supply through low interest rates, low reserve requirements and purchases of treasury bonds and other financial assets. The abundance of "easy cash" and low interest rates allow consumers to buy everything from homes to consumer goods. Businesses use the money to expand. Financial investors and banks borrow to purchase stocks.

The increased demand for houses, equipment for businesses and financial assets leads to slowly but steadily increasing prices — in other words higher inflation. Over time, this results in an asset price bubble.

To "fight" high inflation and deflate price bubbles the Fed now starts to incrementally increase the interest rate. This makes it less profitable for banks to keep investing in the stock market with borrowed money. As a result, banks start to sell stocks and use the receipts to repay their loans. Commercial banks pass on the higher discount rate to consumers and businesses. This makes it more difficult for some people and businesses to pay their loans — leading to defaults. Defaults in turn reduce people's demand for goods and services, decreasing other businesses' profits. This easily leads to a chain reaction of lower demand, lower profits and more defaults.

The stock market sell-off started by banks can easily lead to panic sales. Rapidly declining prices cause financial trouble for heavily invested banks, as the value of their loans starts exceeding the value of their assets. Smaller banks usually fail — 140 US banks did so in the year 2009 alone — while "too big to fail" banks are rescued through government bailouts. In the 2008/2009 financial crisis, the Fed provided $9 trillion in emergency loans to big banks, with Merrill Lynch, Citigroup and Morgan Stanley receiving $2 trillion *each*. Smaller banks which do not qualify as "too big too fail" are often acquired by their much larger rivals, further concentrating the power of large banks.

As economic growth collapses, the Fed again opens its flood-gates of easy-cash — starting another boom and bust cycle.

I would like to emphasize that it goes against voluntaryism to regulate financial markets. In contrary, the regulations already in place are so strict that they prevent new banks from being established — effectively "protecting" big banks from competition.

Did the Glass-Steagall Act enacted in 1933 (and repealed in 1999) prevent the economic crisis of the 1970s, or of the late 1980s? — Obviously not. The only type of regulation that works is "self-regulation." Banks which take on too much risk should feel the consequences and get bankrupt. Losing their jobs and reputation is the best deterrence for ruthless bankers.

While the Fed caused financial crises in the past, the next catastrophe is already in the making. The current period of artificially low interest rates has fueled a stock market bubble larger than any seen in decades.

While the sub-prime mortgage market was inherent to the 08/09 crisis, the next one may very well be based on a collapse of the derivative market. Just the 9 biggest banks have a combined derivative exposure of $230 trillion, or about 3 times world GDP.

A next crisis may also be the result of unsustainable government debts and unfunded social security liabilities in the US, Europe, and China. Near zero interest rates on treasury notes make it possible for governments to pay their interest obligations at the moment, but once the Fed and other world central banks decide to increase interest rates to "average" levels, countries all over the globe will find themselves unable to serve their debt obligations.

The workings and interconnection of the Federal Reserve with its member banks and the federal government are complex. Following diagram tries to visualize these relationships. Follow the arrows in order from (1) to (10). Feel free to count the money flows quantified by coins and stacks of bills — they will balance out!

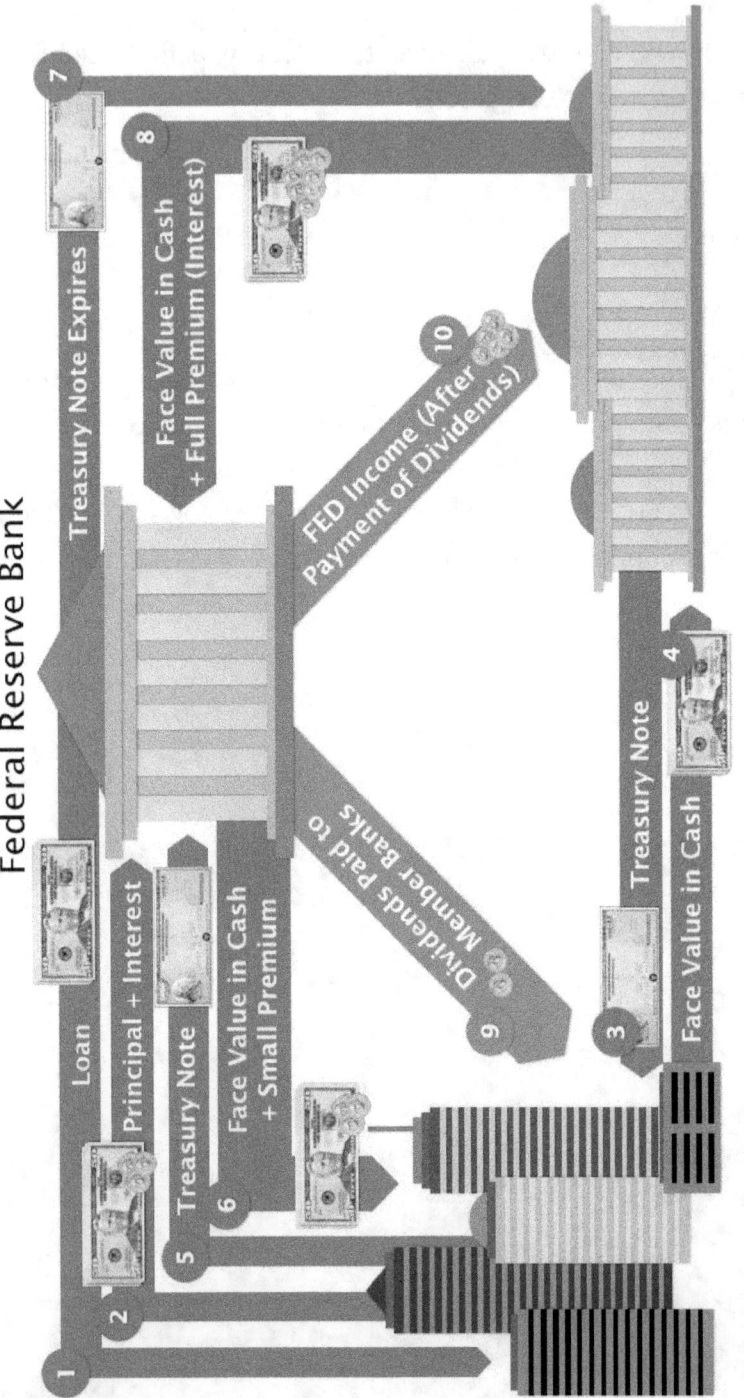

Federal Reserve Bank

Federal Government

Commercial Banks
(38% of Which Are Members of the
Federal Reserve System)

© Lucas Vincent Holding Limited

1

2 Loan

Principal + Interest

Treasury Note Expires 7

8 Face Value in Cash
+ Full Premium (Interest)

10 FED Income (After
Payment of Dividends)

Treasury Note 5

6 Face Value in Cash
+ Small Premium

9 Dividends Paid to
Member Banks

Treasury Note

4 Face Value in Cash

3

Illustration 17.2 How the Federal Reserve System Works (left)
(1) and (2) correspond to commercial banks borrowing from the Fed. (3)-(8) correspond to the Fed buying treasury notes through what is called open market operations. (9) refers to the Fed's payment of dividends to member banks. In step (10) the Fed remits any remaining income to the federal government. Image: own work by author

--- Learn More ---

- [Video] The Biggest Scam In The History Of Mankind / Hidden Secrets of Money (Documentary) - https://www.youtube.com/watch?v=iFDe5kUUyT0.

- [Graphic Visualization] The size of the derivative exposure by the world's 9 largest banks. http://demonocracy.info/infographics/usa/derivatives/bank_exposure.html.

--- Sources ---

1. US Constitution - Archives.gov. http://www.archives.gov/exhibits/charters/constitution_transcript.html. Retrieved July 28, 2015.

2. "Central Bank Transparency and Independence by Country." N. Nergiz Dincer and Barry Eichengreen. Sept 04, 2013. The Bank of Korea Working Papers. http://www.bok.or.kr/contents/total/eng/boardView.action?menuNaviId=1941&boardBean.brdid=12594&boardBean.menuid=1941&boardBean.rnum=1. Retrieved July 28, 2015.

3. Thomas Jefferson and Andrew Jackson Quotations - "Famous Quotations on Banking." The Money Masters. http://www.themoneymasters.com/the-money-masters/famous-quotations-on-banking/. Retrieved July 28, 2015.

4. Who Owns the Fed? - Brooks Jackson. FactCheck.org. http://www.factcheck.org/2008/03/federal-reserve-bank-ownership/. Retrieved July 28, 2015.

5. "The Fed's $3.5T QE purchases have generated almost half a trillion dollars for the US Treasury since 2009." Mark J. Perry. American Enterprise Institute. https://www.aei.org/publication/since-2009-feds-qe-purchases-transferred-almost-half-trillion-dollars-treasury-isnt-gigantic-wealth-transfer/. Retrieved July 28, 2015.

6. List of Failed US Banks in 2009 - Federal Insurance Deposit Insurance. https://www.fdic.gov/bank/individual/failed/banklist.html. Retrieved July 28, 2015.

7. "Fed Made $9 Trillion in Emergency Overnight Loans." Chris Isidore. CNN Money. http://money.cnn.com/2010/12/01/news/economy/fed_reserve_data_release/. Retrieved July 28, 2015.

8. "The Glass-Steagall Act Explained." Reem Heakal. Investopedia. http://www.investopedia.com/articles/03/071603.asp. Retrieved July 28, 2015.

9. Derivative Exposure by 9 Biggest Banks in the World - "Derivatives: The Unregulated Global Casino for Banks." Demonocracy. http://demonocracy.info/infographics/usa/derivatives/bank_exposure.html. Retrieved July 28, 2015.

FIAT CURRENCIES

CHAPTER 17 - SECTION 2

The vast majority of the world's currencies are fiat currencies. A fiat currency is accepted by a population due to government decree, with fiat meaning "decree." Government backing gives a fiat currency its value.

A gold-backed currency, on the other hand, obtains its value from the underlying gold. Currencies may also be backed by various other metals and resources — as long as they are valuable.

Many currencies have historically been backed by gold rather than other precious metals such as silver due to gold's relatively stable value over time, with silver prices tending to be more volatile. In the past, gold-backed currencies often included the gold in physical coins which were usually made out of gold alloys.

Modern gold-backed currencies, including the US dollar until 1973, were mostly backed by gold reserves stored in a central location, with paper currency and coins made out of cheaper metals "representing" the stored gold's value.

The downside of having the gold that backs a currency stored at a central location is that this allows government to slowly dilute the value of the currency, as happened with the US dollar. A government can easily increase the supply of paper money, while keeping gold reserves the same — essentially reducing the amount of gold that backs every unit of currency.

In 1973, under Richard Nixon the US removed the gold standard entirely, allowing unrestrained increases in the money supply without the Fed having to acquire new gold reserves. The main reason for eliminating the gold standard was the US government's need for funds to finance its Keynesian deficit spending. As would be expected in such a situation, the average annual inflation rate increased to more than 7% in the 1970s. In comparison, average annual inflation between 2010 and 2015 was less than 2%.

After the fall of the gold standard, the Petrodollar System was introduced to ensure the dollar's continued world dominance as a reserve currency for foreign governments. The Petrodollar System is based on an agreement between the US and Saudi Arabia to price oil only in US dollars. Under this system, which is still in place today, the US purchases oil from Saudi Arabia and other OPEC oil producers in dollar, while Saudi Arabia promises to use the oil sale receipts to invest in US treasury notes. The deal had following advantages for the US:

1. Pricing oil in US dollar ensured continued demand for the currency, as any country wishing to purchase oil had to exchange its own currency into dollar. This demand increased the dollar value compared to other currencies. A US dollar that is worth more allows Americans to enjoy higher purchasing power abroad while reducing inflation, as imported goods priced in foreign currencies become relatively less expensive. The Petrodollar System helped to

Illustration 17.3 Introducing the Gold Standard in the Islamic State

The Islamic State has started to introduce its own gold- and silver-based "Islamic Dinar" to (using the Islamic State's words) "emancipate itself from the satanic global economic system" (see "Learn More" section at end of chapter). Image: ginasanders, Bigstock

boost the value of the dollar in light of its decreasing attractiveness without gold backing.

2. Because oil is priced in dollar, the US can increase its purchases of oil simply by printing more money. If the UK increased its money supply, it would see its exchange rate fall vs the USD as there would now be more pounds per dollar. The decrease in the value of the pound would be equivalent to the increase in money supply

and, as a result, would *not* allow the United Kingdom to buy more oil.

3. Saudi Arabia's use of oil revenues to purchase US treasury notes increased demand. Increased demand for treasury notes meant the US government could lower the interest rate it offered on new bond issues. This has saved the US billions.

The main problem with fiat currencies is that they allow governments to infinitely increase the money supply, potentially leading to hyperinflation. Contrary to popular belief, there have been dozens of cases where governments printed money to the extent that those with currency savings lost nearly everything. To end this chapter, the following table presents some of the more severe cases of hyperinflation — ordered by date.

Chapter 17 - Section 2: Fiat Currencies

Country	Period	Highest Monthly Inflation Rate (%)
France	1789–96	143.26
Germany	1920–23	29,525.71
Austria	1921–22	124.27
Poland	1921–24	187.54
Soviet Union	1922–24	278.72
Hungary	1923–24	82.18
Greece	1942–45	11,288
Hungary	1945–46	1.295×10^{16}
Taiwan	1945–49	398.73
China	1947–49	4,208.73
Bolivia	1984–86	120.39
Nicaragua	1986–89	126.62
Peru	1988–90	114.12
Argentina	1989–90	196.6
Poland	1989–90	77.33
Brazil	1989–93	84.32
Yugoslavia	1990	58.82
Azerbaijan	1991–94	118.09
Congo (Zaire)	1991–94	225
Kyrgyzstan	1992	157
Serbia	1992–94	309,000,000
Ukraine	1992–94	249
Georgia	1993–94	196.72
Armenia	1993–94	438.04
Turkmenistan	1993–96	62.5
Belarus	1994	53.4
Kazakhstan	1994	57
Tajikistan	1995	78.1
Bulgaria	1997	242.7
Zimbabwe	2007–09	2,600.2

*Last official monthly inflation figure provided by the Zimbabwean government in July 2008. Other estimates are higher.

Source: adapted from "Hyperinflation Rates by Country - 2011 Annual Report, Federal Reserve Bank of Dallas." Original data source: Monetary Regimes and Inflation: History, Economic and Political Relationships, by Peter Bernholz, Northhampton, Mass.: Edward Elgar Publishing, 2003, Table 2.1.

--- Learn More ---

- Islamic State mints its own 'Islamic Dinar' coins - http://www.telegraph.co.uk/news/worldnews/islamic-state/11694838/Islamic-State-mints-its-own-Islamic-Dinar-coins.html

--- Sources ---

1. US Gold Standard - Federal Reserve Bank of Richmond. https://www.richmondfed.org/faqs/gold_silver. Retrieved July 28, 2015.

2. US Inflation by Decade - InflationData.com. http://inflationdata.com/articles/charts/decade-inflation-chart/. Retrieved July 28, 2015.

3. Hyperinflation Rates by Country - "2011 Annual Report." Federal Reserve Bank of Dallas. https://www.dallasfed.org/assets/documents/institute/annual/2011/annual11.pdf. Retrieved July 28, 2015.

INFLATION VS DEFLATION

CHAPTER 17 - SECTION 3

It is the Fed's stated target to generate 2% inflation every year. Why does the Fed want to create inflation? And why is the target rate set at 2%? Let us answer these questions below:

Changes in an economy's price level are measured through various price indices. The most common of these is the Consumer Price Index, or CPI. There is also a wholesale price index, a manufacturer price index and many others. The CPI for a given year measures by how much prices of a pre-defined basket of consumer goods increased over the past 12 months. An increase in the price index (i.e., the value of the goods in the basket) is equivalent to a rise in the economy's price level.

Inflation is the "persistent increase in the price level of an economy." With "persistent" we mean that the price of goods has permanently increased and, for example, was not due to a drought or some other temporary factors.

Similarly, deflation is the "persistent decrease in the average price level in an economy."

In simple terms, inflation means that prices in an economy are permanently increasing, while deflation means that prices are decreasing.

As inflation increases prices, every dollar buys less. We say that inflation reduces the purchasing power of money.

What is the Fed's rationale to target a 2% inflation rate, and to what extent is it valid? Let's find out!

1. A 2% Inflation Rate Supports the Economy

This common argument goes as follows: when consumers expected prices to decrease in the mid-to-long-term, they would delay their purchases, in turn hurting the economy. A 2% inflation rate can prevent this from happening.

There are several problems with this claim:

First: many, if not most products already get cheaper during their product life cycle. Other products may not get cheaper, but improve their value once a new version is released. This includes a wide range of goods, from electronics to appliances and vehicles. Shortly before a new car model is launched, the old one is usually sold at steep discounts. And while different generations of a cell phone are often priced similarly, their features improve over time — increasing value for money.

When you put predictable short-term sales events such as Black Friday aside, most consumers will buy a new fridge or vehicle whenever their old one breaks down — not when the price is lower in a year's time. If the majority of consumers delayed purchases to save, then why are iPhone or car sales highest shortly after their launch, when prices are highest? Many consumers simply buy products when they want and need them, and not several years down the road to cash in a 20% discount.

Prices for many products, or at least their value for money, get more attractive despite the Fed's efforts to the contrary because productivity improves by more than the decline in the US dollar's purchasing power.

Even more telling that deflation does not hurt the economy is the fact that the industry in which prices have decreased the fastest — the electronics and technology industry — is also one of the largest, fastest-growing and most profitable.

Demand for necessities and commodities is even less affected by deflation than electronics are. For example, assume consumers expected the price of gasoline and electricity to decline in the coming year. By no means would they cut back on gasoline and electricity use today. To the contrary, knowing that energy prices will decrease would assure consumers that there is little risk in upgrading to a larger SUV or a fourth air conditioning unit. In this context, deflation would actually increase demand for large cars and energy-intensive appliances and, as a result, boost the economy.

Nonetheless, we have to assume that there are always some consumers who rather wait to buy in a deflationary environment. However, even in this case deflation is unlikely to hurt the economy. While people may postpone a vacation for the moment, they will still spend their money at some point in life. When purchases are delayed, demand decreases today but will be higher in the future. People would have more savings to spend during their retirement, for example, boosting demand in several decades to come. Averaged out over half a century, all these effects mean that deflation would make little to no difference to the total amount of money spent.

Along with decreasing prices for goods and services, deflation would likely result in declining wages. Yet even when wages decrease, productivity improvements and declining consumer prices mean that people's purchasing power increases — or at least remains constant.

Under deflation, companies try to counter declining market prices for their products. One way to do this is by offering more value to consumers, for instance, by delivering better product features. Other companies may try to offset declining sales revenues by purchasing modern machinery to improve productivity and cost efficiency. From this perspective, deflation can be an incentive for firms to improve productivity — allowing us to produce more with fewer resources.

Decreasing prices would also incentivize people to start businesses. Why? Because decreasing prices mean that a fixed amount of money (e.g., $100) can more easily be earned today than in ten years from now. This business incentive may improve economic activity, rather than stifling it.

2. Deflation Is Bad for Government Debt

This is probably the government's number one (and most valid) reason for inducing inflation.

Even if the number of goods and services we produce every year remained constant, increasing prices (inflation) mean higher taxes. Increasing property values mean higher property taxes, higher wages mean higher income taxes, and a higher Consumer Price Index (CPI) means higher consumption taxes. Given that government debt stays constant, these "inflated" tax receipts allow the government to more easily service its debt.

Under inflation, both debt and savings slowly lose their value. This is why inflation is generally advantageous for borrowers, while disadvantaging lenders. The opposite is true for deflation, which favors lenders, but harms borrowers. In effect, inflation redistributes wealth from those that save to those that borrow.

Because governments around the world are notoriously indebted, it makes sense for them to encourage inflation. The morally questionable aspect about this is that governments use their direct and indirect control over the money supply to induce inflation and thus benefit themselves. Other people and businesses who happen to owe a lot of debt also benefit — at the cost of lenders and savers.

In fact, institutionalized inflation is nothing else than institutionalized discrimination, against those that are disciplined and save. This discrimination along with the forced redistribution of wealth makes inflation a major violator of the law of liberty and voluntaryism.

3. Deflation Would Result in Bankruptcies

This common argument assumes that deflation increases a borrower's debt burden, makes it more difficult to repay debt and increases defaults. This is definitely the case for sudden, unexpected decreases in prices, as was the case during the house price collapse of 2008/2009, when house values dropped to levels below the underlying mortgages (this is called being "under water" or "upside down"). In effect, people had more debt on a house than the house was worth. On the other hand, it remains open for discussion whether consistent, moderate deflation has the same effect, as evidenced by the relationship between interest rates and inflation.

As shown in following illustration, lower inflation is usually accompanied by lower interest rates. Any negative effect lower inflation has on borrowers tends to be balanced out by the positive effect of lower interest rates.

Both inflation and interest rates for treasury notes peaked around 1980 and reached a low in 2015.

In the long term, deflation would result in significantly lower interest rates, thus reducing the supposed threat of deflation to indebted businesses.

Illustration 17.4 Relationship Between Interest Rates and Inflation

Interest Rates and Inflation

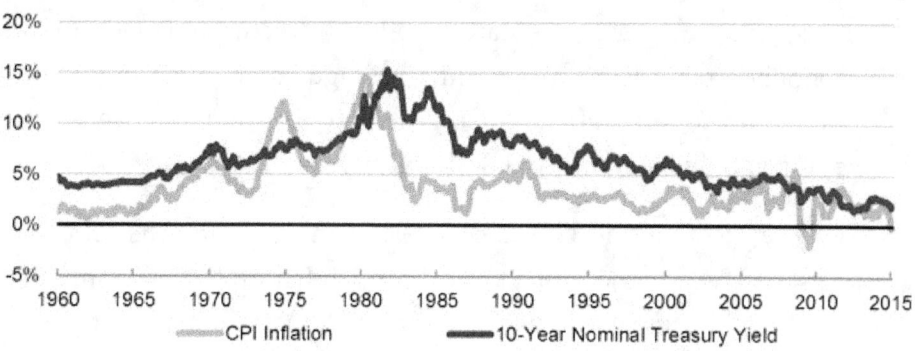

Source: Federal Reserve Board, BLS.

BROOKINGS

Lower inflation or even deflation correlate with lower interest rates. Image: The Brookings Institute

4. A 2% Target Inflation Rate Is Ideal

The argument that the Fed's 2% inflation rate target is optimal for the economy has two flaws:

1. The 2% target rate is completely arbitrary. The Fed's official website states that the 2% inflation target is what the Federal Open Market Committee (FOMC) "judges" to be "the most consistent over the longer run with the Federal Reserve's mandate for price stability and maximum employment."

   No information is given on the methodology used to derive this rate.

   How does the Fed know that 2% inflation is better than a 2.1% rate?

2. The Fed's methods used to measure inflation, including the CPI index, are misleading — hardly reflecting actual changes in the economy's price level. When inflation figures are "doctored," it is impossible to compare them to a target inflation rate and make appropriate judgements and policy decisions.

   Many argue that the CPI *underestimates* inflation, as the CPI only measures what the Fed calls "core inflation." Core inflation excludes changes in energy- and food prices, while measuring price changes of electronics, cars, and other manufactured goods. The argument to ignore energy- and food prices is based on the assumption that they are too volatile to be useful to compute the *persistent* change in an economy's price level.

   Interestingly, the remaining "core items" used to calculate inflation just happen to be products with naturally decreasing prices such as cell phones. When a new iPhone costs the same as the old one, but includes more features, the Fed actually records a decrease in price. This is because one now receives more value for the same price.

The problem is that both energy and food represent large portions of an average person's expenditure. Their exclusion results in a mismatch between the official inflation rate and the price changes people experience in the supermarket and at the gas station. Just ask anyone to estimate the price increases he/she experiences and compare them with the official inflation rate. The actual perceived inflation rate will almost always be higher than the one that is officially reported.

The discussion about measuring inflation would be incomplete without mentioning the opposing viewpoint. Some claim that the CPI severely *overestimates* inflation. This theory actually assumes that we are experiencing constant deflation — not inflation. And while it may sound counter-intuitive, there is a grain of truth to it:

The official cumulative inflation rate between 1913 and 2015 is 2310%. Accordingly, $1 million in 1913 is equivalent to around $24 million in 2015. So far, so good. Now let me ask you a question: would you rather have $1 million in 1913 or $1 million today?

Based on the official inflation rate, $1 million today has 1/24 the purchasing power of $1 million in 1913. Or in other words, $1 million in 1913 is worth 24 times more than $1 million in 2015.

Nonetheless, many people would prefer to have $1 million today, as it allows them to buy advanced cars, air conditioning, computers, cell phones, plane travel and advanced health care — all of which not a billion dollars could have bought in 1913.

Perhaps you would even prefer 1 million 2015 dollars to 1 billion 1913 dollars.

If that is the case, based on your preferences, we would have experienced cumulative deflation of 99.99% in the 102-year period. In other words, you would value one 2015 dollar at least 1000 times as much as one 1913 dollar.

This compares to the aforementioned official inflation rate of 2310% for the same time period, which assumes that one 2015 dollar is worth only around 0.04 1913 dollars.

The reason for the huge discrepancy between official inflation and the "perceived" long term deflation is technological progress. Basic goods such as wheat or Coke have indeed seen their prices increase by the rate estimated by the Fed. Yet technological advances mean that money today has more far-reaching purchasing power — for products which would have been unimaginable a hundred years ago. Buying a computer in 1913 would have been impossible, even if you had been prepared to spend billions or trillions of dollars.

5. A 2% Inflation Rate Is Low Enough Not to Destroy Wealth

Whenever an economy experiences inflation, people pay a "hidden" tax. The purchasing power of newly "printed" money is always equivalent to the decrease in purchasing power of the original money stock.

Assume there are 10 houses, 10 homeowners, and $1 million dollar. Ignoring the velocity of money, we can divide the money stock by the number of houses to find the average cost of a home — $100,000. Furthermore, assume that every of the 10 homeowners has savings of $100,000.

The government now decides to print $1 million of new money, doubling the money supply. It wants to use the money to acquire as many of the houses it can. Because there are now $2 million in the economy, prices rise, with $200,000 being available for every house. Because the government holds 50% of the money supply, it possesses 50% of all the money's purchasing power. This allows it to purchase 50% of the houses.

The value of the government's freshly printed money came directly from the existing money stock. In fact, the original $1 million lost 50% of its purchasing power. Originally, $1 million bought 10 houses — now only 5. This loss in money value has been "transferred" to the government's newly printed bills. By printing money, the government essentially introduced a 50% tax on the savings of its citizens.

Inflation is a "savings tax" that is used to transfer value from savings to newly printed money.

And while the Fed's 2% inflation target rate is better than a 10% rate, it still redistributes wealth from savers to the money manipulators.

Keep the Money Supply on Par With GDP Growth

Inflation will always bring with it the redistribution of wealth from savers to the money printers. Both the law of liberty and voluntaryism are violated by this mandatory "hidden tax." The only way to end this is by eliminating engineered inflation. This can be done by increasing the money supply by the same rate or less than growth in national output (GDP).

When the money supply is increased by the same rate as national output, prices remain constant, as the number of dollars available for every good and service remains unchanged.

When the money supply increases at a lower rate than GDP, or is kept constant, prices decrease, as fewer dollars are available for every good and service.

Below table illustrates the effects of various changes in money supply on the economy's price level (inflation):

Money Supply	Price Changes	Effect
Money Supply Increases by More Than Output (GDP)	Inflation	Hidden Tax: Wealth Transfer From Savers to Those Who Print Money
Money Supply Increases by Same Rate as Output	No Price Change	No Transfer in Wealth
Money Supply Increases by Less than Output	Deflation	Savers Gain Purchasing Power
Money Supply Stays Constant, Output Increases	Deflation	Savers Gain Purchasing Power

The beneficiaries of money printing include the member banks of the federal reserve system — about 38% of commercial banks — that are allowed to borrow from the Fed at favorably low rates. A question we have to ask is why member banks are allowed to borrow at these preferential rates, while regular consumers and businesses have to accept the marked-up rates offered to them by commercial banks?

The dollar system is owned by everybody and should not merely benefit those that control it.

Again, the value of the Fed-created money that member banks borrow is equivalent to the value loss of the savings of regular people and businesses. Either allow everyone to borrow newly printed money at preferential rates or stop money printing altogether.

Japan and Deflation

Does deflation cause lower growth? No - when looking at real world evidence. Japan, the only major economy that has experienced prolonged periods of deflation during the last two decades is a great example. Let's have a look at Japan's annual GDP growth and inflation rate since 1990.

Illustration 17.5 Japan's Annual GDP Growth and Inflation Rate

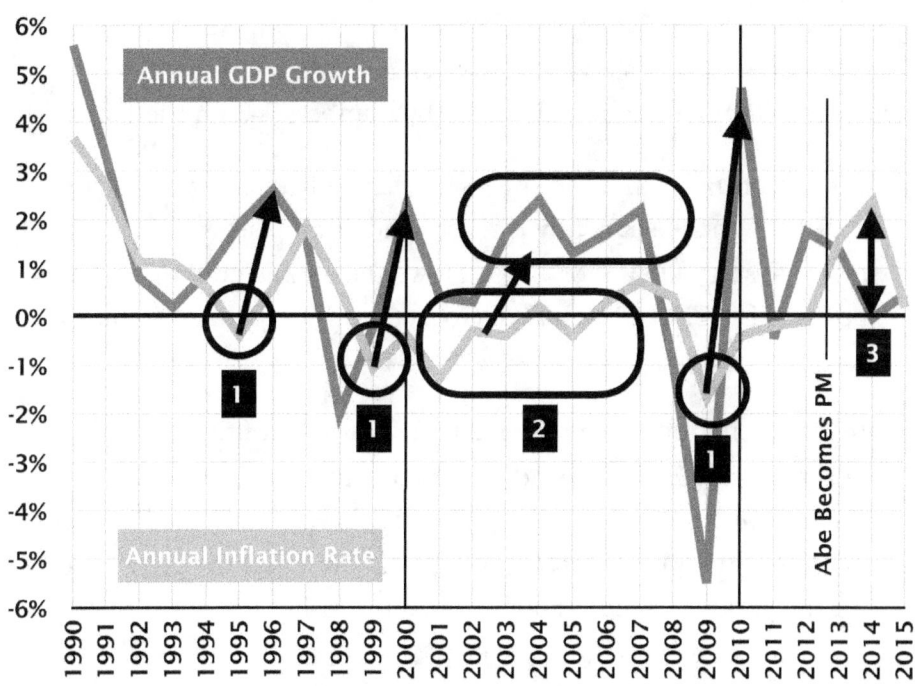

Deflation may not be the cause of Japan's economic malaise. Image: own work by author; data from the World Bank, inflation.eu, and Statista

More than two decades of low inflation and economic growth after the 1989 asset price crash appear to confirm the notion that low inflation/ deflation have prevented Japan from growing at a rapid pace.

According to theory, low inflation (or deflation) today leads to lower investments in machines and construction of property today, and therefore lower economic growth tomorrow.

However, the relationship between Japan's GDP and inflation trends suggests something very different, namely that:

1. deflation does not inhibit GDP growth, and may even promote it

2. high economic growth causes higher inflation, not vice versa as is often claimed.

In more detail, this is shown by three characteristics of Japan's inflation-GDP relationship, identified by numbers 1-3 on the graph:

1. Whenever inflation hits a low (see encircled areas in the chart), GDP growth subsequently picks up and often peaks out just 12 months later. If deflation caused lower economic growth, how is it possible for GDP growth to skyrocket every time inflation hits a low?

2. In 2001 inflation bottomed out at -1.27% and continued to be negative until 2003. Instead of resulting in even lower economic growth, GDP growth started to rise, peaking at 2.2% in 2004. In fact, the low-inflation period up until 2006/7 laid the groundwork for the period of medium and relatively stable economic growth between 2003 and 2007.

   Only after the period of prolonged economic growth did inflation rose to a still low 0.7% in 2007.

3. When Abe Shinzo was elected Prime Minister of Japan in 2012, he introduced "Abenomics," a Keynesian spending spree intended to boost inflation, and thus economic growth. As expected, the Bank of Japan's QE money printing program pushed inflation to a 23 year high. Instead of bringing higher economic growth, however, the rise in inflation led to a crash in economic growth to just 0%. This experiment alone should put the theory to rest that deflation harms short term growth, or that higher inflation promotes the national income.

--- Sources ---

1. "Why does the Federal Reserve aim for 2 percent inflation over time?" Federal Reserve. http://www.federalreserve.gov/faqs/economy_14400.htm. Retrieved July 28, 2015.

2. US Inflation Calculator - http://www.usinflationcalculator.com. Retrieved July 28, 2015.

PRIVATIZATION OF MONEY

CHAPTER 17 - SECTION 4

The Federal Reserve, its member banks, and the US government use their control of the US dollar to their benefit as made obvious by constant inflation and bank bailouts. We have a system in place that is far from compliant with either the law of liberty or voluntaryism.

Privatization of Money is the Solution

The private ownership of the Fed gives the impression that our monetary system is a product of capitalism or free markets. Nothing could be further from the truth. The Fed is evidence of a de facto merger between the state and some of the world's largest financial corporations. The government and banks are deeply interwoven — Congress approves bailouts for banks, while the government depends on banks and the Fed buying treasury notes. It is no wonder that high ranking officials and bankers rotate frequently between government positions and jobs in Wall Street firms. Former United States Secretary of the Treasury Timothy Geithner who now works as president of famed private equity firm Warburg Pincus is a prominent example. Is it a surprise that while he served as part of the Obama administration,

Geithner led the establishment of the $350 billion taxpayer-financed Troubled Asset Relief Program (TARP) that indirectly supported the company he is now working for, along with many other financial services firms?

The merger between state and corporations is exemplary of fascism, not free markets.

I propose the break-up of the government's monopoly of money, and the true privatization and deregulation of our monetary system. We should have a system that allows independent businesses and individuals alike to launch their own competing currencies.

For example, Walmart could introduce the Walmart dollar, backed by Walmart property and real estate.

You yourself could choose to start a company which buys gold for people, stores it and issues a "gold-backed" paper-currency.

In a true free market, people should be allowed to create and use whatever currency they like. It is natural for everyone to have different visions of how an "ideal" currency should look like. Some want to use a gold-backed currency, while others prefer purely electronic money. Again others are wary of inflation and want to keep the money supply constant. Others think moderate inflation is better than slowly declining prices.

The beauty of a fully privatized and deregulated monetary system is that various currencies can co-exist. Just as the free market produces different cars for various niche consumers, so will it offer different currencies for people to choose from.

Allowing privately operated currencies to compete is essential to preserving voluntaryism — the concept that all interactions should be voluntary. Forcing all individuals to use an inflation-prone fiat currency just because some government administrators believe inflation to be "good" violates that principle.

I personally believe that a deflationary, gold-backed currency would be advantageous but, being a libertarian, do not want to force this belief onto others. A privatized monetary system would allow everyone to use the currency he or she desires. No one, including the government, you or me, should have a monopoly over the creation and administration of money.

The parallel existence of multiple currencies will for sure result in market inefficiencies. However, these inefficiencies are *smaller* than the increased trust and satisfaction people receive from using their preferred currency. After all, if you value a universally accepted currency more than one that is gold-backed, the free market allows you to switch. Others are willing to live with the inconvenience of a less liquid currency, as they value certain attributes such as gold-backing more than the associated costs. Free-choice always leads to the outcome that maximizes people's satisfaction. The market mechanism will choose the combination of private currencies which deliver best what people value.

If the "inefficiency argument" was sufficient to ban the existence of many, decentralized currencies, then why do we have thousands of different car models for consumers to choose from? After all, the argument could be made that producing just one model for everyone would be more efficient. The fallacy of this logic lies in the fact that people value the choice of many different car models more than the lower price of a standard vehicle. Otherwise, people would all be driving low-cost, mass-market cars such as the Toyota Corolla. Not to forget that the notion of "banning" companies and people to produce and exchange a large variety of goods for "efficiency purposes" is totally opposed to liberty and people's right to unrestrained, voluntary interactions.

How to Pay for the Upkeep of a Monetary System

The principle of causation states that you should only pay for what you are actively responsible for. Everything about the administration of a monetary system, from the production to the distribution of money, is expensive. How can we pay for this while adhering to the principle of causation?

In a system dominated by private currencies, the free market decides how these costs are paid for. Currency issuers are free to come up with innovative ways to do so, from charging users a monthly flat fee to proportional transaction charges. Consumers are free to choose the currency whose usage fee model they like the most. This stands in stark contrast to today, where every taxpayer is inadvertently forced to pay for the upkeep of a fiat currency.

Bitcoin, probably the most prominent of all privately operated currencies, solved the problem of upkeep costs in an interesting way. By using the currency, bitcoin users store the "blockchain," a ledger of all bitcoin transactions, on their computers.

A subset of users approves all bitcoin transactions before they are stored in the "blockchain." This approval process is also called "mining," as it is rewarded with newly issued or "mined" bitcoins. No central authority is needed.

The approval process becomes more complicated and harder to process over time, resulting in a leveling off of the bitcoin supply. This makes the currency strongly deflationary over time. A bitcoin is divisible into

100,000,000 sub-units, called Satoshi, which allows for small transactions even as the built-in deflation results in ever lower prices for goods and services.

--- Learn More ---

- [Video] How bitcoin mining works - https://www.youtube.com/watch?v=GmOzih6I1zs.

- Eleven examples of local currencies - http://money.cnn.com/galleries/2012/pf/1201/gallery.community-currencies/index.html.

CONCLUSION

CHAPTER 17 - SECTION 5

Our current monetary system is complex. Here is a summary of everything we have discussed in the last five sections:

- In the United States, the Federal Reserve issues money, although this privilege was originally granted to Congress. The Fed does this by adjusting the discount rate, setting reserve requirements and buying and selling financial assets in open market operations.

- The Fed's policy to expand and contract the money supply first leads to asset bubbles, and then to financial crises. Small banks often fail, while big banks are bailed out by government. Every crisis leads to a further consolidation of the finance industry.

- Financial market regulations stifle competition and thus empower big banks. All while bailouts promote reckless investment behavior. The solution to risky speculation is letting careless banks fail, not more regulations.

- The abolishment of the gold standard allows unlimited printing of money. In combination with the Fed's annual 2% inflation target rate, this results in the US dollar being devalued as measured in terms of decreasing purchasing power.

- The decrease in purchasing power as a result of inflation is a "hidden tax" everyone has to pay.

- Deflation is occurring in various industries such as the technology sector, and contrary to public opinion does not harm the economy. Deflation has limited effects on demand, as few people delay purchases of consumer goods to save 10% in one year's time.

- The solution to above problems, and to achieve liberty, is to:

  - Re-introduce the gold standard to prevent governments from printing excessive amounts of money.

  - Abolish the Fed and let Congress issue money directly.

  - Eliminate inflation by keeping the money supply constant, or at least in sync with changes in the amount of goods and services produced in the economy.

  - Allow private currencies to be used in parallel.

Thank you for reading Roadmap to Liberty. I hope you enjoyed it.

You can always email me at <u>LucasVincentHolding@iCloud.com</u>.

Also visit <u>www.RoadmapToLiberty.com</u>.

To get notified when I release a new book, accompanying website or video series >> sign up here: <u>http://eepurl.com/btwL8v</u>

APPENDIX

Appendix

Regarding Chapter 2: Political Ideologies

	Countries Invaded by Nazi Germany	
	Invaded Countries (Borders at Time of Invasion)	Invaded Countries (Borders as of Today)
1	Albania	- Czechoslovakia
2	Austria	+ Czech Republic
3	Belgium	+ Slovakia
4	Czechoslovakia	- Yugoslavia
5	Denmark	+ Croatia
6	Estonia	+Slovenia
7	Finland	+ Bosnia and Herzegovina
8	France	+ Montenegro
9	Greece	+ Kosovo
10	Hungary	+ Macedonia
11	Italy	+ Serbia
12	Latvia	
13	Lithuania	
14	Luxembourg	
15	Moldova	
16	Monaco	
17	Netherlands	
18	Norway	
19	Poland	
20	Romania	
21	Russia	
22	San Marino	
23	Sweden	
24	Ukraine	
25	Yugoslavia	

Appendix

	Invaded Countries (Borders at Time of Invasion)	Invaded Countries (Borders as of Today)
1	Afghanistan	- Czechoslovakia
2	Albania	+ Czech Republic
3	Armenia	+ Slovakia
4	Austria	- Yugoslavia
5	Azerbaijan	+ Croatia
6	Belarus	+Slovenia
7	Bulgaria	+ Bosnia and Herzegovina
8	China	+ Montenegro
9	Czechoslovakia	+ Kosovo
10	Estonia	+ Macedonia
11	Finland	+ Serbia
12	Georgia	
13	Germany	
14	Hungary	
15	Iran	
16	Kazakhstan	
17	Korea	
18	Kyrgyzstan	
19	Latvia	
20	Lithuania	
21	Moldova	
22	Mongolia	
23	Poland	
24	Romania	
25	Tajikistan	
26	Turkey	
27	Turkmenistan	

Countries Invaded by the Soviet Union

Appendix

Countries Invaded by the Soviet Union		
28	Ukraine	
29	Uzbekistan	
30	Vietnam	
31	Yugoslavia	

Thank you for reading Roadmap to Liberty. I hope you enjoyed it.

You can always email me at LucasVincentHolding@iCloud.com.

Also visit www.RoadmapToLiberty.com.

To get notified when I release a new book, accompanying website or video series >> sign up here: http://eepurl.com/btwL8v

www.ingramcontent.com/pod-product-compliance
Lightning Source LLC
Chambersburg PA
CBHW071326280526
45787CB00001B/7